WHERE DIVERS DARE

WHERE DIVERS DARE

THE HUNT FOR THE LAST U-BOAT

Randall Peffer

BERKLEY CALIBER, NEW YORK

BERKLEY CALIBER

An imprint of Penguin Random House LLC
375 Hudson Street, New York, New York 10014

This book is an original publication of Penguin Random House LLC.

Copyright © 2016 by Randall Peffer.
Penguin supports copyright. Copyright fuels creativity, encourages diverse voices,
promotes free speech, and creates a vibrant culture. Thank you for buying an authorized
edition of this book and for complying with copyright laws by not reproducing, scanning, or
distributing any part of it in any form without permission. You are supporting writers and
allowing Penguin to continue to publish books for every reader.

BERKLEY CALIBER and its logo are trademarks of Penguin Random House LLC.
For more information, visit penguin.com.

Library of Congress Cataloging-in-Publication Data

Peffer, Randall S.
Where divers dare : the hunt for the last U-boat / Randall Peffer.
p. cm.
ISBN 978-0-425-27636-5 (hardback)
1. U-550 (Submarine)   2. World War, 1939–1945—Naval operations, German.   3. World
War, 1939–1945—Naval operations—Submarine.   4. Shipwrecks—Massachusetts—
Nantucket Island.   5. Shipwrecks—North Atlantic Ocean.   6. Underwater archaeology—
North Atlantic Ocean.   7. Divers—United States—Biography.   8. Deep diving—United
States—History.   9. Salvage—United States—History.   10. World War, 1939–1945—
Campaigns—North Atlantic Ocean.   I. Title.   II. Title: Hunt for the last U-boat.
D782.U186P44 2016
940.54'293—dc23
2015028313

First edition: April 2016

PRINTED IN THE UNITED STATES OF AMERICA

10   9   8   7   6   5   4   3   2   1

Jacket design by Rita Frangie.
Book design by Tiffany Estreicher.

While the author has made every effort to provide accurate telephone numbers and Internet
addresses at the time of publication, neither the author nor the publisher is responsible for errors,
or for changes that occur after publication. Further, the publisher does not have any control over
and does not assume any responsibility for author or third-party websites or their content.

Penguin
Random
House

For veteran seamen Mort Raphelson, John Hudock,
Robert Ziemer, Albert Nitsche, Hugo Renzmann,
Klaus Hänert, Friedrich Torge, and Robert Wilcox
as well as their shipmates, and their families.
Bless them all.

AUTHOR'S NOTE

The events, the actions of individual men, and the dialogue in this book have been carefully reconstructed from my firsthand observations as well as the stories of the men involved, their families, and eyewitnesses. When necessary and appropriate, I have also relied on an extensive collection of relevant books, websites, military records, and the established protocols of operation and communication on board vessels of the type and vintage of U-*550*, USS *Joyce*, and SS *Pan Pennsylvania*. As with almost all events with multiple witnesses, sometimes the stories about what happened diverge. When such discrepancies arose during my research, I have gone with the story for which there exists the most corroborating firsthand testimony and evidence.

Prologue

A black night on the North Atlantic. Joe Mazraani's eyes feel like they're popping out of his skull as he sits in the steering seat on the dive boat *Tenacious*. The vessel is lumbering westward at 10 knots, giving off the sour scent of diesel exhaust. It's only about 2240 hours, at night, but it feels like long past midnight. Mazraani squints to see beyond the glow of the chart plotter, the depth sounder screen, the radar, and the compass. More than a few people have noted that when he's at the helm of his dive boat, he puts them in mind of George Clooney in *The Perfect Storm*.

He has been peering into the gloom for hours, days. Years, if he has to admit the truth about the depth of his obsession for this hunt. He knows that it's not rational, but at some point tonight he has started to imagine flailing, beckoning arms, the flashes of white life vests among the dark waves. Then German cries of "*Helfen sie mir.*" Help me.

He wonders if he's alone with these ghosts. Or are the other men on *Tenacious* haunted, too? But, of course, they are. Why would they be out here on such a night so far from land if they were not spellbound, caught in the thrall of the dead, the dying, and the mysteries that surround them? Possibly divers Brad Sheard, Eric Takakjian, and Anthony Tedeschi, sleeping in their forecastle berths, are dreaming of the naval battle that took place here, near the edge of the continental shelf, 70 miles south of Nantucket Island on April 16, 1944. It was a day when the Battle of the Atlantic exploded in chaos on America's doorstep.

Maybe sonar operator Garry Kozak, curled on the berth behind the steering station on a short break, is picturing the morning when a torpedo from U-*550* split open the side of the tanker SS *Pan Pennsylvania* on this patch of ocean. Maybe as he snores softly, Kozak's seeing the *Pan Penn* list suddenly 30 degrees to port. Or perhaps he's seeing twenty-five American men from the tanker scrambling into a lifeboat, then seeing the ship capsize.

Maybe divers Steve Gatto and Tom Packer are sharing the same nightmare as they sit side by side on a bench seat, snacking on peanuts and gazing into the sonar monitor on the galley table in front of them. Gatto and Packer have been deep wreck diving buddies for so long, they sometimes feel uncertain where one man's mind leaves off and the other's picks up.

Maybe together they are lost in the moments when depth charges from the destroyer escort USS *Joyce* drive the German sea wolf to the surface. Perhaps they are witnessing the withering attack from three destroyer escorts, hearing the *pock-pock-pock* of 20mm cannons firing as the Americans' shells turn U-*550*'s conning tower into Swiss cheese. Or possibly they are wondering what it must have been like to be one of those German boys who abandoned his sub for the water as the U-boat was sinking. The Americans rescued only thirteen men. That water's so cold. Nobody knows better than divers such as Gatto and Packer how frigid and unforgiving the North Atlantic can be. They've witnessed too many men die in these waters for real, not just in a nightmare hijacked from 1944.

Joe Mazraani hears a groan. It's Pirate, his Portuguese water dog sleeping at his feet. Mazraani shivers a little. But it's not Pirate's groan or the chill of the night air that rattles him. It's this place and its phantoms. If you ask him, he'd tell you that you don't want to ever come to a watery graveyard like this without a serious band of brothers. You don't want to be hunting for a lost U-boat far at sea with bad weather coming without the best of shipmates. You sure as hell don't want to be thinking of diving 300 feet down in black waters unless you have someone you really trust to watch your back.

Ashore he works as a criminal defense attorney in New Jersey, but out here he's the captain of *Tenacious*. Like all of his shipmates tonight, he's not *just* a man starting to face off with ghosts. He's a man on a mission. They all are.

This trip marks their second summer of active searching, and the pressure's building. While Mazraani's team has been hunting for *U-550* in absolute secrecy, another team, led by a respected New England wreck diver, has been publicizing its own search for the *550* with YouTube videos. A recent one shows the New England team laying a wreath on the water over the wreck of the tanker blown apart by the U-boat. And rumor has it that yet another team is also trying to mount a search for *U-550*. Bottom line: if the *Tenacious* divers don't find the *550* on this trip, someone else will probably beat them to the long-lost submarine.

Not even treasure is more compelling to these divers than being the first humans on a wreck. And treasure, of a sort, is definitely important to wreck divers. They bring back artifacts all the time, spend tens of thousands of dollars to restore them and display them at their homes and at museums and dive shows. If this wreck were a commercial ship like the liner *Andrea Doria*, salvaging artifacts from the wreck would be fair game. The U-550 discovery divers have plates, glasses, silverware, and bronze nautical hardware from dives on the *Doria*. Wreck divers see their artifact collections as preserving history, and at times they share their collections with museums. Tom Packer was one of the divers who helped to salvage a bell off the *Doria* back in 1985. Gatto has a helm, a steering wheel, from the liner. He, Packer, and diver John Moyer have filed legal papers in court, which makes them Salvors in Possession of the wreck.

But divers cannot own a warship such as U-*550*. Maritime law unequivocally states that the wreck of a warship forever belongs to the country it served. It's a way of honoring and preserving war graves. The divers aboard *Tenacious* respect that. Instead of harvesting artifacts from the sub, they want to find *550* to get as close as they can to a moment when the Battle of the Atlantic flared right off US shores.

U-*550* is the last unfound German U-boat known to have sunk in diveable waters off America's East Coast. For divers Eric Takakjian and Brad Sheard, the hunt to unravel the mysteries of this submarine goes back twenty years. For others, such as Gatto and Packer, men in their fifties, this dive expedition is another chance to bond with some of the few men who really understand them. They are divers whose names rise from the pages of *Shadow Divers* as some of the most seasoned deep wreck divers in the Northeast.

All of these guys feel the lure of unearthing history. They crave the opportunity to bear witness to the buried time capsule that is a previously undiscovered wreck. They seek the challenge of the search above and below the water, the planning for both the hunt and the deep, dangerous dive. They love the anticipation of a long and sometimes rough boat ride, crossing the water to the middle of nowhere. They thrill to the interface with sea creatures such as lobsters, immense codfish, sea turtles, rays, dolphins, whales, and white sharks. They relish plunging to places few humans see and fewer return from. Finally, they cherish the chance to resurface in the world of the living again with an artifact such as a bell or a porthole that says, "I have been to the underworld, the land of the dead. I have come back to tell you all." Strong drugs.

And, while Packer rarely puts his motives into words, he's here to watch out for his dive buddies, especially the totally pumped younger men whose enthusiasm for their sport can drive them to take terrible risks. Packer knows how easy it is to get lost inside a wreck or trapped by debris. Diving gear has gotten so much better since he, Gatto, Sheard, and Takakjian started diving more than three decades ago, but equipment is never fail-safe. And when you are going as deep as 300 feet, you probably can't make it to the surface and live if you run short of air down there. Every man on *Tenacious* has his own personal collection of almost-died stories. All of them have known men who have died diving wrecks. Several of them have led the way to recover dead divers from the dark corridors of a shadowy ghost ship.

But for thirty-four-year-old Mazraani, and the even younger Tedeschi, danger beckons. Finding and diving the *U-550* is the ultimate adventure, one seductive enough to prompt Mazraani to buy his own dive boat to chase the dream. It's a fantasy so alluring that the young attorney has hired Kozak to use his high-tech sonar "fish" to scan the inky water for a lost phantom.

And right now it looks like Kozak's fish has a problem.

"What the hell?" Packer's voice brings Mazraani back to the present.

"Huh?"

"The monitor just freaking froze," says Gatto.

Somebody wakes Kozak.

"Hold your course," he says groggily, "until I can fix this thing."

For the past fifteen hours the expedition team aboard *Tenacious* has been towing their sonar fish, a 6-foot-long, torpedo-shaped echo sounder on a wire, 440 yards behind the boat, 250 feet below the surface of the Atlantic. The dive boat has been steaming back and forth across an 84-square-mile grid where the divers think *U-550* lies.

This kind of searching is what deep-sea hunters call "mowing the lawn." It's mind-numbingly boring, and yet it demands total attention to every little detail observed by the sonar fish if you want any hope of finding your needle in the haystack. In this case the needle is the wreck of a U-boat sent by Hitler to prey on American merchant shipping sixty-eight years ago. A predator sunk by coast guard and navy sailors. The alleged grave of more than forty men.

"You want me to turn around for the next pass to the east?" asks Mazraani.

"No. Just keep going," says Kozak. *Tenacious* moves beyond the perimeter of the search grid.

Mazraani nods, reminds himself to focus, stick with the program.

It's only a minute or so before the sonar monitor's online again. Mazraani's thinking about turning his boat back to the search grid when one of the guys at the monitor says, "Holy shit. We're going over something."

Instinctively, Mazraani hits the key on the laptop that is his GPS chart plotter to mark the position.

Gatto, Packer, and Kozak are watching a strange bottom anomaly coming into view on the side scan, a mysterious blip. It looks too large to be a submarine, but who knows?

"This could be big," someone's voice cracks. "Wake the others."

It's 2245 hours, July 22, 2012, and maybe these deep wreck hunters have just found their holy grail. But nobody's going down there to see. Not now. Even on the sonar monitor the ocean looks dark as all hell.

PART ONE

A Collision Course

1

Going to War

Ground Zero for U-*550* lies in a barren patch of the Atlantic 70 miles south of Nantucket Island, Massachusetts, but the trail to the death, the mystery, and the glory begins in Kiel, Germany, on February 6, 1944. On this day U-*550* sorties for its first and last patrol from one of the Third Reich's primary U-boat bases, a complex on the southern side of the Baltic Sea.

Bone-chilling, gray. That's the morning of February 6, 1944, in Kiel. The temperature hovers at the freezing mark with a mix of rain showers and light snow in the air. The wind comes light from the southwest. There's about three miles of visibility. Mist freezes to a glaze on the steel rim of the conning tower as Kapitänleutnant Klaus Hänert, the captain of U-*550*, orders his deck crew to loose its lines from the long Tirpitz Pier. Then he gives a command from his perch on the conning tower down the voice pipe to the control room beneath. The submarine's quiet electric motors begin to spin the props tucked deep beneath the stern bustle. The U-boat leaves silently. Stealth is a matter of course in the Ubootwaffe.

Once the boat slips away from the pier and into the shipping channel, Hänert gives orders and the twin MAN supercharged, nine-cylinder diesel engines begin to growl. As the props take a harder bite of the water, a deep vibration starts to shudder through the hull. Hänert must feel the excitement, pride, and dread of taking this new U-boat and his first command on a long and dangerous patrol. It will surely include combat. The captain has been shaking down his boat and training his young and inexperienced crew with the Fourth Flotilla in the Baltic. But now U-boat command has assigned *550* to the Tenth Flotilla at Lorient in occupied France. It's a base it will never see.

Unlike many of the smaller Type VII attack U-boats at Kiel, which are housed in two massive bombproof shelters called Konrad and Kilian, U-*550*, a Type IXC/40 long-distance cruiser, has spent most of its short life, when not at sea, either on a mooring or tied alongside the Tirpitz Pier with other Type IXs preparing for, or returning from, patrols. Hänert is more than a little relieved to get his vessel out of this vulnerable position. In recent months, Allied bombers have pummeled this small city. On January 4 and 5 the Allies hit Kiel with bombs from nearly seven hundred planes. Neighborhood after neighborhood have collapsed into rubble.

At last, U-*550* has broken free of the dock where it has been provisioning for a week, escaping the horror of the bombings. The mission begins. Maybe the weather's harsh, but this leave-taking marks a glorious moment for a U-boat crew. With this overcast, there will be no Allied air raid today. On the pier a band is playing a romantic German folk song called "Muss i' den . . ." The song comes from the Rems Valley, in southwestern Germany. Navy bands always strike up this tune as a send-off for warships leaving on long patrols.

Gray-uniformed soldiers of the Wehrmacht stand at attention in formation along the quay, saluting the departing submarine with the classic *Heil Hitler* and the extension of their right arms. Most of the fifty-six men in the crew of the *550* are lined up on the deck, fore and aft of the conning tower, standing at parade rest, with their hands behind their backs.

Despite the cold, they are not dressed in their winter, leather deck gear, the *U-Boot Päckchen*, or their thick, checkered scarves. The crew, including Hänert, wear their dark blue uniforms. They look smart as a petty officer calls them to attention. Then they salute navy-style—right hand to the brow. Ashore, the red, black, and white swastika flag of the Third Reich waves from a pole above the base commander and his attachés.

It's easy to imagine Hänert feeling a pang of nostalgia in his stomach as the commander and his minions return the salute. During the earlier years of the war, the "happy time" when German submarines ruled the seas, Konteradmiral Karl Dönitz was the father of the Ubootwaffe and commander of the submarines, the *Befehlshaber der Unterseeboote* (otherwise known as *BdU*). He often made it a point to stand by and salute departing boats. No more. For about a year now, Dönitz has been the commander in chief of the entire navy. The U-boat service no longer feels like an elite fraternity of independent hunters who eschewed political ties to the Nazi Party. Now, the Ubootwaffe has more than four hundred new submarines and twenty thousand new men. Many, even some of the officers, are barely twenty years old. And so few of them are coming back. U-boot Command doesn't broadcast its losses, but the submariners have their suspicions. Only one out of four or five boats is making it home these days.

Back in 1942, when Hänert sortied on the first of two cruises as a watch officer aboard U-*68* with the ace skipper Karl Friedrich Merten, the U-boat service had been a tight group of seafaring titans. Hänert felt invigorated, alive, and accomplished during a fifty-eight-day patrol into the Caribbean. Merten and Hänert sank seven ships, a loss of over 50,000 gross tons for the Allies, and the young Hänert snapped photos of the dying ships for his scrapbook. On his second patrol in U-*68* to the South Atlantic and Cape Town, the sub sank nine ships, more than 56,000 gross tons.

The *550*'s captain has the self-confidence of an officer who has served as adjutant of the head of the navy Grossadmiral Eric Raeder as well as a leader who has learned the ways of submarine warfare from the best of the best. But today, as he orders a course change down the voice pipe to bring U-*550* into formation behind a mine-clearing *Sperrbrecher*, and between two smaller attack subs also leaving on patrol, nothing is certain.

Who could blame this handsome, blue-eyed officer with the light brown hair if he has fears? As the U-boat passes the 236-foot-tall tower of the Laboe Naval Memorial off to starboard, the recently completed tower might well touch off strong feelings in Klaus Hänert and his crew. It stands as stark testimony to thousands upon thousands of German naval mariners who have left this port never to return home. In just the past seven months more than 160 U-boats have vanished beneath the waves. The day will come when a memorial at the base of this tower will stand in tribute to over twenty-eight thousand men lost in U-boats during World War II. Great Britain and the United States have been outbuilding Germany in warships for two years. Allied antisubmarine detection systems (ASW) in both ships and aircraft have vastly improved. And from what Hänert has heard in his pre-patrol briefings, British, Canadian, and US antisubmarine aircraft have nearly the entire North Atlantic covered, as if the ocean alone were not hostile enough in February. In addition to his enemy, Hänert's facing a minefield of massive storms and 30-foot seas that can dwarf a U-boat 252 feet long.

But orders are orders. In the past year German forces have suffered terrible losses in Stalingrad, North Africa, and Italy. The general public in Germany, not just the high command, has come to expect a major Allied invasion against the Third Reich in France or Norway this coming spring or summer. The fatherland's losing the war. Still, Dönitz has been telling the Führer that a few bold, well-placed strikes by U-boats, particularly on the shores of America, could turn the tide of combat in Deutschland's favor again. U-boats such as the *550*, under the command of battle-tested skippers and operating as lone wolves, might buy Germany time to bring new superweapons online such as a jet fighter, an astonishingly fast and stealthy Type XXI submarine, long-range rockets, and an atomic bomb. So, as the crews of the U-boats say, "*Westwärts.*" Westward ho.

Still, at a moment like this departure, U-*550*'s commander must think about the family he left back home in Flensburg, near the border with Denmark. His mother and father and sister have suffered so much. They have already lost his two younger brothers, *Wehrmacht* soldiers, in the war. Now he must wonder if his family will ever see him again. Quite possibly the man at his side, the twenty-five-year-old ship's doctor, Friedrich Torge, is having the same dark thoughts. What about the officer on the other end of the voice pipe, the submarine's engineering officer, Hugo Renzmann? The young machinist Johann Rauh standing so proudly on the foredeck? And wardroom steward Albert Nitsche, who is also the gunner on the boat's 37mm cannon? What about all of these boys who try so hard to act like men?

Is their last dive coming sooner than any of them can imagine? Such wretched thoughts for a U-boat commander going to war. Such dark worries for a man who has celebrated his twenty-sixth birthday only five days ago.

2

First Blood

February 22, 1944

"Alaaaarm." First officer Gutram von Lingelsheim-Seibicke has the watch. He's shouting from the observation deck atop the conning tower, shouting down the voice pipe. "Alaaaarm." The same word in Deutsch and English calls men to fight or flee.

It's a clear arctic afternoon, 100 miles south of Iceland. The sun hangs low on the horizon. U-*550*'s steaming west at full speed, about 17 knots . . . and it's under attack. A bell, one of those high-pitched, incessant, electric janglings, rings through the boat. It doesn't stop. It's machinist Johann Rauh's first sign that he's going into combat, maybe looking death in the face at age seventeen. But there's no time to dive and hide. The lookouts have spotted an aircraft. They hear the heavy rasping of its engines even before they see it diving toward the sub, coming at them out of the blazing sun.

Under the clatter of the MAN diesels and the endless clamor of the alarm bell, sailors curse the captain's choice to run on the surface in broad daylight, *Tageslicht*. Standing orders from BdU call for U-boats to submerge during daylight hours, but such a thing is not practical for a boat with orders to proceed across the vast North Atlantic with all due haste.

The *550*'s crew calls Klaus Hänert the Old Man or *Herr Kaleun*, short for *Kapitänleutnant*. Today the Old Man has chosen to take his chances by running on the surface in Tageslicht. The sibilant sound of this sunny word is possibly the first hint in two weeks to remind Johann Rauh to even consider any difference between day and night. The young machinist has not been on deck since his boat's brief stop at the U-boat base in Kristiansand, Norway, on February 9–10 for provisions and fuel. Rauh has become a boy trapped in a fetid, damp cocoon—a pipe where the only light is a brownish haze emanating from a few caged ceiling bulbs or hanging lamps. The air reeks of fuel oil, sausage grease, unwashed armpits, and human waste, *Scheisse*. How he wishes he were home in Munich with his father the brewery worker, sister, stepmother, and two stepsisters.

Only 3 miles away and closing, the attacker seems to be a big, twin-engine vulture to the men on the conning tower of *550*. Just a silhouette. High-winged. With a fuselage that looks like a boat. It's what the Americans call a PBY Catalina, built by Consolidated Aircraft of San Diego, California. The Canadians call it a Canso and build these planes in Vancouver and Montreal. Cruising at only about 100 knots, it's one of the slowest aircraft in any air force. But it can stay aloft for twenty-four hours, has a range of 2,500 miles. And it's a proven sub killer. It packs state-of-the-art radar, sonar, and magnetic detection gear for spotting enemy submarines. A crew of eight-man .30- and .50-caliber machine guns in the nose and side turret blisters. Under the wings hang four 250-pound depth charges for blowing the foe to kingdom come.

On the U-boat men shout, urging Albert Nitsche and the rest of the gun crew into action. To Nitsche, so recently a young naval recruit from the Sudetenland, on the Czech border, it seems only seconds before the sub's pressure hull and the armor shield on his 37mm echo with the rattling of the aircraft's shells tearing at the U-boat. His ears pound from the rumble of the twin 20mm guns firing just behind him on the "cigarette deck" wings of the tower. His single 37mm pounds away at the attacking Canso from the after extension of the tower deck known as the *Wintergarten*.

The first officer orders a sharp turn to starboard right toward the plane. It's a great defensive move, minimizing the submarine to a slender target. The Canso can't correct quickly enough for the submarine's swift change of course and veers away as Nitsche and the other gunners on U-*550* begin to pepper the air with ordnance.

But Flying Officer C. C. Cunningham, piloting Royal Canadian Air Force 9841, aircraft "S," of Bomber Reconnaissance Squadron 162, has no intention of letting this U-boat escape. Long based in Nova Scotia, the squadron has seen little action until moving to its new base at Reykjavik, Iceland, just a few months ago. From Iceland, the amphibious Cansos are in an excellent position to intercept U-boat traffic intent on hunting convoys off the North American coast, and today Cunningham has a "live one." Before the war ends his squadron will claim five U-boat kills, the most of any RCAF unit.

The pilot wheels his Canso into a steep turn and lines up for another attack out of the sun. The plane dives to just 50 feet off the waves, gaining speed as it takes aim on the submarine's port beam. Nitsche's fully engaged now. The flash of tracer bullets zips all around the Canso. But then his gun jams after firing just 50 rounds. He watches in horror as the Canso roars toward him. The engines sound like a swarm of wasps. The first officer is barking down the voice pipe for the engineer to crash dive the sub, barking to Nitsche and the other men on deck to secure their weapons and get below. Already Rauh and the rest of the U-boat crew are sprinting forward through the vessel toward the bow of the submarine, launching themselves through low and narrow doorways in the watertight bulkheads as they aim to shift the crew's weight into the bow and help the sub submerge more quickly.

Type IX U-boats take about 35 seconds to dive below the surface, but that's not fast enough to escape the Canso. The deck crew has not yet dropped down the tower hatch when the Royal Canadians release four depth charges, bracketing the sub to port and starboard. The explosions of the shallow-detonating charges kill one of the gunners outright, blow a second off into the sea, and wound a third. Albert Nitsche grips the ladder below in the tower, gasps for breath, and remembers that today is his birthday. He's twenty. Eighteen-year-old Eberhard-Josef Bensberg and twenty-year-old Heinrich Kluge are dead. Kapitänleutnant Klaus Hänert has his own men's blood on his hands. What a miserable feeling.

As U-*550* heads down, the hull groans from the depth. The needle on the *Tiefenmesser*, the depth gauge, passes 160 meters, 170, 180. The sub must get out of reach of new Allied depth charges that can be set to detonate as deep as 200 meters. All of his life Johann Rauh will remember this day, tell his son the story fifty years later. Who could forget the moaning of the pressure hull? The chill? The terrible hollowness in the guts? The tightening of the air in the chest? The shallow breathing of shipmates? One of the dead is a boy beloved for playing his guitar, treasured among the crew for the music he has brought them. They liked to gather around him and sing.

Now the singer's gone. In the blink of an eye. Nothing's left but an old guitar stashed behind a spare torpedo. And the boat is diving deep to lick its wounds. It seems like the Old Man wants to take the sub and himself to the limit. Even if the *550* emerges again from the depths, there will be no more singing on this boat. Johann Rauh knows that.

But what neither he, his captain, nor U-boat Command know is that by the spring of 1943 Britain has broken the Enigma code, nicknamed "shark," that the submarines use to communicate with BdU. British and American intelligence units are now tracking every U-boat in the North Atlantic and passing on the information to Canadian counterparts. The *550*'s patrol is a known entity. It is not just bad luck that has brought the Canso down on the sub's head and is driving it toward the bottom of a very deep ocean. Its enemies are on the alert, hunting the gray wolves. Hunting the hunters.

3

Mission to America

March 17, 1944

A screech erupts from the submarine's public address system. It has been broadcasting American swing songs such as the Glenn Miller Orchestra's "In the Mood." Almost everybody on watch feels his skin prickle with the shrill and piercing sound. In the so-called House of Lords, the forward torpedo room, men groan in their berths and cover their ears with their dirty blue and white gingham pillows.

The Old Man has ordered the engineer to advance his engines to *grosse Fahrt*, full ahead, and the sudden surge into steep North Atlantic seas has caused the needle on the phonograph in the radio room to skid off the disk. For the first time in two weeks the sub is seriously under way again, and it feels as if it may have a real mission at last. Running like this in rough weather, there can be no more phonograph music. The needle won't stay in the record grooves. From here on out, the speakers of the boat's public address system will be offering up folksy or heroic music by the likes of the Potsdam Garrison Chapel carillon from Radio Berlin, broadcasting to *550*'s Telefunken receiver over a low-frequency band.

After about two weeks of weather reporting duties at 53 degrees north, 40 degrees west, U-*550* has new orders at last. No matter what the orders say, they bring an escape from this purgatory. Since relieving U-*802* two weeks ago, Hänert's boat has been stuck about 600 miles south of Greenland, catering to the needs of the Führer's growing fears of a massive Allied attack against German forces on their Western Front. It may come as soon as the spring. Since the beginning of 1944, BdU has been dispatching its U-boats to maintain a network of weather reporters across the North Atlantic as a means of forecasting when the Allies might have good meteorological conditions for an invasion. During the first five months of 1944, twenty-nine U-boats have been given weather reporting assignments as their primary duty, placing them out of the mix for both offensive and defensive actions.

Two or three times a day, the *550*'s crew has recorded wind, sea, and cloud information as well as temperature and barometric pressure. But the information has seemed far from accurate, especially since the barometer used on deck has never agreed with the other two inside the U-boat. Nevertheless, the *Funker*, radioman, has sent his weather report back to BdU during the middle of every night.

What miserable duty, trying to hold the submarine in position against constantly buffeting seas. In his memoir *Escort*, Denys Arthur Rayner, who served in the British convoy escort service, writes that the winter of 1944 had "quite stupendous seas" and was the "worst of the whole war." Winter storms are scattering convoys, sending escorts running for home with storm damage and, to Rayner's trained eye, rendering U-boat operations virtually out of the question.

He doesn't know the resolve of Klaus Hänert and his crew. Despite the arctic temperatures and storms, they keep soldiering on in their little boat. U-*550*, a Type IXC/40 long-distance cruiser, is known to its crew as a *Seekuh*, a sea cow. Its keel was laid down at the Deutsche Werft shipyard in Hamburg as Werk *371* on October 2, 1942. Launched eight months later, it is 252 feet long, nearly 23 feet abeam. It displaces 1,100 long tons and has a range of over 11,000 nautical miles.

After World War II, a number of *550*'s sisters will surrender to American forces and will be thoroughly evaluated at the US Navy submarine shipyard in Portsmouth, New Hampshire. Given the high level of fear and mythology surrounding the sleek and mysterious U-boats, it's surprising that the US evaluators will give the Type IXC rather mediocre marks as a weapon of war.

True, the pressure hull in the Type IX will prove in combat that it can return from dives of as much as 900 feet, exceeding its predicted crush depth. But while Type IXs can descend a bit deeper than American submarines of the same era, American inspectors will write in their evaluation for the Department of the Navy: "The hull is conservatively designed, and is believed to offer nothing currently constructive. While certain aspects are novel, it is believed that they are heavy and expensive solutions to the particular design problem."

The inspectors will also notice that quite a few of the details in the construction of the submarine had been hastily done or accomplished by less than expert shipyard workers. This, of course, makes sense because by the time *550* is under construction, late 1942/spring 1943, Germany has already begun to feel as if it's running short of time, basic resources such as tin, and skilled labor to prosecute the war.

Even though the Ubootwaffe has equipped *550* with a few state-of-the-art T5 acoustic torpedoes for use against attacking destroyers as well as the offensive T3 torpedoes, it is already obsolete for fighting a modern deep-ocean war. Its design derives from a U-boat called the Type 1A, which was conceived in the early 1930s for long-distance cruising.

Only the newest U-boats, the Types XXI and XXIII, which are not yet available to the fleet in the winter/spring of 1944, can run for long periods beneath the surface. U-boats of the older Type VII and Type IX designs, like the *550*, can only run submerged on their electric motors for a few hours before their battery power gives out, and they can only move forward underwater at speeds of less than 7 knots, a terrible disadvantage against destroyer escorts and sub chasers that can steam at more than 20 knots.

To call the *550* and its sisters *Unterseeboote* or "submarines" is a bit of a misnomer. They spend more than 85 percent of their time traveling on the surface. Often they even attack on the surface. Diving is usually only for moments dictated by the need for stealth or by extreme fear. Not a good situation when the air is full of what the U-boatmen call "bees," antisubmarine, hunter-killer aircraft.

A careful look at U-boats such as the *550* and its sister Type IXs and Type VIIs suggests that the mythology surrounding the U-boat service owes more to the endurance, stoicism, persistence, dedication, bravery, and fraternity of the crews than to technical advantages in the vessels themselves. These men constitute a special breed. Where they go one, they go all. Like deep-wreck divers, they hold their emotional breath, push their fears to the back of their minds, and count on their brothers to carry them into the unknown and back safely.

So it is aboard U-*550* at the moment when the Old Man's voice echoes from the public address system. *"Achtung."* Attention. Hänert tells his men that the boat has received orders from BdU. U-*550* is to start heading south. Destination, New York City. They will be hunting for the biggest, fattest targets of opportunity they can find departing the refineries on the New Jersey side of New York Harbor. They aim to cover the beaches of Long Island with oil spilled from Franklin Roosevelt's tanker fleet. They will make America fear the U-boat once again.

There is no shouting or cheering among the crew. Just a sense of steely determination and private fears. Except for the rumble of the diesels and the crashing of waves over the rolling deck, U-*550* rings with silence and purpose. These submariners can only wonder about what shadowy events the Fates are weaving for them. All that the crewmen of *550* know is that quitting is not an option.

4

New York Night

April 9, 1944

After two weeks of ducking and hiding from the bees, U-*550* arrives at a quadrant on chart 1970G, North Atlantic Ocean, marked "CA." U-boat Command has divided the chart into squares with 486 nautical miles per side. "CA" embraces the coastline of New England, New York, and New Jersey. Tonight, on the bridge, Klaus Hänert shows his first officer the glow in the sky over Long Island and New York City. They can't believe that the Americans are so cavalier that they have only blacked out the lights of houses and businesses along the shore, not the whole metropolis.

Two years ago U-boats first came hunting along the American coast during the "happy days" when they sank more than a hundred ships in six months. Many German submarine crews had only chart 1970G and travel brochures of New York to steer by. No detailed charts. But since those days U-boot aces such as Reinhard Hardegen have mapped the area for U-boats patrolling in his wake. Hänert and his navigator know the location of key landmarks on the shipping lanes, such as the Nantucket Lightship area and the Ambrose Light buoy at the entrance to New York Harbor. They know the shoals and minefields that await them off the entrance to New York, Cape May, and Norfolk. And they know underwater coves and canyons on the edge of the continental shelf where a U-boat might run and hide.

After two months of winter storm upon winter storm, April offers up a few precious promises of spring, brief moments of calm seas. A day when the sky is as blue as the Danube River. A day when flocks of seabirds wheel over great, silvery schools of bait fish. A day pregnant with the return of whales like the clownish humpbacks. A day followed by this starlit night watch when the air is mild, the sea is glass. The Germans can actually smell the potato fields of Long Island and the clam beds in Great South Bay. It's a night when it is good to hear the siren song of America's Billie Holiday's "God Bless the Child" playing in the back of one's head, good to feel that husky voice lifting you away from the obligations, fears, and the squalor that lie in the boat beneath your feet.

U-boat sailors sometimes disparage their boats as "iron coffins," especially since the survival rate of U-boats on combat patrols has dipped to 20 percent during the winter and early spring of 1944. Not only is it dangerous to sail into combat aboard an Unterseeboot, but also life is a constant challenge in a hundred irritating ways. Working, eating, and sleeping with more than fifty other men for months at a time in a metal tube that is only 15.5 feet across at the widest, a tube with only two toilets, is no picnic. Here at 41 degrees north, 72 degrees west, the inside of the hull sweats and drips with condensation. When the sea temperature is as cold as it is this April, about 40 degrees Fahrenheit, the air in the submarine is about as cool as the seawater, except in the engine room and within about 6 feet of a few space heaters.

The crew wears all manner of clothing to keep warm, including sweaters knitted by their grandmothers. Some sleep with gloves or mittens. Most of the seamen wear a blue, woolen hat called a *Schiffchen* day in and day out. The Old Man wears his *Schumütze*, the peaked officers' cap. Like all U-boat captains at sea, he wears the white tropical cover as a symbol of his service, but it must seem something of a joke to Klaus Hänert in the frigid weather of the past two months. Almost all the men are growing beards because there is no fresh water for shaving or bathing. The desalinating plant aboard makes only 63 gallons of water a day, which is used for cooking and keeping 60 tons of batteries topped off. At this point everyone's skin has turned a ghostly pale. It itches constantly, and every time a sailor rolls out of a berth to go on watch, his epidermis presents him with a new mosaic of rashes, pimples, and boils.

Tonight, on top of all of these little miseries, BdU has sent the men of the *550* something quite a bit scarier, a mission right into the heart of the enemy's homeland defenses. Before he shares the Funker's recently decoded message from U-boat Command with his first officer, Hänert may think about the otherworldliness of the place where this message began. It might as well have come from a cave on Mount Olympus; the senders may as well be gods. They live and work in a secret U-boat command center called Lager Koralle, in the rural outskirts of Berlin.

Originally intended as a naval intelligence school in 1939, the Lager Koralle is a bunker buried under the forest north of Bernau, Germany. Fearing Allied bombing attacks on Berlin, Admiral Dönitz and the leadership of the German Navy, Oberkommandos der Kriegsmarine or OKM, moved their headquarters here in early 1943. Shortly thereafter, the principal radio station for the Ubootwaffe began operating from a warren of connected underground bunkers 25 feet below the surface, hidden beneath a few conventional buildings that functioned as barracks and an officers' mess. Soviet occupation forces and the East German military will use the bunkers after the war until the Lager Koralle is abandoned following German reunification. Even in ruins, the Lager Koralle will seem a weirdly aloof and threatening place. A maze of tunnels, mysterious electrical equipment, bombproof steel doors, and signs warning, *BETRETEN VERBOTEN*, trespassing forbidden. An underworld command center for a legion of undersea warriors. Such a place oozes not just secrecy, but also a titanic malevolence.

Especially on this night in April. On watch off the coast of New York, Hänert shares the new orders with his first officer. The U-boat captain may well feel a subtle stabbing in the belly and possibly fears that he and his boat are pawns in a game played by shadowy forces. BdU, the gods in the forest bunker, want 550 to proceed inshore of the 100-fathom line, to cross onto the waters of the American continental shelf and close with the coast. The sub has orders to patrol the eastbound shipping lanes departing from New York. When a convoy comes, the U-boat must use its torpedoes and guns to wreak havoc on the Americans. Heil Hitler. Happy hunting and *viel Glück*. Good bloody luck.

The coming days may be the worst yet for the crew of U-*550*. After the last two months at sea, the men have just about reached their limit. Even though no one talks about it, the death of the guitarist still haunts them. The endless, incandescent light in the pipe has brought a hollow glaze to the men's eyes. Conversation these days on the boat—always a place where quiet is prized and idle chatter only tolerated in the House of Lords—is all but a lost art. Something must be done to buoy these young men's sagging spirits before they go into combat . . . because that moment is surely coming.

So it is that the captain of a U-boat, contemplating the battle ahead, has been known to order the cook to distribute a round of schnapps for the boys as their leader announces the orders. Or on a rare spring night like this off New York, he might bend to the voice pipe and tell his engineer, "Open all the hatches. Ventilate the boat. And let the men in groups of six come on deck to the Wintergarten to share the peace of God's natural world for a while."

Only after they all have inhaled their fill of this starry night will he tell them to prepare the boat and themselves to engage the enemy, that somewhere not so far ahead lie deeply laden American tankers that must not reach Britain. He will not say that stopping one of those tankers may well bring on the fight of their lives.

5

Tanker

1600 Hours, April 15, 1944

The sky clots over New York Harbor. It is late afternoon, but it feels like night. The air looks the color of blurry charcoal in the thick fog. After the predeparture convoy conference briefing, Mort Raphelson, a veteran merchant mariner and radio officer from West Philadelphia, boards the water taxi with his seabag and shoves off for his ship. He's a slender young man with dark hair, a kind face, and a twinkle in his eyes as if he finds life constantly amusing. This convoy will be his third voyage in recent months aboard the tanker SS *Pan Pennsylvania*. By the way the water taxi has begun to jink port and starboard to avoid ships looming up suddenly out of the fog, Raphelson can tell that the poor visibility portends a miserable night to put to sea. He's surprised that in this fog the water taxi is able to deliver him to his ship anchored among a maze of other vessels. In recent months there have been more than five hundred merchant ships at anchor in New York Harbor at one time. But arrive he does, and he's delighted.

This convoy promises to be a great trip for him because his ship is one of the command ships in the convoy, and he has a new commercial radio operator and two navy operators to assist him. He will not have much to do on this trip. The commercial operator, Mark Zeller, is fresh from radio school, and this is his first voyage. He wonders aloud about the danger from U-boats, but Raphelson tells him that things have been quiet. Fear not.

But how can a man with Raphelson's experience not worry? His ship has just loaded the equivalent of 140,000 barrels of 80-octane aviation fuel to deliver to Londonderry, Northern Ireland. He's about to cross the ocean on a floating bomb, a very big bomb. One of the largest American tankers of World War II, the *Pan Penn* is only five months old. It registers 11,016 gross tons, is 515 feet, 11 inches long, and is 70 feet abeam. Two steam turbines drive a single propeller, giving it a top speed of about 20 knots.

Raphelson's ship is the first of five sisters built for the US Maritime Commission. They are a special variation of the T3-type tankers. Designated T3-S-BF1 USMC, all five have been fabricated in Norfolk, Virginia, by Welding Shipyards, Inc., the company-owned shipyard of National Bulk Carriers, Inc. To many observers, the ship looks a bit odd because the poop deck extends about half the length of the ship. The raised poop gives the after tanks more volume but also creates the illusion, when the tanker is fully loaded, that the front half of the ship is submerged. More than one aerial antisubmarine reconnaissance aircraft and surface patrol have mistaken the *Pan Penn*, seen at a distance, as an immense U-boat. Sometimes Raphelson wonders if these mistakes could lead to an attack on his ship by friendly fire.

But such thoughts are far from the front of his mind as he finds his familiar radioman's cabin near the captain's quarters in the midship house at the middle of the *Pan Penn*. It's a bare-bones, steel cabin— nothing glamorous for National Bulk Carriers—but it is a private space close to the radio room and the bridge deck where a man can sleep, read mystery novels, smoke his pipe, and be alone with his thoughts. During the past year, Raphelson has literally sailed around the world and crossed the North Atlantic eight times. He's feeling a little bit like a man of the world these days. Tonight he's sailing with a collection of pipes purchased at his different ports of call, from England and Panama to Australia, the Persian Gulf, and Brazil.

So it is that before he turns in for some shut-eye, Raphelson takes his evening pipe of Edgeworth tobacco. As a boy, he dreamed of going to sea, and now he is. In 1940 Raphelson took a written examination with the hope of getting an appointment to the newly formed Merchant Marine Academy where he would graduate as a deck officer. He passed the exam, but his parents would not give him permission to attend.

But now circumstances have changed. With the war going on, Raphelson's parents have become more agreeable to his joining the war effort. In 1942 the government began making a big push to train civilians for all types of war-related jobs. One of the programs taught young people the fundamentals of radio theory and operation. Raphelson quit his job as a clerk in an insurance company and enrolled.

His teacher told him about the US Maritime Service Radio Training Station on Gallops Island in Boston Harbor. It was an eighteen-month program that trained the students in radio techniques with the goal of getting a radio telegraph license to become an officer on board an American merchant ship. To get more radio operators on board the ships, the government cut Raphelson's course to eight months. The merchant service was in dire need of trained radio officers. In 1942 German submarines were sinking American ships and killing crews faster than the United States could replace them.

But on the night of April 15, 1944, Raphelson isn't worrying much about U-boats, despite having heard at the convoy conference that the US Navy's Eastern Sea Frontier (ESF) submarine trackers detected a U-boat's radio transmission off the coast of New York and New Jersey on both April 14 and 15. The sub trackers tending the wall chart at ESF's Joint Operations Control headquarters have dubbed the

U-boat "Red George" and placed it "within 600 miles of Cape May [New Jersey]." Still, in the past four Atlantic crossings Raphelson's convoys have not been bothered, and he has the utmost confidence in this ship and his captain.

"The captain of the ship was named Delmar Leidy," Raphelson will recollect sixty-eight years later. "He was the nicest skipper I had on any ship. Another good feature was that the ship traveled as part of a high-speed convoy. This convoy moved at close to 15 knots, which means that the trip across the North Atlantic to England would take about seven days. Because of the speed, the U-boats could not catch up to us and this meant a safer trip."

That's the theory. But it doesn't account for the initiative of Klaus Hänert and the crew of U-550.

There are moments when Raphelson's alone with his pipe that some of his natural buoyancy vanishes and he pictures a large dark shape like a shark tracking the *Pan Penn*. Sometimes he thinks about his voyage on a tanker called *Sinclair Opaline*. The trip marked his first convoy across the North Atlantic, and he felt scared the whole way. The slow convoy designated HX228, with *Sinclair Opaline*, left New York on February 28, 1943, as the second of four convoys totaling more than two hundred merchant ships and military escorts.

German intelligence had broken British codes and knew the locations of the convoys. BdU ordered three wolf packs of thirty-eight U-boats to lay in wait for these convoys in an area known as the air gap, a patch of ocean southeast of Greenland not protected by shore-based antisubmarine aircraft until later in 1943. Beset by severe gales for more than a week, the convoys had their first brush with the U-boats on March 6–7. The attacks persisted until March 19. When the U-boats withdrew, the Allies had lost thirty-three ships and about five hundred men. Three U-boats made their final dives.

German propaganda called this sprawling battle the "greatest convoy battle" of World War II, and Mort Raphelson saw the whole thing go down. On the night of March 11, the freighter *William C.*

Gorgas was leading the thirteenth column of HX228, sailing immediately to the starboard of Raphelson on the *Sinclair Opaline* in rough seas. At 0242 hours the *Gorgas* took a torpedo from U-557. The survivors abandoned ship. The sub fired another torpedo two hours later, which detonated the explosives stored in the number-one hold and shattered the night sky. The British destroyer HMS *Harvester* picked up about fifty of the *Gorgas*'s crew, but only twelve survived after the *Harvester* took a torpedo from another U-boat.

Raphelson saw ships exploding all around him. But a man has to put such dark memories aside, especially before he goes to sea again. And on the evening of Saturday night, April 15, 1944, the hour has come for the radio officer to free his mind of ghosts and curl up beneath the blankets to get some sleep while a fellow can. The *Pan Penn* will sail at some point later this evening with nine officers, forty-one crewmen, and thirty-one naval armed guards to man the deck guns.

The fog and the dark are going to raise hell for all the ships in the convoy as they try to negotiate the swept channel through the minefields protecting New York Harbor. God help them as they try to form up into columns while heading east along the southern coast of Long Island. Even though the *Pan Penn* will be observing radio silence, Raphelson expects to be busy when he takes the morning watch, 0400 to 0800 hours, in the radio shack. He knows that on black and foggy nights offshore, anything can happen.

6

Escort Duty

1900 Hours, April 15, 1944

As the fog thickens and the evening turns pitch dark, the six destroyer escorts of Task Group 21.5 assigned to shepherd CU-*21* to Londonderry cast off their lines from various wharves and piers in New York Harbor. The command ship USS *Poole* leaves from Staten Island, while USS *Peterson, Harveson, Kirkpatrick, Gandy,* and *Joyce* get under way from places such as Pier 35 in Manhattan and the Brooklyn Navy Yard. Three escorts proceed to sea through the mineswept channel leading southeast out of the harbor in the vanguard of the merchant ships they aim to protect, while the *Peterson* and the *Joyce* wait in the anchorage area at Sandy Hook, New Jersey, as "tail-end Charlies" until all the ships, including the *Pan Penn*, have headed to sea.

Lieutenant Commander Robert Wilcox, captain of the *Joyce*, paces the open-air flying bridge of his DE a little after midnight. He's thirty years old, with the fine facial features and slick blond hair of a film-star sailor like the actor Kirk Douglas. A native of Portland,

Maine, and Baltimore, he is the son of a coast guard officer who died when Wilcox was in high school. The captain of the *Joyce* grew up hearing stories from his father, Lieutenant Commander George E. Wilcox, about being aboard the USS *Morrill* in Nova Scotia on December 6, 1917, when the infamous Halifax explosion occurred after a French ammunition ship exploded and took two thousand civilians and a big chunk of the town with it.

Such war stories have instilled Wilcox with an almost preternatural alertness. He should be getting some rest before he returns to the bridge to oversee the morning watch, but he can't sleep. He's feeling cautious and on edge as he watches his executive officer and the quartermaster guide their destroyer escort to sea. He can't stop thinking about what he heard at the convoy conference briefing. There's a U-boat that navy trackers are calling Red George hunting out here somewhere.

All the lights on the bridge deck have been turned off or dimmed to improve night vision as the *Joyce* takes to the ocean swells. The lookouts and officers on the flying bridge squint into binoculars and try desperately to keep the shadow of the ship in front of them in sight. The ships in the convoy are using the high-frequency, portable, battery-powered TBS (talk between ships) radio for ship-to-ship communication. Messages from the convoy commodore and escort command on the *Poole*, coming to the *Joyce* over the TBS, dictate that all vessels in CU-*21* head due east, with the merchant ships steaming at fourteen knots. Ships should hold their relative positions in a two-column line tonight after clearing the swept channel. The chances for a collision are far too high to have ships in this pea soup searching for their spots in a half-dozen designated convoy columns of five ships each.

It's another month, another convoy to chaperone to the United Kingdom for Bob Wilcox. And like Mort Raphelson on the *Pan Penn*, Wilcox is wrestling with ghosts. In this case, missing comrades and their missing ship USS *Leopold*. This escort group has had six DEs manned by US Coast Guard crews like the men on the *Joyce* as its contingent. But tonight the navy's USS *Gandy* is replacing the coast guard's USS *Leopold*. Five weeks ago, when Wilcox was just eight days shy of his thirtieth birthday, he witnessed U-*255* sink the *Leopold*. That night he came face-to-face with the brutality of war and excruciating moral choices.

The *Joyce* and the *Leopold* were patrolling on the flanks of the twenty-seven-ship convoy CU-*16* on March 8, 1944. As it approached an area of the North Atlantic that the sailors called "Wolf Pack Alley" or "Torpedo Junction" in stormy weather, Leopold's HF/DF radio detection gear, known as "Huff-Duff," intercepted a radio transmission from a U-boat lurking along the route of the convoy. The convoy changed course as per standard practice. But the next night, March 9, south of Iceland, the *Leopold* reported radar contact south of the convoy. Ordered to back up the *Leopold*, Bob Wilcox on the *Joyce* changed course to intercept the U-boat and called his crew to general quarters. The *Leopold* launched two flares and caught a glimpse of a submarine submerging. No sooner had the *Leopold* opened fire than U-*255* fired a T5 acoustic torpedo at the DE, catching it with a devastating explosion near the bridge. The crew of the *Leopold* immediately began to abandon ship.

Wilcox's ship closed with the wounded *Leopold*'s port side, where he saw a large hole. He circled to assess how badly it was damaged and discovered that it had a hole in its starboard side as well. The DE appeared in immediate danger of breaking in half. At this point one of the *Joyce*'s lookouts reported sighting the wake of a torpedo in the moonlit sea tracking toward the *Joyce*. Wilcox wheeled his ship to face the torpedo. According to some of the men on the *Joyce*, it barely escaped being hit as Wilcox conned his DE clear of the oncoming torpedo.

Passing the *Leopold*, the *Joyce*'s captain could see its crew signaling him with a flashlight and starting to abandon ship. He hailed them and said, "We are dodging torpedoes. God bless you. We'll be back." He thought that at any moment his ship would become a casualty as well.

All his life the memory of leaving the crew of the *Leopold* to save his own ship will bring Bob Wilcox to tears. By the time the *Joyce* returned and rescued 28 men, all of the Leopold's 13 officers and 158 of its complement of 186 enlisted men had been lost. Some of these were friends of Wilcox and the crew of the *Joyce*. Off duty, between convoys, the men of the escort group had partied together. Little wonder that the captain of the *Joyce* chokes up at the thought of losing two of the *Leopold*'s men just in the midst of rescuing them. At that instant his lookouts reported another torpedo heading for the *Joyce*. Wilcox ordered his ship to flank speed, and the rope holding the *Leopold*'s survivors parted. One of the lost men was the executive officer of the *Leopold*, Lieutenant B. P. "Pete" Cone.

It's a name and face forever stamped in Bob Wilcox's mind. He has learned from his father and the coast guard that coming to the aid of a fellow mariner is a seaman's highest duty. There is no more compelling bond between men than what author Joseph Conrad called the "bond of the sea and the fellowship of the craft." It's an old-school notion in a modern war. But Wilcox never joined the coast guard to fight a war. He joined to save lives. Some nights he doesn't sleep, thinking about Pete Cone and all those other men from the *Leopold* that he could not save.

7

Collision

A tanker's breaking radio silence four minutes early. That's what has the officers on the bridge of USS *Joyce* suddenly in a fuss. CU-*21* is one of the first convoys in which the navy has distributed the portable TBS radios to every vessel for ship-to-ship communication. New toys for the boys. But at the convoy conference the merchant ships were charged not to break radio silence except after dark and only between the top of the hour and 10 minutes after the hour. U-boats might be able to track these transmissions, so communications are to be kept to a minimum.

But now someone from the tanker SS *Sag Harbor* is raising holy hell. He's saying he just hit another ship. It's the kind of news to make Bob Wilcox pound his fist against something and say "Goddamn." The kind of news that makes him want to reach for his pipe and tobacco pouch. He has a certain affinity for Heines Blend tobacco laced with a little amphora for that rich fragrance of oranges, raspberries, and flowers. It calms his nerves, gives him a chance to think before doing or saying something rash or impulsive. Above all things, a skipper must keep his cool . . . so he heads to his quarters and packs his pipe.

It takes minutes to sort things out on the scratchy radio messages, but eventually the situation grows clearer. The *Sag Harbor* has collided with the Honduran-registered freighter SS *Aztec*. No one has been hurt. Both ships are safely afloat and under their own power, but both have enough damage that neither feels capable of continuing across the North Atlantic. One of the DEs will have to screen these ships while they return to the swept channel and proceed back into New York Harbor. It's not worth taking the chance of letting them return without an escort. All the skippers heard it at the convoy conference: there's a U-boat designated Red George out here somewhere.

The TBS radio on the *Joyce* goes silent for a while . . . and so does the bridge deck. The men on the bridge of the *Joyce* know that escort commander Captain William Kenner on the *Poole*, at the van of this ragged line of ships, is deciding which of the two tail-end Charlies, the *Joyce* or the *Peterson*, gets the job of baby-sitting the two wounded ships as they limp back to New York. It will be wretched duty in this fog. A setup for another possible collision in pea soup visibility with so many ships running in and out of New York without lights or much radio communication.

There was a time as recently as a year ago when the greatest danger to a ship entering or leaving New York was attack by a U-boat. But as both Mort Raphelson and Bob Wilcox know, those days are pretty much gone, even if there is a lone wolf out here somewhere. Now the greatest danger, by far, is collision. Although exact statistics are hard to come by, Wilcox knows that during the spring of 1944 a ship in the waters near New York has at least a seven times greater chance of being sunk or damaged by a collision with another Allied ship than by taking a torpedo from a U-boat.

Wilcox and the bridge watch on the *Joyce* remember all too well the deadly collision suffered by the destroyer USS *Murphy* in these same waters while heading out of New York Harbor one night just six months ago as a convoy escort. On October 21, 1943, the *Murphy* left New York with a convoy to follow the same basic route as CU-*21* across the North Atlantic. While tracking an unidentified radar contact feared to be a U-boat, the *Murphy* found itself in close quarters with the tanker SS *Bulkoil*. Startled by the sudden, close, and shadowy appearance of the destroyer, the tanker skipper imagined that a U-boat might be in the area and have the *Bulkoil* in its sights. The tanker took immediate evasive action per the skipper's antisubmarine training, but turned accidentally onto a collision course with the *Murphy*.

Before the destroyer could fully respond, the *Bulkoil* rammed the *Murphy*'s port side between its bridge superstructure and forward exhaust funnel and cut the destroyer in half. Due to the effectiveness of watertight doors, the stern section of the ship survived with most of the crew. It was towed back to New York and eventually rebuilt. The bow sank almost immediately, killing thirty-eight officers and men.

Tonight, the men on the *Joyce* can only hold their breaths and hope that their group commander on USS *Poole* does not pick their ship to try to locate the *Aztec* and the *Sag Harbor* in this fog and shepherd them home. There are far too many ships out here for a ship's crew to be at ease. With the range on the newest version of surface-search radar set at 12 miles, the watch on the *Joyce* can see several dozen targets clustered around them.

Wilcox and his men pace, stare out into the pitch, cast furtive glances at the TBS set, and hope for an answer from the *Poole*. They hope that tonight the fickle finger of Fate will not point their way . . . the way it did at those men in the bow of the *Murphy* or at the men aboard the *Leopold*.

Finally, the TBS crackles. Buzzes. Everyone eyes the radio and listens.

It's the briefest of messages. Escort command on the *Poole* is hailing the *Peterson*. It is to rendezvous with the *Aztec* and the *Sag Harbor*, escort them back to the swept channel . . . then catch up to CU-*21* again with all haste.

A collective sigh rises from the bridge of USS *Joyce*. Like the time when the ship dodged suspected oncoming torpedoes during the *Leopold* rescue, the lieutenant commander's luck is still holding. Maybe the *Joyce* and this skipper lead charmed lives. Bob Wilcox is sure of it when he pictures his beautiful wife, Alice. Goddamn if he didn't marry a model . . . and the kindest, sweetest woman. She has given them their four-year-old son, Dick. Both son and mother are living with Alice's parents at 803 West Highland Street, Deland, Florida. What Wilcox wouldn't give to be with them in Florida now. But duty calls, and for the captain of the *Joyce*, a man is nothing if he does not do his duty. Tonight that means protecting this raggedy-ass parade of merchantmen heading for Northern Ireland. If Red George is out here somewhere, it had best steer clear of DE-*317*.

8

Enemy Contact

0500 Hours, April 16, 1944

"*Kontak.*" The Funker's voice echoes from a cubicle just forward of the control room in *U-550*. Klaus Hänert has the morning watch.

After running on the surface most of the night to recharge its batteries, *550* has descended to periscope depth, to hide underwater and listen on the Balkon/GHG passive sonar for the heavy hum of a large propeller that could announce a fat prize heading east along the shipping lanes toward Cape Cod and Europe.

Since the air attack, Hänert is taking no more chances exposing his ship and his men on the surface. He quizzes the radioman, who has one hand pressed to his headset over an ear, listening to a ship's propeller and the thumping of its machinery coming from the array of hydrophones positioned around the bow of the U-boat.

"Kontak?"

"*Jawohl, Herr Kaleun.*"

Bearing?

The Funker says he has a *Horchpeilung*, a sonar echo, to the west.

Type IXC/40 U-boats have both attack and sky observation periscopes aboard, and Hänert calls for the raising of the attack scope out of its well. He climbs from the control room into the tower, where he settles onto something like a bicycle seat attached to the scope housing and peers into the eyepiece. The Old Man looks to the west, to the U-boat's *Bachbord* (port), sees nothing but fog. He questions the GHG operator again on the likely range.

The target is about 1500 meters away, possibly closing, possibly not. But definitely worth scrutiny if not a shot. The *550*'s captain has not brought his boat this far to miss a chance at striking a blow for the fatherland because of a little fog. He tells his engineer, Hugo Renzmann, to blow some water from the ballast tanks, adjust the diving planes, and take the boat up for a better look. Experience has taught Hänert that shooting while surfaced always gives a better chance of bagging the prey.

It's only a minute before the U-boat's captain and the deck watch have put on their leather coats, gloves, and scarves, pulled their hats down around their ears, climbed the aluminum ladder in the conning tower, and whirled the locking wheel to free the deck hatch overhead. The captain is on deck, his 7x50 binoculars in hand, even before the last of the remaining water from the observation deck has finished splattering down through the hatch.

The first light of false dawn is just starting to spread through the fog, to merge with the faint glow of New York and Long Island to the northwest. Aside from this spectral glow, the sub captain can see nothing. He and the watch face to the west. The U-boat is still in silent running mode, propelled by its quiet electric motors, not its diesels. The men on watch cup their ears for the sound of a ship's engine, but they hear nothing. The wind is almost calm, seas no more than a meter high.

Hänert calls down the voice pipe to the Funker. Where is that ship now?

It's fading, comes the answer. The target has moved past the U-boat . . . is gone to the east. Everything is silent. In the Funker's headphones. On the observation deck. Everywhere in the boat. The only noise is the low growl of the electric motors and the slapping of waves against the bow of the boat. From the galley comes the scent of ersatz coffee and sour buttermilk soup heating as the cook prepares for another breakfast. The adrenaline that has been dosing the arms and legs and chests of the men on watch evaporates with a nearly silent curse.

"Now what, Herr Kaleun?" That's the question machinist Johann Rauh wants to ask, Albert Nitsche wants to ask, Dr. Friedrich Torge wants to ask. All the crew wants to ask. But no one will. Questioning the skipper is not their right.

"Open the vents," Hänert calls down through the pipe to Renzmann. "Take her down."

U-550 will not get caught on the surface with the sun rising. If there is one ship in the area, there will probably be more . . . and these days the American ships don't go anywhere without their destroyer escorts.

The U-boat descends to 30 meters. Quietly. The commander does not want to run afoul of escort destroyers and the tons of depth charges that the DEs can release, twelve at a time, on an enemy submarine. "Wabos," the German sailors call these killers. Wasserbombes.

Nun warten wir. That's what the men tell each other. Now we wait. You won't need the Funker's headphones to hear the convoy passing overhead. It will sound like rolling thunder.

PART TWO

The Battle

9

Damn Fog

0600 Hours, April 16, 1944

For the first time in 24 hours Captain Delmar Leidy can actually see slightly beyond the bow of his tanker SS *Pan Pennsylvania*. He can make out the silhouette of the ship that he's following. The sun will be up in about 15 minutes. The fading fog looks like a swarm of diamonds hovering over the seven bombers lashed down on the foredeck.

Leidy heard about the collision between the *Sag Harbor* and the *Aztec* when he came on the bridge this morning. Bad business. It's the kind of story to make a seasoned mariner shiver to think about. A ship's master and his bridge crew have to be at their sharpest in this kind of weather. The warmer moist air of early spring always spells fog when it settles over these cold waters. But there is also a little comfort in it. U-boats can't see to attack a convoy in the fog. A good thing because at the convoy conference someone said that there's a lone wolf, Red George, out here.

CU-*21* has been heading east at about 14 knots all night, steaming blindly through this weather. The ships are traveling in two long lines. *Pan Penn* is the second vessel in the left-hand line. Now, with the visibility lifting, Leidy must hope that soon the convoy commodore will order the convoy to form into a half dozen columns. *Pan Penn* is designated "ship 21." This means that when the convoy forms, Leidy's ship will be at the head of the second column, flanked to port by one column of ships, to starboard by four more columns. Those to port and starboard will act as shields to protect the *Pan Penn* from any U-boat that might pop up on either side of the convoy. No doubt, Leidy wishes he had those shields right now. What tanker master would like having his port side exposed to an attack from an enemy submarine now that it might actually be able to see him? With the ships in just two lines, there is no way the escorts can patrol these long lines of ships, especially now that the *Peterson* has gone back to New York with the *Sag Harbor* and the *Aztec*. That leaves only five DEs to sweep for U-boats.

One of the concepts giving value to convoys is Delmar Leidy's sense that ships traveling in a tight block, only a few hundred yards apart, offer exceptional protection to the vessels at their core. A second benefit of convoys is that by concentrating a lot of shipping in a very small area, ships traveling in convoys are harder for predators to find than individual ships traveling known routes along which a U-boat can wait until its prey comes along at predictable intervals. This benefit holds particularly true when convoys avoid well-known shipping lanes.

The convoy system roots in ancient marine practices, but it gained modern prominence during the Napoleonic Wars, when Britain had its merchant ships travel in defined groups to hide and protect them from French warships. One challenge to convoy travel has always been regulating the speeds of dozens of ships sailing in formation, and at the outset of World War I, some naval strategists complained that convoys were a waste of time, especially since a convoy's speed was limited to the speed of its slowest member. For a while England rejected convoys in favor of armed warship escorts for short-haul merchant traffic across the English Channel. Only after the growth of the German U-boat fleet, and the subsequently high number of torpedo sinkings of British merchantmen, did England return to the convoy concept. Shipping losses to U-boats dropped from 10 percent to less than 2 percent after the English began forming ships into tight blocks accompanied by squadrons of dedicated escort destroyers.

Shortly after Nazi Germany showed its intention of European domination by invading Poland in September 1939, Britain, France, Australia, New Zealand, India, South Africa, and Canada declared war on Germany. World War II was under way. Having battled with Germany just twenty-odd years earlier, England knew that Germany would use its navy, especially a U-boat force that the Third Reich had been building in secret, to neutralize England by cutting off the island nation from ships carrying all manner of raw materials necessary for sustaining a war. A return to convoy formations was essential.

But England found itself desperately short of destroyers to escort convoys, especially the crucial North Atlantic convoys bringing materials from the United States and Canada. The Americans, who were at the time maintaining neutrality in regard to the war, agreed to lend Britain fifty mothballed World War I destroyers, nicknamed "four pipers" for their four funnels, in exchange for ninety-nine-year leases on land to build bases in British territories in the western Atlantic and the Caribbean such as Newfoundland, Bermuda, the Bahamas, Jamaica, and Trinidad. With the help of the American destroyers, which became known as the "town class" (most were renamed after towns in England), the Royal Navy began shepherding a constant flow of convoys between points in eastern Canada, such as Halifax, to and from Britain.

After the United States entered the war in late 1941, most eastbound convoys, such as CU-*21*, departed from New York. And as

British, Canadian, and American shipbuilders maxed out production of faster merchant ships, fewer convoys were limited to a slow speed of only seven to nine knots, typical of World War I convoys. After 1943 many convoys, such as CU-*21*, were fast convoys capable of steaming at 14 to 15 knots. At these speeds conventional U-boats like the Type VII attack submarines and the Type IX cruisers could barely keep up with the merchant ships and could be overrun by new, faster American escort destroyers.

Like the other convoys leaving New York weekly in 1944, CU-*21* will become a tightly packed unit, its six columns measuring less than 8,000 yards diagonally across, with the escorts patrolling another 3,000 yards off to the sides. Such a unit, traveling at 14 knots, is hard for a U-boat to find and penetrate, not to mention stalk and torpedo, once the convoy has closed up. With such facts locked in his mind, Delmar Leidy, like his radio officer Raphelson, should be feeling confident that SS *Pan Pennsylvania* will have an uneventful voyage to Northern Ireland during the next seven days.

Except for one thing. Leidy has heard from his counterparts on the coast guard and navy escorts that convoys have a curious peculiarity when it comes to ocean warfare. The officers aboard destroyer escorts like to think of convoys as bait to draw U-boats out into the open, where they can be attacked. Leidy knows that in this modern age of long-range radio communication, German spies in New York, and Germans eavesdropping on coded messages between England and America, can too often pinpoint and broadcast a convoy's departure to U-boats. Until the convoy forms into its tight floating fortress, the bait—like a loaded T-3 tanker—is at its most vulnerable. If a U-boat gets word from BdU of a convoy's departure, or is sitting right on the doorstep of New York City, all hell can break loose.

Such thoughts of U-boats must lurch through Delmar Leidy's mind as he listens intently for the low buzzing of the TBS, hoping to hear a message to form up from the convoy commodore, Captain E. H. Tillman aboard MV *Lightning*. But the TBS is silent. It's daylight now. The commodore is observing radio silence. So Leidy grabs his binoculars and trains them on the signal flags aboard the *Lightning*. No form-up signal yet. Lord have mercy. Time is of the essence. As the tankermen heading to the mess deck for breakfast might joke darkly, "What if old Adolf's waiting out here this morning?"

10

The Good Shepherd

The commander of USS *Joyce* may well be gnashing his teeth and yearning for another pipe of his special blend. Bob Wilcox is trying to stay calm on the bridge of the *Joyce*. But things aren't going so well. Signal flags calling for CU-*21* to form went up aboard MV *Lightning* at 0700, and on the *Joyce* shortly thereafter. Since then, the DE has been patrolling the seas for straggler ships, slewing port and starboard in long arcs to pass on the flag message and sweep for enemy submarines.

The sky's the color of iron. Visibility varies from 1 to 2 miles. A light breeze filters in from the northwest. There are no breaking wind waves, but a heavy swell is running. The *Joyce* steams off the starboard rear flank of this confused flock of ships. They are spread out 10 miles behind the van. The lead ships head 90 degrees. They have reduced their speed to 12 knots to let the rest of the ships catch up to them. Some of these ships, mostly tankers, are surging forward, veering away from the easterly course in search of their final place in the convoy. Some appear confused about the flag signals. A couple seem not to have seen the *Joyce*'s signal flags at all. The scene is what the coasties on the *Joyce* call a regular SNAFU. Situation normal, all fucked up.

Wilcox's ship is the shepherd that has to bring order to the SNAFU. Sometimes escorting three dozen merchant ships feels to the captain of the *Joyce* like trying to herd cats. But he's glad that if he has to do this job, he's in this ship, *his* ship. During the past six months Wilcox has grafted his soul to the *Joyce* in the same way that Klaus Hänert has bonded with U-*550*. They have come to trust their lives to their vessels. It's the way with sailors the world over. No doubt, this dependency is one reason why sailors refer to ships as "she." The ocean is a hostile environment. A person's ship is all that stands between a sailor and death. A ship is a mother. And after the nightmare of the *Leopold*'s sinking, Wilcox thinks his ship has carried him to hell and back. The *Joyce* is quite a lady.

Like Klaus Hänert, Wilcox has been with his ship from the moment of commissioning. That day came on September 30, 1943, after DE-*317*'s completion at the Consolidated Shipbuilding Corporation in Orange, Texas. The *Joyce* is one of eighty-five Edsall-class DEs built during World War II, more than thirty of which, like the *Joyce*, manned by US Coast Guard crews and used for convoy escort duty. The ship is 306 feet long and 36 feet, 7 inches abeam, with a draft of 10 feet, 5 inches. Its displacement is 1,253 tons, and it carries a crew of 186 officers and men. At flank speed it can steam at 21 knots, thanks to four Fairbanks Morse diesels. The *Joyce*'s range is 10,800 nautical miles at 12 knots.

Let U-boats beware. This DE has three 3-inch/.50-caliber deck guns, two 40mm cannons, eight 20mm cannons, three torpedo tubes, two depth charge racks, and eight depth charge projectors. As it zigzags to herd straggling merchantmen into position in CU-*21*, the DE carries a hundred depth charges ready to launch over an enemy submarine. In addition, the *Joyce* has a hedgehog array, a forward-firing weapon that launches mortar bombs. They explode on contact with a submarine. The *Joyce* also carries state-of-the-art radar and HF/DF as well as sonar that can detect a U-boat at up to 4,000 yards.

The United States built 563 destroyer escorts for the Allies during World War II. The impulse to design and build DEs arose in the spring of 1939, after Germany invaded Czechoslovakia in March of that year. England and the United States foresaw war and the need for a mass-produced destroyer to escort merchant convoys and engage U-boats. For convoy duty, the navies did not need a full-size destroyer of 2,000 tons, 375 feet long, with a crew of more than 300. They wanted a ship with half that tonnage and crew. Unlike destroyers, the destroyer escorts didn't need to be able to steam at speeds of 35 knots to keep up with a task force of battleships, cruisers, and major aircraft carriers. DEs required only a top speed of slightly more than 20 knots to protect merchant convoys traveling at 8 to 15 knots.

What evolved over the five years following 1939 were six successive classes of destroyer escorts, each with a hull 290 to 308 feet long, a displacement of 1,140 to 1,500 tons, and a crew of 180 to 220 officers and men. Although they did not have the speed or armament of destroyers, DEs were more maneuverable than their bigger sisters and cost two thirds less to build.

Sailors on DEs were mostly younger than twenty years old and largely inexperienced except for a few petty officers. Officer Robert Wilcox was not much older. But youthful enthusiasm served DE crews well and gave them an esprit de corps and an exceptional can-do spirit. Since taking command of the Joyce, Wilcox has thoroughly shaken down his crew with training in Bermuda and Maine as well as two round-trips across the North Atlantic with Task Group 21.5 of Escort Division 22. CU-*21* is the ship's third eastbound convoy. In less than six months of active duty on the North Atlantic, crewmen aboard the *Joyce* have already earned the Navy and Marine

Corps Medals. Wilcox and two others have received commendations for their outstanding performance during their rescue of survivors following the U-boat attack on USS *Leopold*.

Now it's with confidence in his battle-tested crew that Wilcox orders his ship to crowd the sterns of these merchantmen steaming in the haze off to port. He's going to drive the wayward sheep forward into a tight herd before some hungry wolf in his Unterwasserboot code-named Red George comes snooping around with big plans to make a meal of a tanker. Head 'em up, move 'em out. The time for the gnashing of teeth is over.

11

Target Sighted

0800 Hours, April 16, 1944

The Funker's voice breaks the silence of the control room, the hum of *550*'s electric motors. "Horchpeilung, Herr Kaleun." Sonar contact to the west.

U-550 is at periscope depth. Hänert would prefer to hover here beneath the waves and remain totally silent while he waits for the fog to lift and he takes up the hunt. But U-boats are too unstable. They need water flowing over the bow and stern planes to keep level, so *550* has been creeping northeast, the screws turning over at low rpms.

"Large ship," says the Funker with both hands pressing his earphones to his head, "at least one."

Hänert bolts up into the tower. He goes straight to the attack periscope at the back of the conning tower, lowers himself onto the bicycle seat, and peers into the scope. The attack scope rides up and down within a heavy metal casing that makes a thick column between the captain's knees. His feet are on pedals to rotate the periscope around, spinning him with it. He turns his hat backward so its brim doesn't interfere with the eyepiece, looks to the west. Turning the scope 90 degrees left, then sweeps to the right, he can hardly believe his eyes as he faces south. U-550 is in the middle of a disorderly cluster of tankers and destroyers. An aircraft carrier is just about to cross the U-boat's bow. What luck. The gods are good.

Although the 550's skipper doesn't know it, the ship is the British HMS *Premier*, a Ruler class escort carrier, 9,170 tons, 15,160 fully loaded, 494 feet long, 69 feet abeam. It is capable of a speed of 18 knots and armed with two 5-inch guns, eight twin 40mm cannons, dozens of 20mm guns and is carrying fourteen Hellcat fighters, ten Wildcat fighters, and more than thirty Corsair fighter-bombers. Eighteen of the planes are on the hangar deck. The rest are on the flight deck, where Hänert can see them.

He sure would like to blow those aircraft into little pieces. But his crew has got to be fast. That carrier could get away. Hänert has one shot. His best chance for a strike is to fire three torpedoes in a fan pattern. He calls for the flooding of tubes one, three, and four. Arm the T3 torpedoes. *Schnell.* Hurry. U-550 has just seconds to estimate the carrier's course, speed, and distance, then program a solution into the *Vorhaltrechner*, the electromechanical device that sets the gyrocompass steering mechanism of the torpedoes.

The carrier's just about to move across 550's bow. The sub's Old Man squints into the scope, twists its handles to change the angle and magnification for a better view. He sees the deck full of airplanes that the enemy is shipping to the British Isles to bomb his homeland. His stomach tightens when he thinks of the bombing and his family back home, all his men's families. Before he left Germany, he watched as the Allied bombers flattened Kiel, and he knows that the same thing is happening all over Germany. He has heard stories about withered bodies lying in the streets like burned logs. He wants to stop the bombing here and now, wants to kill those airplanes.

There's urgency in his voice when he calls to the petty officer who will program the Vorhaltrechner. The carrier is eastbound. Hänert estimates its speed at about 12 knots, but it seems to be accelerating. It's 45 degrees off the U-boat's starboard bow at about 1,000 meters. Now, right now, the enemy ship is at just about the ideal spot for a torpedo attack. Set the torpedo depth on two "eels" at three meters, one at four.

But *Scheisse*. Shit. The carrier's got company.

Hänert sees two faster and smaller gray ships in the background. DEs. They're sweeping in front of the carrier for U-boats. *Mein Gott*, do they see him? Or hear him? Or is the noise of the carrier and the other ships masking him on the destroyers' sonar?

"Macht schnell." Hurry up. Do we have a solution? Can I fire?

"Soon, Captain," says the petty officer. Then, "Jawohl, Herr Kaleun." Fire when ready.

Hänert squints at the target, finds the word *Folgen*, the command for "fire," on the tip of his tongue. But the carrier has already charged more than halfway across the sub's bow. It's moving away to the east. Out of range.

Too late. Not even a fan shot of three T3 eels is likely to yield a hit now.

Verdamit. The enemy's planes have slipped right through Hänert's fingers.

He slumps with his forearms propped against the periscope. Could it be that the Fates brought him all this way across the North Atlantic to tease him with this chance at victory, only to humiliate him? A passage from the Kriegsmarine's 1943 *Submarine Commander's Handbook* taunts his memory.

> *During every attack, situations may develop in which a continuation of the attack appears to the submarine commander to be hopeless, or impossible. Only if the submarine commander, imbued with the determination to win, and unrelenting toward himself, conquers these feelings, will it be possible for him—in view of the few opportunities of attack which the war at sea will provide—to achieve any success at all.*

Reisst euch zusammen! In other words, shape up and do your duty. Get back in the game, Herr Kaleun, he must tell himself.

He tries to focus on what he's seeing in the scope again. His feet on the pedals are already rotating the scope back to the west. The crew below can feel the tension as they hear the whirring of the periscope motor. But . . . *was ist das?* What's this? A tanker, a plume of dark smoke trailing off from its funnel, lumbering right along in the wake of the carrier. It's the biggest tanker he has ever seen. More than 500 feet long, in excess of 10,000 gross tons. It's so loaded that its bow looks submerged back to the midship house. And look at that. Airplanes. Seven B-25 Mitchell bombers are lashed on the foredeck of the tanker. Maybe the commander of U-*550* will get a chance to kill American airplanes after all.

12

Attack

This really could be Klaus Hänert's lucky day. The tanker steaming toward his bow with those bombers is so exactly on the trail of the aircraft carrier that the petty officer programming the Vorhaltrechner does not even need to enter a new solution for the torpedo gyros. The shot is here to be taken. To hell with those DEs and everything else. It's time to kill airplanes.

"Folgen," says Hänert.

"*Los*," calls the engineer from the control room. Loose. The *Aal*, the eel, blasts from its tube. Two others follow.

The U-boat crew feels the slight jolts as the pneumatic pressure in the torpedo tubes expel three T3s from the bow of the sub.

Part of Hänert wants to wait and watch those airplanes and the tanker go up in a ball of flames. But the engineer says that the boat cannot hold equilibrium here at periscope depth. It is growing unstable and could be an easy target for the destroyer escorts. The Old Man gives the order to dive. Crash dive. Bow planes five degrees down. Stern planes three degrees. Macht schnell.

Hänert slides down the ladder to the control room, counting seconds. At this distance the first torpedo should hit the tanker in less than 50 seconds. These weapons have gotten so much better since the war began. Realizing that its traditional steam-driven torpedoes, with their bubbling wakes, were not stealthy enough for a modern war, Germany developed a battery-driven electrical torpedo known as the G7e for the Battle of the Atlantic.

As Klaus Hänert knows all too well from his previous cruises, the first iterations of this torpedo had significant problems and a failure rate of 20 to 40 percent. Powered by hundred-horsepower electric motors and lead-acid batteries, G7e models share the same dimensions as all World War II U-boat torpedoes. They measure 53.3 centimeters in diameter and 7.16 meters in length. Each torpedo packs a 280-kilogram warhead. Because of the batteries and other intricate parts, the torpedoes need constant maintenance from torpedo room crews to have a chance of functioning on patrol. Furthermore, while the electrically driven torpedoes have the advantage of stealth over the steam eels, the electric Aals have had persistent problems with both types of detonating systems the Kriegsmarine has been using. The early models were also slower and had a shorter range than their steam-driven predecessors.

The good news for Hänert and U-550 on this Sunday morning is that Deutschland's engineers have made significant improvements in their eels during the past year. The T3 version of the G7e torpedoes now rocketing toward the tanker can go faster and farther than the previous designs. With a redesigned detonator that uses the magnetic field of the target ship to explode the warhead, the three eels that Hänert has just launched in a fan pattern can detonate under the keel of a ship and break its back. If these eels connect, their target is most likely doomed.

Time will tell. Another 20 seconds, more or less. Hänert's boat dives through 30 meters. Everyone aboard is counting the torpedoes' run in his head. Johann Rauh and his friend Albert Nitsche brace themselves against a bulkhead and count. *Fourteen, fifteen, sixteen* . . .

The Old Man knows he needs to get deeper fast, make this boat a ghost, before the tanker blows, if it blows, and the DEs come looking for him with a vengeance. He tells Hugo Renzmann to open more vents in the ballast tanks. Put U-*550* on the bottom.

The sub is diving for an additional 20 seconds, slipping beneath 60 meters of ocean. But there's no explosion, and the sub's plunging deeper. The men in the control room catch each other's eyes. *Was ist los?* What gives? And maybe they are all feeling that gnawing in the pit of their stomach that comes with a dark recognition of impending failure, a leaden sense of their own worthlessness and the futility of their mission for a dying state. Verdamit, that's what the crew of this submarine is feeling when the distant thunder of an explosion echoes through their ship and U-*550* takes a deeper angle toward the bottom.

The sound of the tanker fracturing overhead, less than a half mile away, is so loud that the Funker rips off his headphones.

No one cheers. The *Pan Penn* is already groaning, wailing in death above them. And the submariners are hanging on to anything they can as their boat vectors toward hell as if it's on rails.

13

Mortal Wound

0805 Hours, April 16, 1944

The ship shudders, then lurches hard to port just as Mort Raphelson takes a second bite of his biscuit. He's on the mess deck of SS *Pan Pennsylvania*, has just come off the 0400-to-0800 watch, for his breakfast. The steward has taken his order, and he has been musing over the light crispness of this biscuit, thinking, "Oh, boy, this is going to be a great trip" if all the food coming out of the galley is as good as this biscuit. But now, nearly knocked off his seat, staring at a collage of white porcelain plates spilled on the metal floor, and seeing wide-eyed men picking themselves up, he has three new thoughts. One, a boiler just blew. Two, scratch that. Three, the Germans got us this time. *Holy heaven.*

Instinctively, Raphelson heads for the door, aims to hightail it forward to his duty station, the radio room and the bridge. He will be needed. But when he opens the door, he meets a wall of steam from ruptured pipes. He slams the door shut, retraces his route among the tables of the mess deck toward the stern. Now the men who were on the floor a minute ago are rushing in what seem twenty directions. Many are already wearing life vests. At one point a steward sprints past him butt naked. The man runs to the rail, plunges over the side, is gone.

Raphelson goes up a rear stairwell to the poop deck. Crossing the poop on his way forward, he sees a gang of men piling into the number-three lifeboat, which hangs from davits on the starboard side. He barely notices as someone releases the lifeboat's bow falls too early while the boat is not fully in the water. The boat tips forward, spilling more than a dozen men into the sea. And now all those men are in it . . . and being sucked into the churning propeller.

The captain's deposition on the event reads: "The ship was making about 13 knots. I then went to the starboard wing of the bridge and found that some of the crew had become panicky and had attempted to launch the number-three lifeboat without any orders whatsoever."

Sixty-eight years later Mort Raphelson will say, "The sad thing is, no one on that ship had to die." Panic killed them.

But even as the water around the tanker turns cherry red from the dyed gasoline gushing out through a 50-foot hole in the port side, the radio officer doesn't panic. He runs for his post in the radio shack up forward as a misty red cloud rises above the gasoline. It sears his lungs, burns his eyes.

There's no catwalk over the deck, so Raphelson works his way toward the midship house along the starboard rail. The ship is vibrating and making noises like metal ripping apart. The tanker's listing to port, and Raphelson has trouble keeping his footing. He has worse trouble keeping on his feet when the ship suddenly veers 90 degrees to port to get clear of the convoy following behind. If the ship blows, Captain Leidy doesn't want to take other ships with it. Eyes riveted on the wheelhouse, Raphelson doesn't see that the deck has begun to bow and buckle under his feet.

He has watched tankers explode after taking a torpedo. There's usually a minute or two after the strike before the whole ship goes off like a bomb. It's coming, he's almost sure. But he wants to get back to the radio room and transmit the dreaded message "SSSS," Morse code for being under attack by a submarine. In the minds of some macabre jokesters on merchant ships, SSSS is shorthand for "Sighted sub. Shit . . . sinking." It's a dismal message if ever there was one. A last shout in the dark. Part of Raphelson wants to stop in his cabin and grab the watch his father gave him. If he can't live with that token of family, then he'll die with it. But first things first.

In the wheelhouse Captain Leidy says there's no need to send a coded message. He has already hailed the convoy commander aboard the lead DE, USS *Poole*, and the convoy commodore via the TBS, reporting the torpedo strike. Now Leidy and the leader of the naval armed guard aboard are barking orders, trying to bring the general panic on the ship under control. Leidy confronts a gang of men trying to launch the number-one lifeboat and orders them to heave it back in place. *Pan Penn* is wounded, for sure, but might yet be saved. Next, Leidy calls on the gunners to fire their 3-inch gun off to starboard, away from the spilling gasoline, to warn the other ships in the convoy that *Pan Penn* has been struck and is in distress. All communication with the engine room is gone. Leidy blows the torpedo warning signal on the ship's whistle. It alerts the engineers to put the engines in reverse and stop the vessel.

This scene has been and will be repeated hundreds of times before the war ends in 1945. Although statistics vary, about 5,000 Allied ships will sink during the Battle of the Atlantic. Half of those sinkings will come at the hands of U-boat crews. Dead American merchant mariners during the war will number between 5,000 and 9,500. England will lose as many as 30,000 men. Of the approximately 220,000 to 280,000 merchant mariners who will man America's freighters and tankers during the war, about 1 in 26 will not come home. The American merchant marine service will suffer a loss rate of 3.9 percent, the highest loss rate for any branch of wartime service in America, a full 1 percent higher than the US Marines, who will have the next highest loss rate.

Despite their heavy losses, America's merchant mariners will not be considered war veterans or granted veterans' benefits by the US government following the war. During subsequent decades, the government will grant veterans' status to women aircraft ferry pilots, telephone operators, and dieticians. But the merchant mariners will achieve only limited veterans' status following a difficult federal court battle in 1988. Still, because of technicalities, fewer than 100,000 of the sailors who served will be eligible for veterans' benefits. None of them will receive the ritual US flag that vets in other services get for their funeral. None will receive the veterans' grave marker.

But veterans' status couldn't be farther from the radio officer's mind as he stands on the bridge of SS *Pan Pennsylvania* and watches while Captain Leidy finally gets the remainder of the crew to stop panicking, to take a deep breath, and to abandon ship in an orderly fashion. The number-one and number-two lifeboats are now in the water and tied alongside as well as a couple of life rafts. The crew, once numbering fifty merchant mariners and thirty-one navy gunners, is now down to a total of just fifty-six. Twenty-five men are missing. It's clear to Leidy that his ship took a torpedo in the number eight tank. It was three-quarters empty, and the lack of gasoline in the tank has kept the ship from exploding. But now it lists 30 degrees to port.

Leidy stands at the ship's helm, looks out over the long bow, tells Raphelson and an engineering officer that he thinks his ship can be saved. They could restart the engines and head for Rhode Island. The engineer says that he doesn't think this is an option. He has just come up from the engine room. It's starting to flood and awash in gasoline, which has caught fire. The head of the armed guard says that the deck has cracked three-quarters of the way across just in front of the stern house.

"Then her back is broken," Leidy says. He tells the engineer and armed guard to join the lifeboats and cast off.

"I think it's time for us to go, Cap," says Raphelson. "I just want to get my watch from my cabin."

The captain shakes his head. Don't do it.

Raphelson sees that the port rail of the ship is already awash with seawater and a heavy film of red-tinted, 80-octane gasoline. "There's a life raft tied alongside for us."

And so Leidy and Raphelson head for the raft. It's a classic Hollywood exit, and a merchant mariners' tradition. The captain and the radioman are the last off the dying ship, wishing it "Fare thee well."

14

To the Rescue

0818 Hours, April 16, 1944

The TBS radio crackles on the bridge of USS *Joyce*. Escort group commander Captain W. W. Kenner, aboard the *Poole*, is ordering the *Joyce*, *Peterson*, and *Gandy* to sweep for the U-boat and pick up survivors from the *Pan Penn*. Since receiving word 13 minutes ago that the *Pan Penn* took a torpedo, the *Joyce* has called the crew to general quarters. But it has still been patrolling, according to orders, off the tail end of the convoy, trying to shepherd stragglers into formation. Now the orders have changed.

Bob Wilcox is just about to tell the quartermaster to steer due east for the stricken *Pan Penn*, at the front of the convoy, when a lookout reports another convoy straggler looming out of thick haze to the west. Goddamn, this so-called convoy is an errant bunch.

"All ahead flank speed," he tells the officer of the deck. "Put us on that straggler."

It's 10 minutes before *Joyce* can advise the straggler to haul ass for its place in the convoy and warn it about the wounded *Pan Pennsylvania*. Ten minutes before Wilcox can order a course change back to the east toward the sinking tanker. He tells his ASW officer, Lieutenant (j.g.) John Bender, in the sound hut to look sharp, there's a German shark in the water around here somewhere. The bridge crew has started running sub sweeping patterns to screen the starboard side of the convoy.

As the *Joyce* charges toward the *Pan Penn* at 21 knots, the morning haze continues to limit visibility to just 1 or 2 miles. Wilcox is a man who believes deeply in the benefits of preparation. He tries to gather himself for the rescue ahead, tries to remember what went wrong and what went right that night six weeks ago when the *Leopold* took a hit. The night that he tried to rescue his friends between dodging torpedoes. That whole scenario could be about to unfold again.

USS *Joyce* relies on its sonar for detecting a U-boat underwater. Sonar works by sending a sound wave through the water, a "ping." When that sound wave hits something solid, it causes an echo. The sonar operator, or the machine itself, uses the time the echo took to return to calculate the distance to a target. The *Joyce*'s sonar gear functions like a beam of light. It emanates from a sonar head mounted underwater near the ship's bow and scans a small area. The ship's crew has to shift the sonar head manually to scan broadly ahead of a ship. Known as the QGB, the DE's sonar unit keeps company with a tactical range recorder and an attack plotter in the sound hut just forward of the flying bridge.

Bender and his ASW technicians are glued to their QGB, listening for an echo from a shadow somewhere ahead, hiding beneath these heavy swells.

"Any contact, Lieutenant?" asks Wilcox, ducking into the sound hut. The sonar men shake their heads. Nothing yet.

Someone aboard the *Gandy* is on the TBS, reporting that his lookouts believe they have just spotted a torpedo in the water, coming toward them. Time: 0839 hours.

USS *Peterson* reports it's at flank speed. The DE is closing with the convoy and a rendezvous with the *Pan Penn* after escorting the *Aztec* and the *Sag Harbor* back to New York. The hunt is on.

"I want this guy, gentlemen." Wilcox's voice rings firm as steel.

15

Run or Hide

0845 Hours, April 16, 1944

The lookouts on the *Gandy* who thought that they saw a torpedo heading their way must have been mistaken. Men imagine phantom threats in battle all the time. There's only one U-boat out here, and U-*550* has been bottomed out and in trouble since its shot at the tanker and crash dive.

Half an hour ago the sub hit the bottom in about 280 to 300 feet of water with a succession of hard bumps, knocking torpedomen in the House of Lords off their feet. The Old Man and his engineer have the distinct feeling that their crash dive has plowed a furrow with their U-boat into the seabed.

"Wir sind stecken geblieben, Herr Kaleun," says the engineer Renzmann. We're stuck.

Klaus Hänert knows that in this depth of water, he makes an easy target for the destroyers. He mulls over his options. The Funker claims that the U-boat is nearly under the tanker. The wounded ship overhead is releasing an endless medley of creaks and groans as it breaks up. The tanker's death rattles echo through the submarine, making a sad and dissonant chorus. The noise is so shrill that the Old Man is almost sure that the DEs probing for him with their sonar will not be able to detect any small bits of ambient noise coming from the 550. He has secured the boat for silent running. The crew has shut off all but essential electronics, such as the sonar and gyrocompass. The men have even silenced the pumps. But Hänert knows that the tanker's moaning will not cover him from the destroyers' sonar forever . . . and there's also the possibility of his victim coming down right on top of his head.

Wie gehts? What to do?

The Kriegsmarine's *Submarine Commander's Manual* offers counsel.

Do not see danger everywhere and in everything, do not overestimate the enemy, do not always seek to place yourself in his position, do not assume that everything that is going on in the theater of war applies to yourself—these internal reservations and scruples are a sign of uncertainty, and of a negative attitude, which impairs your ability to reach a decision, and endangers the success of the operations.

Audacity and a readiness to take responsibility, coupled with cool, clear thinking, are the pre-conditions and the basis of success.

The message is clear. Be bold, push emotion out of your brain. Focus on the problem. To fight or to run? That is the question. But it can't be the first question . . . because the boat may well be mired in the bottom. How do you get out of here without making a lot of noise or sending telltale bubbles of air to the surface when you blow your ballast tanks? If you do that, the destroyers will be on you with their depth charges like avenging angels.

He asks Renzmann, back from an inspection of the boat after the hard landing, if 550 has damaged bow planes, stern planes, and rudders.

"Nein, Herr Kaleun."

"Then we have a chance."

Renzmann says that if they blow all the tanks and use full power from the electric motors, *jawohl*, they have a chance.

Hänert considers the convoy, turns to the Funker's booth, asks where the convoy is.

It has moved to the east, already out of listening range.

And the destroyers? It's a silly question that the Old Man better swallow before it bursts from his lips. He needs no hydrophone to tell him that the destroyers are still overhead. He can hear the chugging of their screws, stopping and starting. They must be picking up survivors off the tanker. There's nothing he can do right now. To move would be suicide. The destroyers' ASW crews will spot him in an instant. But maybe, just maybe, the DEs will leave after they pick up the tankermen. After all, their first priority is to guard their convoy, and right now it's getting away from them.

For the moment there is nothing to do but wait to see if the DEs leave. The standing order is for all quiet on the boat. Every man not on watch in the control room or in the radio room should be in his berth. Even the captain.

If only the enemy and being stuck were the U-boat's only problems. But not a chance. U-*550* has been on the surface for only a few hours in the past two days. And who knows how long they will have to wait down here until it's safe to move? They must conserve oxygen. A Type IX allegedly has enough air in the boat to stay submerged for up to 72 hours. But Hänert knows that 72 hours is a highly optimistic estimate given his circumstances. The air in the boat already sears his throat with a wicked mix of rotting feet, greasy asses, rancid breakfast butter, and cologne that some clown is wearing to cover his foul breath.

The Ubootwaffe sends aboard cases of Muelhens 4711 cologne for the seamen to mask their fetid odors during long patrols. Most of the men give the stuff away to their girlfriends, wives, or mothers before leaving home. But this morning someone in the control room smells like one of the good-time girls trolling for men on Hamburg's Reeperbahn. It's so strong it hurts the eyes, but it doesn't quite mask the scent of vomit. At least one of the men tossed his breakfast during the crash dive. Fear stinks.

The Old Man steps forward from the control room and drops into his own berth to set an example for the men, to model patience, self-control. With his eyes closed he takes stock of his situation again. Worse than the smell in the boat is the state of the batteries. They have been driving everything aboard the U-boat for more than six hours. They cannot last more than another five or six hours at the most. At some point he might be forced to surface while he still has enough electricity to run the pumps and the motors that turn the screws.

And if he has to surface before the DEs are gone? He will have to come up shooting if he wants even the slightest chance of survival. Probably there will be no way for the gun crews to get on deck, then arm and aim their weapons before the destroyers' gunners mow them down. His only real hope will be the T5 acoustical torpedoes already loaded in one bow tube and both stern tubes. Designed to hone in on the sound of a DE's screws, they can be effective defensive weapons if he has time to fire them. It was likely a T5 that took out the *Leopold*.

But assuming he can break his boat free, should he fight or run? T5s are not much of a defense against *three* destroyers. Stealth is his best ally. He should run. Run deep, run fast . . . while he still has enough battery power. But where? He pictures his chart of the New England seaboard and his navigator's plot of his course over the past day. By this plot he's at about 40.09 degrees north latitude, 69.44 degrees west longitude. The edge of the continental shelf is perhaps a dozen miles south of his position. It's a sheer cliff dropping from about 100 meters in depth to 300 meters, more than 900 feet. And it gets deeper.

If he can make a dash for the edge of the shelf and dive over, he can drive 550 to perhaps 230 meters. At that depth he will be below the deepest setting the Americans can put on their depth charges. And he can lose the DEs by going beneath a thermocline that he suspects exists at about 100 meters below the surface. It's a layer of colder, denser water that the Americans' sonar cannot penetrate, the ultimate natural shield to hide him from his enemy. If they don't hear him, they will soon turn away and chase after their convoy. He can surface to a peaceful and empty April day.

But he has to make his move toward that deepwater shield soon, while the batteries still have power and the crew still has oxygen and not just this stench of fear, feet, and too much 4711. He will take the 550 almost to its crush depth. But somehow it will survive. It's a tough boat, and the crew is as ready as they can be. They have done their duty for the fatherland. Now let the gods smile on these boys, give them a chance to rise from the dead. Once he's sure the DEs have left, he'll break this U-boat off the bottom and run for dear life.

16

Gotcha

"Sonar contact." Lieutenant (j.g.) John Bender's words have a sharp edge.

USS *Joyce* has been running a zigzag pattern in search of the U-boat and plucking *Pan Penn* survivors from the gas-slick sea on the tanker's starboard side for most of the past hour. The smoking light is out for fear of touching off an explosion. With the help of the *Peterson*, the job's complete. *Peterson* has hauled twenty-five tankermen aboard. *Joyce* has picked up thirty-one. Wilcox couldn't be prouder of his crewmen. They have repeatedly descended the scramble net hung on the DE's side for the rescue, some entering the frigid water to help the merchant sailors climb the net to the ship's deck. Many of the *Pan Penn* survivors seem half dead from the gasoline fumes. The tanker captain Leidy and radio officer Raphelson look positively green from near asphyxiation.

"Range and bearing?" Wilcox shifts from rescue to combat mode.

"Eighteen hundred yards, bearing three hundred *twenty* degrees, sir. Submarine."

Wilcox doesn't hesitate. "Head for the center bearing. Commence attack at fifteen [knots]." He orders the two racks, sets of steel rails at the stern, prepared for launching Mark 9 depth charges set for shallow detonation. Then he reports to *Peterson* and *Gandy* on the TBS that he has a solid contact and is attacking.

"Target moving left," says Bender.

Wilcox pictures his enemy's course beneath the waves, tells his quartermaster to adjust his course to lead the target by five degrees.

The sonar operator says that the U-boat seems to be altering course again, possibly swerving port and starboard.

Joyce, at 250 yards off the target, adjusts its course to the right. The ASW sonar holds on to a clear target down to a range of 120 yards. This is just about as close as a DE can get before losing contact. But no problem, the sub lies dead ahead.

"Fire," Wilcox tells the officer of the deck who is standing on the starboard wing of the bridge.

"Charges fired, sir." The Mark 9 depth charges, shaped like giant teardrops in a round, steel cage, roll off the racks and splash into the sea, one after the next.

The clock on the bridge shows 0953 hours when the first Mark 9 explodes and throws a geyser of water as high as the funnel of the *Joyce*. Ten more follow. Two hang up in the racks.

"All ahead flank," says Wilcox. "Reload. Let's hit him again."

17

Depth Charges

The world's blowing itself apart in bass drumbeats coming five seconds apart. That's how it sounds to both the sailors belowdecks on the *Joyce* and the men in U-550. The DE's depth charges are bracketing the U-boat. Decades later survivors will say that it isn't like the depth charge attack in *Das Boot*. No one goes mad or cries or leaves his post or shits his pants. But each time a depth charge explodes, the lights go out for a few seconds. Men close their eyes. If their hands aren't holding them in a death grip to some part of the boat or hanging on to the controls of a piece of equipment, they are clutched together, fingers laced, pressed to their chests, or tucked under their chin. Some of them are praying silently. Others are just holding on to themselves so that as little as possible of them gets blown away if *550* takes a direct hit.

Klaus Hänert knows what he's up against. The US Navy's Mark 9 depth charges launched from the *Joyce* entered service in early 1943.

Each charge has 200 pounds of Torpex explosive. Crews can set the charge to explode to depths of 600 feet. A DE carries about a hundred depth charges, and as they explode, a petty officer on *550* is keeping track of the number of bangs in hopes of knowing when the destroyer overhead will run out of charges. But this tally may well be an exercise in self-torture because the Funker says that all three destroyers are on the hunt above. Mein Gott, what chance has a U-boat of surviving three hundred depth charges?

Slim . . . but the survival is not beyond the realm of possibility. Hänert has heard of U-boats surviving horrendous barrages of depth charges. Before the war ends, the captain of U-*427* will report surviving 678 *Wabos*. Depth charges are not really very good at killing subs. They damage submarines by creating a water hammer effect that radiates through the sea after the charge explodes. The lethal radius of a depth charge depends on the depth of detonation, the amount of explosives, the size and strength of the U-boat's hull. A depth charge like a Mark 9 has a killing radius of only 3 to 10 yards against a Type IX U-boat. Destroyer captains grumble among themselves about the need for absolute pinpoint accuracy to get a kill. Slim chance of that. Instead, they hope that they might disable a U-boat. A Mark 9 can wound a sub at 30 yards.

If Hänert knew that the DEs were still up there, he would have stayed hunkered down on the bottom longer. But the destroyers have played a trick on the Funker. They stopped, shut off their engines, and made themselves invisible to the submarine's hydrophones. As soon as the *550* blew its ballast and started to break out of its trough on the bottom and run, the DEs heard it. And now this. A dull thud shudders through the boat. One of the *Joyce*'s depth charges hits the deck aft of the conning tower, rumbles as it catches on some of the wooden deck treads. The men can hear the metallic clang as it rolls aft and over the side next to the diesel engine room. Most of them are holding their breath when it goes off like a thunderclap.

The shock blacks out the entire boat and throws Johann Rauh and Albert Nitsche to their knees. When they open their eyes, their ears are still ringing. A voice like something from a distant dream seems to be shouting and whispering at the same time. Something about the diesel oil. They can't understand what the voice is saying. And then they can, because they can smell it. Men can feel it gushing onto their faces, their hands, their shoulders. Either the diesel fuel tanks have ruptured or it's the fuel lines. And there's the hissing of high-pressure air and the spraying of water. Broken pipes everywhere. Worst of all, the back of the boat is flooding. The lights are not back on. Flashlight beams are darting around in the shadows. The main motors seem to have stopped. And now another depth charge explodes, rolling the boat almost on its side.

"How bad is it?" asks the Old Man when his engineer, Renzmann, returns to the control room from back aft.

The engineer shakes his head. No good. The engine room is a disaster zone, the stern torpedo room's flooding.

Hänert knows this is his moment of truth. Renzmann and all the other men in the control room are looking at him, wide-eyed as the lights flicker back on. The mission can no longer be completed; *550* will never make it back to its assigned base in France. The patrol ends here. Either with U-*550* settling back to the bottom, where depth charges will eventually disable it to the point that all these men drown or suffocate to death. Or . . . the boat blows the rest of its ballast now, makes an uncontrolled ascent, and fights for its life.

Hänert grasps for Plan B, which he formulated more than an hour ago after crashing into the bottom. He orders his crew to arm the T5 eels in tubes two, five, and six. He will rise and fight. Such is the obligation of a man his son will describe as a "correct Prussian officer." It's the boat's duty. It's the men's duty, whether they know it or not. They will not die down here in the dark like dogs.

"Take her up," he tells Renzmann, "and open the outer doors on tubes two, five, and six."

There's swearing from seamen at the controls for the torpedo tube doors.

What's wrong?

Another depth charge rocks the boat.

"Outer doors are jammed in five and six, Herr Kaleun." The damage back aft has prevented the firing of the two stern torpedoes.

The lights have started flickering again.

"Prepare to fire tube two." The Old Man's voice struggles for firmness.

18

Shooting Gallery

1000–1003 Hours, April 16, 1944

USS *Joyce* leans in a tight turn. It's jockeying amid the *Peterson* and the *Gandy* for a second run on the sub, and Bender's ASW team is struggling to get another lock on the enemy when someone on the bridge says, "Holy shit."

U-*550* broaches, bow high, 2,000 yards astern, right in the *Joyce*'s wake. The sub breaks out of the water like a cork popping up or, to Wilcox's way of thinking, like the whales he used to see in the Gulf of Maine. Green water from the dye the *Joyce* left in the water to mark its enemy's position foams off the sub's deck. Bob Wilcox knows by this graceless appearance that the U-boat has surfaced out of control. The German has problems with his propulsion, steering, and dive planes. Instead of steering to the surface, the sub's skipper must have blown his ballast tanks and hoped for the best.

U-*550* has hardly settled back into the water on an even keel when all three destroyers start firing at it with 20mm and 40mm antiaircraft guns as well as 3-inch/.50-caliber deck guns. Someone says on the TBS that the sub has opened fire. All his life Bob Wilcox will tell anyone who asks that the U-boat opened fire so fast that he thought they must have a deck gun controlled from somewhere inside the boat. In other words, Wilcox never saw a gun crew on the U-boat.

Aboard the destroyers a lot of scared and eager gunners are hammering at the U-boat. More than once Wilcox has to call a cease-fire to his crew for fear of hitting one of the other DEs with his guns. Shells from the *Gandy* go so far astray that they ricochet off the *Pan Penn* about a half mile away. They set the tanker and all the spilling gasoline around it aflame.

The *Joyce* veers away to stay clear of this storm of gunfire as the melee erupts around the U-boat. Meanwhile, the *Gandy*, despite having blown one of its main engines 90 minutes earlier, charges at the sub with guns blazing. Ramming is among the US Navy's recommended ways for subduing a U-boat on the surface, and the *Gandy*'s clearly on a mission. It's steaming for the sub's Wintergarten area and its guns. But its aim is not perfect, and it strikes U-*550* about 25 feet from the stern, in the area of its aft torpedo tubes. Even from hundreds of yards away the deck crew of the *Joyce* can hear the screech of steel against steel as the *Gandy* rides right up over the stern of the *550*, settles back into the water, then backs away. Its gunners don't let up for a second. The air fills with the scent of the burning *Pan Penn*. Time: 1002 hours.

"Goddamn. Goddamn it." Wilcox, standing on the wing of his bridge, beats the rail with his fist. It's not that he's angry exactly, or jealous—although he will always tell the world, "I thought that was *my* sub." He's mostly surprised by the *Gandy*'s bold move.

And now here comes the *Peterson* for a piece of the action. As its 20mm and 40mm guns unload on the U-boat, it fires two depth charges from its starboard K-gun launchers as it passes the *550*. The charges, set for shallow detonation, hit on either side of the submarine, shattering air and sea. As soon as the *Peterson* clears the range, the *Joyce* brings all its guns to bear. So much ammo is hitting the conning tower that it's surrounded by a cloud of disintegrating steel.

19

Abandon Ship

U-*550* wallows on the surface, virtually defenseless.

Aboard the submarine, it's as if the men in the U-boat are already dead, know it, and are preparing themselves for a trip to the Norse warriors' afterlife in Valhalla. The lights in the sub have gone out again. Nobody remembers when. Perhaps the engineer killed all power to the boat to prevent stray currents or sparks touching off a fire from the leaking fuel or hydrogen off-gassing from damaged batteries. The ear-shattering clanging and banging of the ceaseless barrage hitting the tower and hull have obliterated everyone's sense of sound and time.

Blood drips from the tower hatch into the control room. Hänert was up there when the sub first started to take fire, but he fell back down the ladder headfirst with shrapnel wounds to his head, arm, and leg. He can't see out of his right eye. Word is circulating through the boat that the battle helmsman and the boatswain are dead or wounded in the tower; one of them may be cut in half. The shelling continues without a break. No one risks going up to look after the fallen seamen. The stern torpedomen and the engine room machinists have abandoned their posts. The boat's flooding badly aft. Spilling fuel continues drenching the engines and machinery spaces.

Wounded but still in control, Hänert orders the crew to prepare to abandon the boat. They must put on their warmest clothes, life vests, and underwater escape lungs. The men press close to the control room and the one open exit to the world outside, preparing physically and mentally to abandon ship. Someone heads up the ladder of the tower with a flare pistol in his hand. Possibly he's the first watch officer, Gutram von Lingelsheim-Seibicke. But no one can be sure. The men are starting to panic and push amid the jerking beams of flashlights.

Before the Old Man fell, he succeeded in opening the deck hatch in the tower. Men can smell the fresh air mixing with the acrid scents of pulverized steel and exploding warheads fuming through the boat. The man on the ladder eyes the source of this tainted air, the bright gray circle of sky at the top of the tower. He intends to try to shoot a signal up through the open hatch. Maybe if the Americans see his distress flare, they will show a little mercy.

Nobody really believes the man with the flare pistol will have success. What can he do? He's just a boy, like them. Just another dreamer in this collective nightmare. Has he forgotten Karl Dönitz has sealed their fates?

In 1939 Dönitz declared War Order #154 to the Ubootwaffe, which reads in part:

> *Weather conditions and proximity of land are of no consequence. Concern yourself only with the safety of your own boat and with efforts to achieve additional successes as soon as possible. We must be hard in this war. The enemy started the war in order to destroy us, and thus nothing else matters.*

In 1942 he underscored his take-no-prisoners policy with what is known as the *Laconia* Order:

> *All efforts to save survivors of sunken ships, such as the fishing out of swimming men and putting them on board lifeboats, the righting of overturned lifeboats, or the handing over of food and water, must stop. Rescue contradicts the most basic demands of the war: the destruction of hostile ships and their crews.*
>
> *The orders concerning the bringing in of captains and chief engineers stay in effect.*
>
> *Survivors are to be saved only if their statements are important for the boat.*
>
> *Stay firm. Remember that the enemy has no regard for women and children when bombing German cities!*

If this is the way that German submariners have been ordered to treat their enemy, how can they expect the Americans to treat them any differently?

But some of the men on U-550 have hope. They have listened to the unbridled cries for mercy in American jazz, watched the rugged individualism and nobility of cowboys in American movies. Maybe there are still Americans like Roy Rogers and Gene Autry. Maybe one of them will see this distress signal.

20

Cease Fire

1003–1015 Hours, April 16, 1944

As the USS *Joyce* churns closer to the sub, its guns pounding away, Wilcox sees a white flare rise from the U-boat's tower.

If he had his pipe, this would definitely be a moment for a puff and a short think. But the smoking lamp is still out on this DE, as per his own order, so the skipper must improvise, take command without the use of his prop. He must make the right decision. So what has he just seen? That's not just a distress flare from the U-boat, that's a *surrender* flare. It's a plea for clemency.

"Cease fire!" he tells his gunners. "Cease fire!" his talker repeats on the TBS to the other DEs.

The *Joyce*'s guns fall silent. The *Gandy*'s firing stops soon after.

But some gunners on the *Peterson* are still pounding away at the sub. In 1984 a crewman from the *Peterson*, Radarman Second Class

A Coast Guard photo of the tanker *Pan Pennsylvania*,
U-*550*'s only victim, before her fateful battle.

The conning tower of U-*550* breaks the surface as the
Pan Pennsylvania burns in the background.

The crew of the U-*550* crowd the conning tower as the boat begins to sink on April 16, 1944. Shell holes can be seen in the conning tower.

Another view of the dying U-boat with additional survivors in the water. Many of them would drown.

The discovery team poses in front of *Tenacious* with the sonar fish.
(L to R: Joe Mazraani holding Pirate, Eric Takakjian, Tom Packer, Steve
Gatto, Anthony Tedeschi, Garry Kozak, and Brad Sheard)

Looking aft at the incredibly intact starboard bow of the U-boat.
COURTESY BRADLEY SHEARD

Mark Nix swims over the bow.
COURTESY BRADLEY SHEARD

Mark Nix hovers over the conning tower.

Looking forward to the conning tower as Mark Nix lights up the scene.
Note the extended attack periscope.

The crew with Albert Nitsche, one of the last surviving crew members of U-*550*. (L to R: Joe Mazraani, Andreas Schalomon, Tom Packer, Anthony Tedeschi, Nadine Nitsche, Steve Gatto, Norman Nitsche, Albert Nitsche, Randy Peffer, Eric Takakjian, Brad Sheard, Harold Moyers)

Collingwood Harris, will tell a US Coast Guard oral historian about what he called the hysterical "euphoria" that pervaded his ship.

> *We were firing everything that we had and finally the order came to cease fire. And something that bothers me to this day was nobody ceased firing and the guns kept firing and the orders had come in screaming, "Cease fire! Cease fire!" Those twin forties were going "kaboom!," rhythmically pounding away. I guess that order was given five or six times before the guns began to let up. They didn't just stop. It just let down and finally died down and a voice kept screaming, "Cease fire! Cease fire!"*

Despite the firing from the *Peterson*, Wilcox sees the Germans streaming out of the conning tower and onto the deck with the intent of abandoning ship. Years later the sub's doctor, Friedrich Torge, will tell his family that panic rules during the last minutes aboard U-*550*. The after compartments are flooding fast. Men rush to escape the sinking vessel, pushing officers to the back, after the captain tells men to escape the sinking U-boat however they can. Torge considers how to face the freezing water that he will surely have to enter. He fortifies himself by clothing himself in his heavy dress uniform complete with its Red Cross armband, gobbles a bar of butter from the galley, and fills a flask with schnapps.

Engineer Hugo Renzmann sloshes through water to confirm that everybody is out except a dead man in the tower. When the water is above his waist in the control room, he blows what's left of the sub's compressed air into its ballast tanks to keep it afloat a few more precious minutes while the men evacuate. Finally, he manually opens the water vents to sink the sub. It's his last duty. The Ubootwaffe requires scuttling the boat as the final act of the engineer before leaving the vessel. The sub has to be sunk before the Americans can ransack it for intel, especially the boat's Enigma code machine and the current codebooks.

Contemporary accounts of the battle will tell of thirteen to fifteen Germans who climb out the conning tower hatch, assemble on the observation deck and Wintergarten, and hope that the Americans might rescue them. Among the men, the wounded Klaus Hänert, flanked by Dr. Torge. But for the next seventy years little will be said outside a small circle of survivors and veterans about the fates of more than forty other seamen from the U-550.

21

Life and Death

1015 Hours, April 16, 1944

Waves surge around the base of *U-550*'s tower. The boat's flooding so badly that the slate-gray seas swirl over the decks fore and aft. Growing ever more unstable from the flooding within, the boat's bow first submerges, then rises high above the waves. The men in the tower cast desperate stares at the *Joyce* as it nears their sinking U-boat's starboard side. Perhaps they are wondering if the destroyer escort intends to open fire on them.

But it doesn't. Its guns are silent.

Wilcox knows how fast 40-degree water can disable and kill. He saw death's terrifying speed on the night he tried to rescue the crew of the *Leopold*. Just a jump into 40-degree water can be fatal. When you fall into cold water, receptors in the skin trigger an array of physiological responses. The first is a gasp reflex. If this happens when your head is underwater and you inhale, you are well on your way to drowning.

If you are lucky enough to not draw water into your lungs, you have other issues. You will begin to hyperventilate. Your heart rate and blood pressure will spike. At this point panic may well set in, amplifying your cardiopulmonary problems. These events can bring on cardiac arrest. But even if your heart keeps beating, without a flotation device that cradles your head and face above the water, you will have difficulty breathing while experiencing the shock of cold water.

Cold shock peaks during your first minute of immersion. If you are still alive and conscious after a minute, your body will begin to shiver to keep itself warm. But it is fighting a losing battle. Water cools your body twenty-five times faster than air. Within a few minutes, the muscles of your limbs will grow dysfunctional. Bodily fluids will start to congeal in your tissue. First you will lose sensation in your fingers and hands, toes, feet. Then your legs and arms will go numb.

You will lose your ability to grasp things or even move your limbs. Trying to swim during the early stages of cold shock and hypothermia will only hasten your body's loss of heat and accelerate the paralysis of limbs. As your core temperature drops below 95 degrees Fahrenheit, you will become disoriented. You may hallucinate. Eventually you will become unconscious and die. Like most of the crew of the USS *Leopold* and the men from the *Pan Penn* who spilled into the water when their lifeboat overturned, you are literally or functionally dead in less than 10 minutes.

Maybe it's this knowledge and guilt over the men from the *Leopold* whom Wilcox couldn't save that informs his next decision. Surely his strong sense of duty and his ardent belief in the brotherhood of the sea drive his ensuing order, too. For better or worse, he's going to choose to take what some other captains would call an unacceptable risk with his ship and crew. What happens after this moment will forever change the trajectory of his life. If things go to hell, he will be dead or standing before a court-martial.

So be it. Wilcox goes with his gut and tells his crew to bring the *Joyce* right alongside the *550*. He orders his sailors to lower scramble nets from the starboard side and to dangle ropes.

Collingwood Harris, listening and recording the TBS transmissions on the *Peterson*, hears Wilcox tell the *Gandy* and the *Peterson*, "I am going in to pick up survivors. If this son of a bitch torpedoes me, I want you to kill every goddamned one of them." What a message, laced the way it is with a strong mix of nobility, fear, a sense of fairness, and a heavy dose of bravura.

Years later, when his son and stepsons ask him why he picked up the Germans, Wilcox will say, "Once those men were in the water, they were no longer my enemy. They would have died if we didn't get them."

While the other destroyers screen him, Wilcox moves the *Joyce* so close to the U-boat that he can look down the open hatch in the tower from the wing of the *Joyce*'s flying bridge. Fifteen minutes later he has thirteen Germans on the *Joyce*. One of the German boys, Heinrich Wenz, is severely wounded. The last two men to enter the water from the raised bow of the sub are Torge and Hänert. The doctor is standing by his wounded commander to the end. Like Leidy on the *Pan Penn*, the U-boat skipper is the last to leave his ship.

Wilcox has a boarding party primed. They aim to go into the 550 and try to keep it from sinking or at least to grab the codebooks and Enigma machine. But the swim of less than 10 yards from the U-boat to the DE is enough to virtually paralyze the Germans. Torge, Rauh, and Nitsche will tell their families that their hands were too frozen to grab the scramble net on the *Joyce*. Coasties have to come down the net to help the sub survivors. The first black man that Albert Nitsche has ever seen is a sailor from the *Joyce* who enters the water to help him up the net. Renzmann sees the doctor wrap a dangling rope from the DE around Klaus Hänert to keep him afloat after his life vest, damaged by the earlier shelling and shrapnel, disintegrates.

Meanwhile, the sub's already sinking beneath the waves. It's too late, too dangerous to put anyone on that boat. Wilcox orders his ship to back away from the derelict. As the Germans lie exhausted on the deck of the *Joyce*, coasties wrap them in blankets. Dr. Torge passes among his shipmates, offering them sips from the flask of schnapps that he brought off U-*550* with him. For Nitsche, the schnapps tastes like life itself. On the *Joyce* the Americans don't think about what has happened to all but this small clutch of rescued Germans. It is as if all those other young men from U-*550* just vanished or never were.

At 1030 hours U-*550* heaves its bow sharply above the waves as CPO O'Hara, who has been taking photos of events from the *Joyce*, clicks a final picture for posterity. The sub slides with a hiss stern-first below the North Atlantic into more than 300 feet of water. Aboard the *Joyce* Wilcox faces an uneasy complement of guests, thirty-one men from the *Pan Penn*, thirteen from the U-boat. Among these survivors are the captains of both ships, so recently mortal enemies. Now what?

22

Strange Bedfellows

Later on April 16, 1944

The clock on the bridge of the *Joyce* has almost reached noon, eight bells. The *Pan Penn* still fumes nearby. It's down by the stern, the after-house submerged. Bender's calling from the sound room that his ASW team hears pings from a solid contact, possibly another sub. *Goddamn*. Wilcox must be wondering, "When does this drama end?"

Since the U-boat sank, some of the *Joyce*'s crew have been attending to the wounded Germans. Others are trying to keep the Germans and the tankermen separated for fear of a brawl. Still others are getting the prisoners into warm, dry clothing before being placed under armed guard. Meanwhile, the deck crew continues sweeping the area for other U-boats. Since the mayhem began four hours ago, the *Joyce*, *Peterson*, and *Gandy* have suspected that there may be another U-boat nearby. Wilcox orders a depth charge attack on Bender's new target and requests a screen from *Gandy* and *Peterson*.

But in the midst of the attack run, Bender tells his skipper there has been a mistake. His sonar men have not spotted a second U-boat. Their target is the wreck of *550*. This is the last time anyone will know the U-boat's actual location for sixty-eight years. Red George can be scrubbed from the plotting board of the sub trackers at ESF headquarters. Nobody writes down the position. Why would anyone? U-*550* belongs to Neptune now . . . like the souls of her crew who never made it aboard a DE and those twenty-five men who died leaving the *Pan Penn*. Aboard the *Joyce* a boatswain's whistle echoes from the DE's public address system. "Now hear this . . ." Finally, DE-*317*'s crew stands down from general quarters and their battle stations.

At about 1300 hours, USS *Joyce*, USS *Peterson*, and USS *Gandy* turn east in search of their convoy. Later aboard the *Joyce* Bob Wilcox retires to the wardroom on the 01 deck for dinner. The room is dim for night running. Dinner is roast beef, fresh green beans, and baked potatoes. Wilcox sits at the head of the table with junior officers on his flanks. There's not much conversation, just the clanking of silverware against plates, the fuming of aromatic tobacco, and some small talk about the Germans. How young most of them are, how scared, how grateful. The *Joyce*'s medical man, the pharmacist's mate, has reported that Klaus Hänert will survive, his wounded crewman probably will not.

The room goes silent.

The officers of the *Joyce* must be thinking about how and when they will tell their families the story of all that has happened today. Bob Wilcox may be wondering what he will leave in the tale and what he will leave out when he finally sees his Alice and son, Dick, again. Mort Raphelson, eating with the sailors on the mess deck, may be having similar thoughts.

And the Germans? They will have stories to tell and edit as well. They are now prisoners of war headed for Ireland. Klaus Hänert, Hugo Renzmann, and Friedrich Torge, Albert Nitsche, and Johann Rauh can expect interrogations. What will they say to the Americans or the English interrogators? Will engineer Renzmann confess every detail that he knows about the new torpedoes and electric U-boats being tested back in Germany? Torge signed a contract with the Nazi Party to get help in paying for medical school after his father, a Protestant minister, died in 1939. Will he soon be regretting his choice to link himself with a totalitarian, bellicose, racist regime? Hänert knows that he will have to answer for his unprovoked attack on the *Pan Penn*. But can he ever tell the captain of the *Joyce*, the man who has rescued him from certain death, that he intended to fire T5 torpedoes at Wilcox's ship? Will he be accused of war crimes?

23

Burial at Sea

April 18, 1944

Wilcox looks agitated. He says that Heinrich Wenz could not be saved.

Hänert listens from his berth in an officer's cabin in USS *Joyce*. His head, shoulder, and leg remain bandaged and weeping blood. It has been two days since the battle, and CU-*21* has rejoined its convoy and plowed more than a third of the way across the North Atlantic. The weather continues exceedingly calm. Something about the moistness of the air feels like spring is finally breaking out over the world.

Wilcox tells Klaus Hänert that he wants to give Wenz a proper burial. Military honors.

The German admires this American's sense of military propriety and something deeper, a guarded empathy, perhaps. He thinks about all the letters that he will be writing to the families of these lost boys.

Each death tears at his heart. Is it enough to say that they died bravely in the service of the fatherland?

Wilcox wonders if the U-boat skipper has a scripture that they might use for the burial service. Neither man is particularly religious, but both are confirmed Christians. They know the Bible.

Conforming to traditional naval burials at sea, they choose a reading from the Book of Psalms. The Twenty-Third Psalm. It has a healing message. Couldn't everyone on this ship use such a message about now? And what about a second reading?

It's late morning on the sunny but cool Tuesday when Wilcox slows his DE. He gathers his ship's company—coast guard sailors, tankermen, U-550 survivors—at the port rail of USS *Joyce* just aft of the bridge. The navy and coast guard have a protocol for burial at sea, and Wilcox intends to do his best to follow it. The pallbearers, a mix of American seamen and Germans, lift the body of Heinrich Wenz on a pallet and balance it on the rail of the *Joyce*. To the dismay of some of the tankermen and coasties, the Stars and Stripes cover the body. Wilcox stands aft of the flag-draped remains in his dress blue uniform, Bible in hand and open. A mix of his own sailors and officers, as well as the men from the *Pan Penn*, surround him. On the other side of the body stand Klaus Hänert and his men alongside a rifle squad.

A boatswain blows his whistle, then calls, "All hands bury the dead . . . attention." A flag crew lowers the colors to half mast overhead. The men stiffen.

"Parade rest," says the boatswain.

Wilcox begins speaking in such a low and reverent voice that Mort Raphelson can hardly hear him. The coast guard skipper says that they are gathered here today to commit the mortal remains of Seaman Heinrich Wenz to the bosom of the sea.

For a few seconds he pauses. The engines of the *Joyce* murmur a low dirge as the captain of the *Joyce* launches into the first scripture reading. "The Lord is my shepherd. I shall not want. He maketh me to lie down in green pastures: he leadeth me beside the still waters. He restoreth my soul . . ."

After a pause, Wilcox reads again. The passage is from Psalm 107. It's a naval favorite for both him and Klaus Hänert, for their men, too.

> *Those who go down to the sea in ships,*
> *Who do business on great waters,*
> *They see the works of the* Lord,
> *And His wonders in the deep.*
> *For He commands and raises the stormy wind,*
> *Which lifts up the waves of the sea.*
> *They mount up to the heavens,*
> *They go down again to the depths;*
> *Their soul melts because of trouble.*
> *They reel to and fro, and stagger like a drunken man,*
> *And are at their wits' end.*
> *Then they cry out to the* Lord *in their trouble,*
> *And He brings them out of their distresses.*
> *He calms the storm,*
> *So that its waves are still.*
> *Then they are glad because they are quiet;*
> *So He guides them to their desired haven . . .*

"Amen." The word echoes from the assembled men, soars over the waves.

After the recitation of the Lord's Prayer, the boatswain blows his whistle, calls the men to attention and to salute.

Wilcox nods to the pallbearers. They tip up the pallet. The remains of Heinrich Wenz slide into the deep blue North Atlantic.

"Parade . . . rest." The group bows their heads.

Seamen fold up the flag. When the flag is folded, the boatswain whistles and calls for one last salute. The rifle team fires three shots into the air. More than a few of the men assembled here must be reflecting on all that has happened since April 15 and wonder if such a thing as "normal" will ever be possible again.

24

Farewell

April 27, 1944

The sky couldn't be bluer, the vegetation couldn't be greener, the air couldn't smell more fragrant with blossoms and flowers here on the banks of the River Foyle in Lisahally, Northern Ireland. But hardly anybody on USS *Joyce* is noticing the Irish spring unfolding at the moment. The ship's astir with rumors. This morning the Germans will be going ashore, going to prison.

Joyce arrived yesterday afternoon here at the river that flows into Lough Foyle. It's rafted portside to USS *Poole*, which lies at a wharf on the eastern edge of the city of Londonderry, "Derry," as it is commonly called. As the westernmost port of the British Isles, Derry has grown into a military outpost of considerable size. There are thirty thousand British and Canadians based here. Six thousand Americans, too. Many of the North Atlantic convoys begin and end at wharves on the river or in the huge protected anchorage of Lough

Foyle. At the beginning of the war, U-boats stalked the shipping lanes leading here. Not so much these days. English ASW vessels and aircraft sweep the area constantly.

Already Mort Raphelson, Delmar Leidy, and the *Joyce*'s other survivors off the *Pan Penn* have gone ashore to be met by consular officials with vouchers for clothes, meals, and hotels as well as plans for repatriation. The scuttlebutt on the *Joyce* claims that a detail of American marines is on its way for the twelve submariners from *U-550*. The men of the *Joyce* are lurking near the gangways that lead from the *Joyce* to the *Poole* then to shore. Guys are taking bets on whether the Germans will leave in handcuffs.

Some of the Americans would definitely like to see that, at least as it relates to one of the Germans. He's Friedrich Torge, the *550*'s young doctor. Since he came aboard the *Joyce*, he has been something of a spectacle in his uniform and Red Cross armband. A few nights ago, some of the *Joyce*'s sailors pulled a prank on Torge. While he was sleeping, they lifted all the badges and insignias from his uniform. Wilcox has had to threaten the crew with no liberty in Derry to get Torge's possessions returned. Respecting the badges, medals, and insignias of a prisoner of war is a matter of observing the Geneva Conventions for the treatment of POWs.

None of the other U-boat mariners has distressed the crew. The German sailors are just boys like themselves. Some speak English. Some claim to be Norwegians. Many have been drafted into the service. Quite a few have hoped that upon capture they would be taken to the United States and as far from the war as possible. Several have confessed sadness and fear about ending up in the United Kingdom. They were hoping to go to the United States. During the crossing the men of the *Joyce* and the Germans have shared clothes and cigarettes. They have talked of home, family, girlfriends. Scuttlebutt has it that Lieutenant Commander Wilcox has given up his cabin to Klaus Hänert and Hugo Renzmann. It's common knowledge that the skipper of the

Joyce has invited the German engineer Hugo Renzmann to take a pipe with him. He has given Torge and Hänert cigars, too.

Sometimes Hänert and Renzmann and Wilcox just sit and talk in English while seated in the captain's cabin. After more than a week aboard the *Joyce*, the Germans no longer feel like strangers or enemies. Now they are headed to a prison camp. Such is the lot of losers who do not die in war. But surely this conflict must end soon. *Nicht wahr?* Right? According to the Germans, the Allies' bombs are demolishing Deutschland. The Third Reich is bleeding U-boats. About sixty boats and crews have been lost since *550* left Kiel on February 6. One boat a day is simply vanishing.

"The marines are here." Word passes among the crew of the *Joyce* and the curious coasties on the *Poole*. The armed guards have come for the Germans. To a lot of people's surprise, there's no sign of handcuffs when the marines assemble the survivors of U-*550*. As the Americans look on, the German seamen gather dockside next to the *Poole*. They are joined by their officers, who have been led from their cabins by Bob Wilcox.

"Time to go," the marine in charge tells his prisoners.

The men look anxiously toward Hänert. It's just about the first time that they have seen the Old Man since he slipped off their U-boat looking half dead. He's wearing sunglasses to protect his damaged right eye. But he's standing erect, looking fit for service again in a knit seaman's sweater. He cuts a dashing figure even to the eyes of the Americans as he lines up his men in two columns of six to face Robert Wilcox. Hänert is at the left end of the front column, flanked by the other two surviving officers, Renzmann and Torge. Someone clicks a picture from the deck of USS *Poole*.

"Good luck," says Wilcox.

"Fair winds, Captain," says Hänert.

Wilcox nods.

An awkward pause settles over the gathering. Then U-*550*'s skipper turns to his men, "Achtung."

The Germans snap to attention as they face the captain of the *Joyce* and salute with their right hands to their brows. The submariners hold their salute. Hänert takes two steps toward Wilcox, looks him in the eyes, salutes too.

Before Wilcox knows it, he's saluting the Germans as well.

25

Loose Ends

The Postwar Years

Their moment as players in the Battle of the Atlantic over, the survivors of SS *Pan Pennsylvania*, the officers and men of USS *Joyce*, and twelve submariners from U-*550* take their exits from the world's stage . . . at least for a while.

Mort Raphelson will continue sailing as a radio officer in the merchant marine service until the war ends. Later, he will attend Villanova University, train as an electrical engineer, fall in love, get married, and raise four children in the Philadelphia area. He won't totally leave the water. Small fishing boats on Delaware Bay will always have a place in his life. For relaxation he will continue to smoke his pipe and build all manner of clocks. Occasionally he will see Mark Zeller, who was his assistant aboard the Pan Penn when it sank. Only then will Raphelson talk about April 16, 1944, but not much.

Bob Wilcox will rise to the rank of captain in the US Coast Guard and spend more than thirty years in the service. He and Alice will have a second son after the war and settle in suburban Baltimore. During the postwar years, he will correspond with Hugo Renzmann, Friedrich Torge, Klaus Hänert, and other survivors of the 550. He will send them CARE packages to help them through the lean times as a divided Germany tries slowly to rebuild. The former skipper of USS *Joyce* will survive Alice in retirement and marry twice more. He will spend his final years in Delray Beach, Florida, lending a hand to various charities and service organizations. Although he will serve in many ships, he will always think of the *Joyce* as "my ship," and he will attend DE veterans' reunions until his death in the mid-1990s.

Johann Rauh, that boyish machinist from Munich who sailed on U-*550*, will finally get his dream of landing in America. He will immigrate to the United States in the 1950s, master English, attend college, and earn an engineering degree. Rauh and his wife, Helga, will raise their family on Long Island, where he can look out to the east at the Atlantic and imagine the day a DE numbered *317* plucked him from those freezing waters.

Albert Nitsche will return to Germany and meet the love of his life, Rosina, an ethnic German from Yugoslavia. He will work at all manner of jobs. As a talented carpenter, he will build houses and commercial buildings to restore a bomb-ravaged Germany. He and Rosina will father a son and live the rest of their lives south of Frankfurt in the same house as their son, his wife, and two grandchildren. All his life he will keep in contact with his old shipmate Johann Rauh and Rauh's wife, Helga, visiting the United States several times to see them.

Years after the war Friedrich Torge will tell his children and grandchildren that April 16, 1944, is the day when he was given a new chance at life. He will be the last of the U-*550* crew to be released from Allied prisoner-of-war camps and will not return to Germany until 1948. When he returns he will have deep regrets about his association with the Nazis and a yearning to help the world. For the next fifty years he will work as a dermatologist and gain a reputation for his high moral standards, at one point challenging a major German manufacturer for exposing its employees to lead poisoning.

Klaus Hänert will return home after prison camps in England and Canada and write long, heartfelt letters to the families of his lost shipmates. He will also create a booklet honoring his crew and mail it to their families. He will marry, and settle in Kiel near his former engineer, Hugo Renzmann. Both men will raise families and join the new West German Navy, the Bundesmarine. They will serve as captains aboard German-manned NATO destroyers built in America, training with their former enemies in the United States. For the rest of their lives, the survivors of U-*550* will think of Klaus Hänert as Herr Kaleun and treasure his presence at their reunions. Eventually Hänert's son Wolf and his grandsons will following in the Old Man's wake and join the German Navy as officers, sometimes serving in submarines.

One thing all of these men will share in their lives after the war will be a reticence to talk about the specific details of what happened on April 16, 1944, even with each other. And it is likely that those details would have been lost with the deaths of the survivors. Except for one thing. Deep-wreck divers, energized by the technological advances in scuba, will become fascinated with finding the drowned submarine, intrigued—no, *obsessed*—by the opportunity to sort out the facts from the mythology surrounding the *550*'s last hours.

These questions about "what happened here?" have the seductive power of a siren's call to deep-wreck divers. They yearn for the chance to find a virgin wreck, swim among its ghosts, and plumb the secrets of their lives as well as their deaths. Nothing is more fascinating than the chance to revive forgotten legends and uncover the truths at their cores. And the more expense and danger involved in the quest? Bring them on.

You want adventure? Try looking for a German sub lost somewhere near the edge of the continental shelf in water more than 50 feet deeper than the liner SS *Andrea Doria*. Scuba divers rank the *Doria* as the Mount Everest of wreck dives. If you could find U-*550* and then actually have the courage to dive it, the adventure would be like what? Like finding a peak higher than Everest and climbing it for the first time? And maybe if you can get back to the land of the living, if you don't die, you will come trailing secrets that the gods have been keeping to themselves.

PART THREE

Deadly Ventures

26

Panic Attack

July 1983

Death stalks deep-wreck diving. Like high-altitude mountain climbing and air racing, deep-wreck diving means laying your life on the line every time that you suit up. There are a hundred ways to die beneath the sea, and some are ever-present. All that a diver can do to protect himself after he yields to the passion of wreck diving is to buy the best gear possible and maintain it. Then train to learn how to manage the risks . . . and train some more. Because if he does this sport long enough, sooner or later death will snag him or the guy next to him. Everyone who dives deep wrecks knows people who have died. One wreck alone, the _Andrea Doria_, has claimed at least seventeen divers. Recovering bodies of fellow divers is something that comes with the territory.

A deep-wreck diver faces several constant dangers on a dive. The first three relate to the depth. If something goes wrong for a diver 170 feet underwater, he cannot just shoot to the surface. Every 33 feet deeper that a diver descends into the water the pressure on his body increases incrementally. These increments of 33 feet are called "atmospheres of pressure." If you are on the surface, your body is functioning in one atmosphere of pressure. Thirty-three feet down, you are experiencing two atmospheres of pressure.

At the top of the wreck of Italian luxury liner SS *Andrea Doria*, about 250 feet in depth, a diver feels seven atmospheres of pressure. He doesn't feel this like weight on his body, but his lungs, capillaries, and tissues sense the difference because the air he's breathing from his tanks is seven times more compressed than the air he breathes on the surface. At this depth he uses seven times as much air for each breath as he would on the surface. And if he's anxious or panicked, he uses much more. Running out of breathing gas is every diver's number one fear.

Air is 21 percent oxygen, 79 percent nitrogen. Oxygen, of course, fuels our tissues. Nitrogen is an inert gas and has basically no effect on the human body at one atmosphere. It's just along for the ride with the oxygen during our respiratory cycle. The nitrogen travels in solution, like the gas in a bottle of seltzer water, through our bloodstream and off-gasses through our lungs when we exhale. The deeper a diver goes, the more nitrogen gets absorbed in the solution of his bloodstream (because of increased pressure). If a diver tries to ascend too quickly to the surface, then the nitrogen bubbles up, like the gas in a shaken can of Coke. The bubbles build up in tissue outside the blood. Depending where nitrogen bubbles occur, they can cause anything from excruciating pain to blindness, paralysis, stroke, or death. Divers refer to such trauma as "decompression sickness" and, more commonly, "the bends" or "getting bent."

To avoid the bends, deep-wreck divers make decompression stops on their way back up the anchor line to the dive boat. Until the advent of dive computers in the late 1980s, many divers carried laminated copies of the US Navy decompression tables with them to tell them at what depth and for how long they had to stop and "hang" on their way up to the dive boat.

In addition to having to manage a safe decompression before returning to the surface, a diver also has to manage the physiological phenomenon of nitrogen narcosis. This usually begins to affect a diver when he or she descends below 66 feet, and it grows more intense the deeper you go. Divers call it "getting narked." Everyone experiences getting narked differently. Some divers get clumsy, some forgetful, some paranoid, some euphoric, some hallucinate. Many divers compare being narked to being drunk. Diving to extreme depths can be like balancing on a narrow beam high above the ground after several martinis. It's frighteningly easy to crash and die even when your equipment is functioning perfectly . . . and sometimes gear fails. A minor problem, such as a leaky face mask or a finicky regulator, can snowball into a catastrophe for a narked diver.

A third demon that deep-wreck divers face is oxygen toxicity. Below a depth of 200 feet, oxygen (because it is under so much pressure) becomes poisonous to the body. High-pressure oxygen can attack the central nervous system and the pulmonary system in a diver's body, causing anything from tunnel vision, disorientation, and seizure to breathing problems, blackout, and—often—death. When divers experience these symptoms, they call it "taking an oxygen hit." For some divers just the thought of experiencing an oxygen hit or being narked is enough to turn them away from this sport.

But not the few hundred men and women who call themselves deep-wreck divers. They relish the challenge. They know that going into a wreck, sometimes called "penetration diving," is like entering a haunted house at a theme park. Except here the things that go bump in the dark don't just spike your blood pressure, they sometimes kill you. There are dozens of ways to get trapped or lost in a wreck. The boogie man waits not just in gear failures, decompression sickness, nitrogen narcosis, and oxygen toxicity, but also in currents, the sudden loss of visibility, and all manner of ship debris that can grab ahold of you and never let you go. The boogie man also lurks in the darker twists and turns of a diver's mind.

Wreck diver Brad Sheard doesn't tell many people this story. It's too sad, too scary. The date and the place have stamped themselves in his mind. July 12, 1983. He's 35 miles southeast of Fire Island, New York, 170 feet above what divers generally call the Virginia Wreck.

The morning starts sunny, hot, and hazy, with the dive boat rocking gently on a sea of glass. Divers roll out of their berths one by one, visit the head, brush their teeth, brew coffee, spoon bowlsful of cereal, and check over their gear as they slowly prepare for their first dive of the day. But despite the lazy morning and the benign weather, Sheard's getting a bad vibe. He's twenty-five years old in 1983. Tall, lanky, blond. A man who will one day grow a long ponytail that he wears like a Native American. His dive buddies will tease him about being a hippie. But he is anything but a drugged-out leftover of the counterculture. His low-key chill comes from a quiet skepticism and an intense intellectual curiosity about how things work, be they aircraft, submarines, or political systems. Sheard also loves to read and research history. He's two years out of graduate school in aeronautical engineering and working for Grumman Aerospace in Bethpage, Long Island. His job is just a few miles from where he grew up on Great South Bay in Sayville and started scuba diving at age nineteen.

This trip to the Virginia Wreck is his first trip offshore to dive a sunken ship in deep water. He has only 165 dives to his credit. But it's not his relative inexperience that has him a little on edge. It's the anxiety of one of the other divers on the boat and the knowledge that a year ago to this very day the veteran diver John Dudas died out here. He was diving this same wreck from this same dive boat, a converted swordfisher called the *Sea Hunter*, out of Freeport, Long Island.

Veteran divers Gary Gentile and Jon Hulburt and two other divers, Mike McGarvey and Jerry Rosenberg, are on the trip with Sheard. The boat has been at sea for more than 24 hours. Yesterday the divers descended for two dives on the bones of the *Coimbra*, then anchored over the Virginia Wreck for the night to wait for sunrise and a chance to dive again. For the past hour this morning, while the divers finish their breakfasts and coffee and start sliding into their thermal long underwear and dry suits, Rosenberg's anxiety has really started to spike.

He keeps telling Sheard and McGarvey, who will be his diving partners, that he has heard that this wreck is such a pile of rubble it's easy to get lost. When they descend to the wreck they need to always keep track of where Gentile and Hulburt have tied in the anchor line to the debris. The anchor line will guide the divers back up to the boat. At the least, losing the anchor line means that a diver has the additional task of making an ascent on his own, away from the relative safety of the anchor line that will bring him to the surface next to the boat and other divers, where he might be able to get help if he needs it.

During an ascent independent of the anchor line, a diver must use the line on his safety reel clipped to his tank harness or other piece of equipment. The first thing he does is to inflate a buoy, either a lift bag or a "safety sausage," which he carries with him. The buoy is attached to the nylon line on his safety reel. After the diver inflates and releases the buoy to the surface, he pulls the line taut so it is as vertical as possible between the surface and the bottom. Once the line is taut, he cuts it off his reel and ties the line to debris on the bottom. Then he starts his ascent with the line to guide him.

But maintaining a horizontal position relative to the dive boat, especially if there is current, is difficult. Current may tug the buoy quite a distance from the boat. And maintaining vertical control while stopping at the correct depths for decompression can be more challenging on a safety line that is not attached to something as stable as an anchored boat. In addition, sometimes the combination of a diver's weight and a strong current can pull the buoy scores of feet underwater, leaving the diver in a precarious situation short of the surface in a place where neither he nor the buoy can be seen by lookouts on the dive boat.

Sheard would rather not think about the challenges of such an ascent right now. He's starting to feel a little freaked out by the prospect. Rosenberg's worrying, and he couldn't be happier to pull his hood over his head, lock his mask over his face, slip off the stern of the *Sea Hunter*, and slide underwater, where there is nothing to listen to except the hiss of his regulator as he inhales and the burbling of his exhaled bubbles. The visibility is astounding, 50 feet or better, and Sheard's loving the vista beneath him, loving being alone in a watery world that looks the way he imagines the Caribbean must look. Long shafts of sunlight probe the crystal, blue water.

All too soon McGarvey and Rosenberg swim up beside him and signal that it's time to start down the anchor line to the wreck as a trio of dive buddies. One of the first things you hear when you start developing an interest in deep-wreck diving is that unlike shallow-water sport scuba divers, many deep-wreck divers shun diving with a partner unless that diver is someone they trust with their life. An unreliable partner can get himself into trouble and end up killing you both in the time it takes to think, "Oh, crap." For this reason diving with Rosenberg today doesn't make Sheard feel all that comfortable. He barely knows this man, has never dived at all with him.

But it's goddamn amazing down here, with the columns of golden sunlight making it look to Sheard as if he's descending into a temple. The bones of the wreck appear below like the ruins of the lost continent of Atlantis. Very cool, thinks Sheard. He pushes his concern about having an unfamiliar dive buddy to the back of his mind and just soaks up minute after minute as they slowly drift like a trio of oddly shaped fish over a chaotic jumble of twisted steel hull plates and broken beams. It's as if time stops and the three of them are locked into a Jacques Cousteau moment with the cod, the pollack, and the lobsters. This is only Sheard's third dive into six atmospheres of depth, and he's feeling what the old TV shows such as *Sea Hunt* called the "rapture of the deep." He's narked, and probably so are his dive buddies.

"This is really awesome," he tells himself as he watches the play of surface light over the mangled wreck, watches an immense codfish hovering like a blimp over the prop shaft of what was once a freighter.

The Virginia Wreck is just a nickname. No one knows for sure the name of the ship that lies here. But Sheard and others have speculated that this is the wreck of the SS *Sommerstad*, a 340-foot Norwegian freighter. A German submarine, U-*117*, torpedoed the freighter in these waters in August 1918. Swimming over the wreck, he can imagine the moments after the torpedo struck. He can almost hear the shouts of men as they scramble into the lifeboats, picture the *Sommerstad*'s captain, George Hansen, jumping from the ship's rail at the last instant, spraining his ankle as he lands in a lifeboat.

Sheard's still soaking in the shadowy bones of this ruined ship and imagining the *Sommerstad*'s last moments afloat when he notices Rosenberg swimming erratically above the wreck. He's searching left, right, twirling to look behind him as if he thinks that something like a big shark is about to attack. Looking on, Sheard realizes that he and the other divers have almost chewed up all of their bottom time. Rosenberg's searching for the anchor line to start back up, but he doesn't see it. Come to think of it, Sheard doesn't see it either, and he feels that "Oh, shit" jab of adrenaline shoot through his chest.

He's stopping to slow his breathing and think when he sees his partners beginning to tie the lines from their safety reels to the wreck. They intend to make free ascents, including deco stops at 20 feet and 10 feet on these safety lines. McGarvey and Rosenberg have tied into the wreck only 5 feet apart.

"That ain't good," thinks Sheard. "They are too close together." They could get tangled in each other's line or obstruct the other guy's ascent. He checks his air, sees he has plenty, but decides that looking for the anchor line isn't worth the risk. He'll make a free ascent, too.

But to be safe, he ties off his line more than 20 feet from the other guys and starts up.

He's busy. When a diver's making a free ascent, especially a diver with limited experience, he needs to devote a lot of attention to managing the changing buoyancy in his dry suit so he doesn't find himself in an out-of-control rush to the surface. Sheard adjusts his buoyancy by venting air through an exhaust valve on the chest of his suit. Every time he needs to vent air, he has to roll onto his back, let out some air, then roll back over again. At the same time he's trying to keep track of his depth and checking the pressure gauge for his air tanks to make sure he has enough air to complete his ascent and deco stops.

Halfway to the surface, he looks over to see how his two dive buddies are doing 20 feet away, and he sees Rosenberg reach over to McGarvey and rip the regulator out of his partner's mouth. Now McGarvey is punching Rosenberg and trying to take back his regulator. Both men keep throwing punches and fighting over that regulator. Tugging, pushing, slugging. Tearing at each other's faces and gear. It is by far the most violent thing that Sheard has ever witnessed, *Fight Club* brutal. Body-jarring, head-snapping brutal. A fight to the death.

Almost instantly, Sheard realizes what has happened. Rosenberg started to panic when he discovered that he could not find the anchor line. Panic led to a raised heart rate and rapid breathing. Then the diver started gulping air like a racehorse. Now he's out. Or thinks he's out. He may have a spare pony bottle of air that he has forgotten about. But instead of signaling to McGarvey that he needed to buddy-breathe and share a regulator, Rosenberg just grabbed for McGarvey's air supply and threw his partner into a fight for his own life.

For an instant, Sheard considers trying to swim to the two fighters to offer them air from his spare pony bottle, but on second thought he knows better. Everything he has ever learned in diving classes tells him that if he gets involved with two panicked, air-deprived divers, he will get sucked into a life-and-death struggle and end up an additional casualty. Clearly, Rosenberg and possibly McGarvey are not thinking rationally. These guys are slugging it out for the one working air supply, and the violence of what's going on is frightening.

"Stop!" Sheard hears himself shouting into his regulator. "Stop!"

It's almost as if the other men hear him, because within seconds McGarvey has his regulator back in his mouth and Rosenberg has gone limp. He's sinking on his back down through the columns of sunlight. Sinking, getting smaller now.

"Holy fuck, he's dead," Sheard says to himself.

Meanwhile, McGarvey has started clawing his way to the surface as if he's climbing an invisible vine. Sheard continues up, too, telling himself to forget what he just saw and focus on managing his free ascent.

At between 30 and 20 feet below the surface, McGarvey starts swimming toward Sheard. The eyes in his partner's mask look as big as hockey pucks to Sheard, and for a second he feels a huge stab of fear as he wonders if the other diver is about to attack him. But McGarvey doesn't attack. He slashes his index finger across his neck. It's the universal diving signal that he's out of air. Sheard doesn't hesitate. He passes the regulator that's in his mouth to McGarvey and finds his backup regulator from his pony bottle.

The two men are buddy-breathing like this at their 20-foot deco stop when suddenly McGarvey spits out Sheard's reg and bolts for the surface. The loss of McGarvey's weight puts Sheard's buoyancy out of control. His suit has too much air now, and he, too, is rocketing to the surface, blowing right through his scheduled 10-minute deco stop at 10 feet and forcing him to drop the safety reel and line.

Luckily, both men pop up within 30 feet of the dive boat.

"What's wrong?" calls the boat captain.

"Jerry's fucked!" Sheard hears himself shouting.

"What do you mean?"

"He's dead. The guy's dead."

Sheard can see that the dive boat captain is becoming distraught.

He keeps saying that he's cursed (having lost John Dudas here a year ago) as he helps McGarvey aboard. But Sheard can't stick around to explain what he has seen. He knows that he must beat it to the anchor line and pull himself back down to 20 feet to finish his deco stop or risk getting bent.

When Gentile and Hulburt come up the anchor line from their dives to hang at their deco stop with Sheard, they have the look of satisfied pro divers returning from a great trip on a wreck. It appears to Sheard that they have no idea what has just happened. This is one of those moments that every diver has experienced when he or she feels completely stifled in the ability to communicate with fellow divers underwater because hand signals just cannot express complex experiences. Sheard wishes like hell that he could tell Gentile and Hulburt, because now his mind has begun cycling over and over what he has witnessed. Two words are beating through his head like the roll of timpani drums. "Holy shit. Holy shit."

After everybody is aboard the dive boat except Rosenberg, and McGarvey is recovering from missing his deco stops, the divers make a plan. Gentile and Hulburt must go down to look for the body. These men are all too familiar with the drill and accomplish their gruesome task in short order, sending up Rosenberg on a lift bag full of air. Sheard has to swim out to the body once it surfaces and tie a line on it to haul it back to the dive boat. Before he starts his swim, the boat captain tells him, "Don't look at the guy's face. You don't want to see that blank stare in your dreams for the rest of your life."

Eventually, a coast guard helicopter arrives and takes the body. Ashore Sheard and McGarvey have to give statements to a police detective. Later they meet with Rosenberg's young wife, because they were with her husband when he died, and they feel that she has a right to know what happened to him. They don't tell the story in much detail, for obvious reasons. It is a difficult meeting that has to be done for a fellow diver and his next of kin.

Sheard feels shell-shocked. He tells himself that if he doesn't make another dive almost immediately, he may never dive again. So . . . three days after the accident, he dives on the wreck of the SS *Oregon*. During the dive he shies away from other divers. His regulator seems to have some sort of problem. It feels like the reg is never giving him enough air. His shyness around other divers and the regulator problems persist for six months. Then one day they both disappear, and he realizes that his reclusiveness and the reg problem have been symptoms of panic attacks that have been hitting him in waves every time he dives. Today he would call it PTSD.

Three antidotes for his trauma are to bury himself in work at Grumman, to keep on diving to face his fears, and to plunge into historical research about the shipwrecks of the mid-Atlantic coast. Many of the wrecks that he hears guys talking about at his dive club meetings are ships sunk by German U-boats. More than a hundred ships met their ends off this coast in World War II. A lot of these torpedoed ships lie out near the edge of the continental shelf, undiscovered. Two of these wrecks played major roles in a dramatic battle. A tanker called the SS *Pan Pennsylvania* and the sub that sank it, U-*550*.

Virgin wrecks. Every diver's dream. Definitely better things to wrap your mind around than the death of a fellow diver. Seven years after the accident on the Virginia Wreck, Sheard will write a book titled *Beyond Sport Diving*. At one point in this book he will say, "Dive stories can sometimes be like fish stories. . . . They tell of mounds of china stretching as far as the eye can see, and of sending up goody bags full of treasures. Such tall tales often extend to secret wreck sites. . . . These ancient wreck sites lie undisturbed on the bottom, waiting for someone adventurous enough to visit them and discover the secrets they still hold." At the end of his book he speculates about some of these legendary lost wrecks. The final and most seductive wreck that he mentions is U-*550*.

Sheard closes his book by saying that the German submarine is an untouched prize. "She lies in deep water, however, and a visit to her realms at a depth of 310 feet would require advanced diving techniques.

Perhaps someday a future generation of divers will brave the treacherous depths to explore the time capsule from an era when traveling on the high seas was far from safe."

Humans are a curious species. Sometimes the very events that traumatize us give birth to magnificent obsessions.

27

Body Search

March 1993

Despite the long johns that Steve Gatto's wearing inside his dry suit, the 34-degree water bites at his skin as he reaches the recently sunken tugboat *Thomas Hebert*. He's trying hard to keep this dive all business, trying hard to hold his emotions in check. That's the way it has to be if you want to be safe on a body recovery dive, especially if you know the men who died in the wreck. And that is definitely the case with Gatto today. He once worked with some of these guys.

Since the *Hebert* went down mysteriously a few weeks ago, leaving the barge it was towing to mark the wreck site, the coast guard and the insurance companies have put more than a few hurdles in front of Gatto and his dive partner Tom Packer's voluntary mission to recover the dead, but their persistence has paid off. The coast guard has no divers for this kind of work, and now the partners are coordinating efforts—using other veteran wreck divers they have recruited—to recover the dead for the families and Gatto's former employer who co-owns the tug. Gatto and Packer dove on the *Hebert* a week ago to get the lay of the land, but a horrendous northeast blizzard sent them running for cover before they had time to go deep into the wreck and find any of its crew.

With the storm gone after five days of howling gales, the divers are back. Today they have a plan to penetrate the sunken tug and do a systematic search, but as they reach the wreck on their descent down the anchor line, Gatto spots a light flashing at him from the bluish-green darkness here at 140 feet. Possibly the light is a warning or a call for help by other divers from the team already on the wreck.

Gatto's a first-responder kind of guy. That's one of the reasons why he volunteered to dive this wreck in search of the lost crewmen. He can't ignore the call of that light. Someone could be in trouble, and Packer, already heading toward the wheelhouse, should be fine on his own . . . for the moment. So, with a wave to his buddy, Gatto turns and swims toward the flashing light. The cold water pricking at his skin is more than just noticeable, and Gatto thinks about how most mariners consider sinking into water this cold as sudden death, but here he is volunteering to submerge himself beneath 140 feet of frigid ocean. His regulator has begun spitting ice down his throat.

At the stern of the 94-foot tug lying nearly upside down in the sand, Gatto finds two other divers . . . but no danger—well, at least no diver in trouble. The light's a signal that the other men have found something. They're beginning to rig a body to be sent to the surface with a lift bag. Gatto tells himself that he should feel some satisfaction. Thanks to this search operation, here's a dead mariner who will be going home to his family.

But back to the mission. Four men are still lost in this wreck, and Packer's alone up forward at the wheelhouse. Gatto gives a couple of hard kicks with his legs and fins. He wants to get back to his buddy before Packer starts into the *Hebert* by himself. For more than ten years he and Packer have been watching out for each other's back. Called the "most formidable deep-wreck dive team on the eastern seaboard" in the best seller *Shadow Divers*, these two men have made thousands of dives together. And they have faced the death of men before. Too many men.

Kicking back toward the wheelhouse of the tug, Gatto gauges the visibility at about 20 feet, but he can't actually see that far because drops of fuel oil are rising off the wreck like a swarm of little black bees. When they hit the lens of his mask, they shatter and leave distracting smudges. Squinting through the smudges, he searches for his buddy in the gloom. It seems like minutes pass. Despite the swimming, he feels the cold water pressing in on his body . . . until he spots a silhouette, hovering like an astronaut in a spacesuit outside the wheelhouse.

Packer waves, and Gatto feels the tension in his chest ease just a smidge. Sticking with the motto "plan your dive, and dive your plan," he drops down into the wheelhouse to look for the lost crew. He wants Packer to spot for him, wants Packer to wait at the doorway while he swims deeper into the wreck. During the divers' previous trip to the wreck, Gatto spotted for Packer when he went into the wreck. That's how it goes with these guys. They take turns assuming the worst risks.

Over a decade of making penetration dives together, Gatto and Packer have learned the importance of having one partner station himself near an exit from the wreck. If the diver going deeper into the wreck stirs up too much silt or debris and the vision goes to hell, he wants to be able to home in on his buddy's light and have his partner lead him out of the wreck. No question, Gatto's putting his life in his friend's hands. It's cold and dark in here.

Born in 1961, Gatto grew up in South Jersey as a competitive wrestler, and the sport left him with a broad-shouldered and restless body looking for outlets. As a young adult, he started competitive drag racing, but it didn't meet his physical needs. Then, enthralled by the TV series *The Undersea World of Jacques Cousteau*, Gatto decided to take a diving course. After being down on his first wreck with the schools of silver-sided fish and the bones of a ship to stir his imagination, he became hooked. Shortly thereafter, he gave up racing cars and started sinking a lot of his income from a series of jobs into buying dive gear and paying for boat rides to deeper wrecks almost every weekend.

By 1981 he had met Tom Packer, and they began diving with top-of-the-line wreck divers such as Gary Gentile and Jon Hulburt. Two years later Gentile took Gatto with him to dive the wreck of the *Andrea Doria* for the first time. Soon Gatto, Packer, Brad Sheard, and a few other close friends formed the nucleus of young and gutsy underwater explorers who called themselves the Atlantic Wreck Divers. They regularly pushed the physical and technical limits of sport scuba diving, following their mentors Gentile and Hulburt in a quest to find new wrecks often untouched by previous generations of divers. They were on a quest to discover wrecks that Gentile wrote about in his popular diving and nautical history books, wrecks that he labeled "depth unknown, location unknown."

But this dive on the *Hebert* is something altogether different. It's a way for Gatto, Packer, and the other divers whom they have recruited to serve a greater good. It seems right that they should help bring the crew of this tug home to their families. A shipwreck makes a cold and lonely grave.

In this wreck, at the moment, Gatto's passing a door, a chair, and other gear back to Packer to push out through the broken wheelhouse window. Then Gatto disappears into a hallway. In clearing some of the corridor from the wheelhouse into the galley and berthing area of the tug, Gatto has stirred up a cloud of debris as well as silt swept into the wreck by the recent nor'easter. Now he's in zero visibility inside a tomb. There's danger all around him that he can't see, and he doesn't like it. From somewhere inside that cloud, he finds Packer's hand and squeezes. It means "I've had enough. Get me out of here."

With half of their bottom time gone, the partners swim free of the wheelhouse and head back to the engine room, where they hope to find an alternate route into the crew's quarters and galley. The divers who recovered the first body have already started up to their deco stops. Gatto and Packer are alone. With the hull of this topsy-turvy wreck poised overhead, Gatto feels like he and Packer are entering a cavern that funnels toward a dark doorway. Once inside the engine room, the men face chaos. What was once an orderly space for the tug's machinery has now become a rat's nest of tumbled gear. Brushing aside dangling towing hawsers, rope, buckets, and large plastic tubs of motor oil and hydraulic fluid, Gatto and Packer swim forward to another doorway leading into the crew's quarters.

The engine room has changed since their visit here before the nor'easter. The storm has freed a massive red tool chest that blocked the doorway leading forward. A welder partially dislodged from a floor plate still hangs over the door. But Gatto reasons that if it hasn't fallen yet, it might not fall for a while. Packer must be thinking the same thing because he darts under the welder and through the door into the galley and berthing area.

This time Gatto spots for his partner, watches the beam of Packer's dive light and the diver's shadow moving away into the guts of the tug. He can tell that Packer's nervous by the way he looks cautiously around every corner before swimming forward, knows that Packer doesn't want to meet a dead mariner eye-to-eye in that tight space.

While hovering near the sill between the engine room and galley, Gatto's eyes catch something at the edge of his dive light's beam. Among the wreckage beneath him, he spots a pair of boots sticking out from under masses of ropes. Sinking closer, he sees that the boots are attached to jeans. And legs. A missing crew member.

Gatto kneels over the body. It crosses his mind that maybe he knows this man, but once again he tells himself that safety down here depends on focusing on the mission. There are two problems at hand. One, how to get the body out of the debris without turning the visibility to shit in an area that Packer will have to transit. And two, they have already overstayed their bottom time. Now they are going to have to make longer deco stops in this cold-ass water.

He's resolving not to free the body on this dive and willing his buddy to reappear when Packer emerges from the darkness, looks at him face-to-face, bright eyes reaching out through the lens of his mask.

He raises one finger in front of Gatto's mask. It means that Packer has found one body. Gatto signals his own find. He can't think about how these discoveries make him feel. Maybe a sense of accomplishment will hit him and Packer once they are back on the dive boat. Surely a sense of sadness and horror will rock him when he thinks about those guys' last moments drowning in a tug as it plunges toward the bottom of the ocean. But for now he's focused on keeping his partner and himself safe. Time to start up.

During one of their deco stops, Gatto and Packer watch two other divers pass them on the way up. The other divers are not breathing air. They are breathing mixed gases known as trimix, a blend of helium, oxygen, and nitrogen. It helps divers avoid getting narked, and in this case the increased oxygen has an added benefit of speeding up the decompression. Shivering in his suit and watching the trimix divers disappearing above him on their way to the surface, Gatto thinks, "I've gotta get whatever they're using."

But cold water or not, a wreck fraught with potential entanglements or not, trimix or not, Gatto knows that he and Packer will be coming back to the *Hebert* as soon as they can. There are still four dead men down here to be brought home. The mission isn't complete, and finishing the job is what these partners do. On subsequent trips using trimix, Gatto, Packer, and their team will make a clean sweep of the *Hebert* and recover all of its crew. They will also gather and document evidence about what caused the accident for the National Transportation Safety Board as well as the coast guard.

If Gatto could look further ahead into the future, he would see trimix gas as the key new tool in his and Packer's compulsion to solve undersea riddles and bring home the dead. Inevitably, the potential for deep diving on trimix will draw Gatto and Packer to a mother lode of festering broken dreams, human misery, and mystery. Klaus Hänert's vanished U-boat waits for these divers. And so does Mort Raphelson's lost tanker.

28

Diving the Moon

Injuries and death related to deep diving on air have been known phenomena since the nineteenth century, but the effects from narcosis were not fully proven until 1939, when US Navy divers were working on the submarine USS *Squalus*. It lay disabled on the ocean floor in 243 feet of water off Portsmouth, New Hampshire, after a valve failed on a test dive. During the rescue of the sub's crew and salvage of the vessel, divers proved that they could avoid the debilitating effects of nitrogen narcosis by breathing a gas mixture of helium and oxygen called heliox, a blend that the navy had been experimenting with since the 1920s.

Because of its atomic structure, helium can off-gas through human tissue faster than nitrogen. And unlike nitrogen, helium has no known narcotic effect regardless of depth. When helium is mixed into a diver's breathing gas, the gas can help divers maintain peripheral vision, coordination, and motor skills in a way that is not possible when breathing normal air below 66 feet. Another advantage of using helium is to reduce the percentage of oxygen in a diver's breathing gas and inhibit oxygen toxicity.

But during the decades following the *Squalus* rescue and recovery, US Navy divers discovered that heliox has problems, too. For one thing, helium conducts heat at six times the rate of air. Divers using breathing gases with high helium content have found themselves freezing when using the gas to inflate their dry suits to adjust for buoyancy. Still, heliox has its uses for extremely deep diving because it takes the narcotic effects of nitrogen out of the mix.

Florida cave divers began experimenting with mixed gases in the late 1980s, and by 1990 respected wreck diver Gary Gentile and tech diver Ken Clayton proved the value of mixed gas when they dove to the German battleship SMS *Ostfriesland* in 380 feet of water off the Virginia coast.

Over time, a trimix of oxygen, helium, and nitrogen became a preferred alternative to air or heliox for dives of more than 150 feet. For divers the term trimix has come to stand for a variety of breathing gas blends. The one thing that all of these variations of breathing gas mixtures have in common is that they replace some of the nitrogen in air with helium. Divers usually refer to trimix varieties by their oxygen percentage and helium percentage. For example, a blend of "trimix 20/50" has 20 percent oxygen, 50 percent helium, and 30 percent nitrogen. For really deep exploration in more than 300 feet of water, divers use a "bottom mix" that has much less oxygen than air to avoid oxygen toxicity. Such a low percentage of oxygen would not support life on the Earth's surface. Someone breathing it at the top of the water column would black out, so a diver going deep also needs to carry a "travel mix" with a higher oxygen content to breathe while near the surface.

In the fall of 1990, Steve Gatto invited Gentile and Clayton to meet in his basement rec room with him, Tom Packer, and a group of other avid wreck divers. Most of the divers at the meeting were enthusiastic about trimix as well as nitrox, and in 1992 pioneering wreck and technical diver Billy Deans from Florida flew to New Jersey and stayed with Gatto while he taught the wreck divers a course in using trimix as a bottom gas for deep dives, and nitrox (which has a higher oxygen component than air) as a deco mix to speed up deco times during ascents. The only things holding back Gatto and Packer were the limited availability of trimix and nitrox, the challenges in blending the gases, and the difficulty in developing trustworthy decompression tables for divers using these exotic gases.

But necessity, like recovering the bodies of lost crew on *Thomas Hebert*, propelled Packer and Gatto into the world of blended gases, and by 1995 the dive team started planning an extremely deep dive on mixed gas after Gentile and Clayton asked Packer and Gatto to join them on a dive to the World War I German warship SMS *Frankfurt*.

One of ten ships (including the *Ostfriesland*) known collectively as the Billy Mitchell Wrecks, the *Frankfurt* sank after US military aircraft used it for an aerial bombing target in 1921. Its sinking was a successful test proving Colonel Billy Mitchell's theory that airpower, not sea power, would be the deciding factor in future wars. Many of the ten target ships, such as the *Frankfurt*, were war prizes claimed from Germany following World War I; some were obsolete American ships. Aircraft bombed and sank almost all of these target ships in more than 300 feet of water, 75 miles off the Virginia/North Carolina coast, in what at the time had been considered water too deep for diving.

But divers with mixed gases, looking for virgin wrecks, began to search out these hulks in the early 1990s. They considered the *Frankfurt*, a light cruiser that is 477 feet long, as the crown jewel. Unlike many of the other Billy Mitchell Wrecks, she sits right-side up on the bottom, resting 415 feet beneath the surface of the Atlantic. For men who once considered diving SS *Andrea Doria* at a depth of 250 feet like climbing to the top of Mount Everest, diving the *Frankfurt* would be like an expedition to the stratosphere if not the moon.

And so it is that on a June morning in 1995, Tom Packer finds himself on the deepest dive of his life. He's sinking into a dark void with the anchor line of the dive boat *Miss Lindsey* slipping through his hand as the weight of his gear drags him toward the bottom. Adjusting the gas in his dry suit and tank-mounted buoyancy wings, he tries to manage his buoyancy to allow a slow descent. The last thing he wants is to sink too fast and become a human submarine in a crash dive, or what divers call a "mud dart." Looking down, he can see the silhouette of Gary Gentile 15 feet below him outlined by the glow of the diver's light. Somewhere above him, Steve Gatto and Jon Hulburt follow.

Packer checks his digital depth readout, reminds himself that he and Gatto have planned to stop at 150 feet beneath the surface and switch from their travel mix of air to the 10/60 (oxygen/helium) trimix they carry under their right arms. Months of planning have gone into this dive. There have been numerous dress rehearsals, including one this morning before he and Gatto started down. Every detail has been analyzed and reanalyzed. Now the script for the dive is written on a laminated card attached to the back of Packer's gauge console. Three years ago the dive buddies made experimental mixed gas dives, along with Brad Sheard and Gentile, to the wreck of the *Ostfriesland* on this same patch of ocean, and they don't want to revisit the anxiety and difficulties of that 380-foot dive.

If Packer would let himself reflect after he switches to his trimix at 150 feet, he might well recall the long, gut-clinching wait for the current to abate before finally starting down to the *Ostfriesland*. He might recall the nearly interminable deco hangs at very deep depths because they had chosen to breathe heliox. He was underwater for three and a half hours, and there was no way to pee. He would definitely recall arriving at his 130-foot deco stop on the way back up to meet a support diver bringing him bottles of gas for the rest of his decompression . . . only to find that the diver and the bottles were not there. He would recall waiting for 15 minutes before the diver arrived, recall trying to take slow and shallow breaths to conserve the gas he had left. He would recall wondering if he was going to run out of air hanging on to the anchor line. He would recall Brad Sheard scratching a message on his slate that read, "Deep, dark, and frightening."

But these are memories that Packer would rather not revisit. The mission on this dive is to do things differently than on the *Ostfriesland* dive. Packer doesn't care about setting a personal depth record or gaining bragging rights in the dive community for this extreme dive. His aim is to prove to himself that he and Gatto can plan and execute a deep and dangerous dive flawlessly while being completely self-sufficient. They aim to dive to the *Frankfurt*, which is 35 feet deeper than the *Ostfriesland*, and make the trip an hour shorter than their mission was to the German battleship. Not only have the choices of travel, bottom, and deco mixes presented challenges, but also arriving at safe limits for bottom time and deco stops have taken countless hours of planning and discussion. And then came the choice for Packer and Gatto of what to carry while not burdening themselves with excessive gear that could task-load them far beyond their usual dive routine, to the point of jeopardizing their safety.

Packer has piled on 300 pounds of gear. It started with putting on dive underwear (insulated long johns), then zipping into his dry suit and strapping a knife to his leg. Then he sat on a bench at the back of the dive boat and eased into a backpack harness holding two steel tanks, called "120s," holding 120 cubic feet of bottom mix. The two back tanks have two separate hoses to two separate regulators, one for backup. There's an isolation manifold connecting the two tanks. In case a regulator fails and starts to free-flow, Packer can isolate the two tanks from each other to prevent the loss of all of his gas, or he can shut down whichever regulator is having the problem and still access the gas in both tanks through the other regulator. Between the 120s is a 40-cubic-foot pony bottle of compressed air for emergencies and a travel mix to breathe down to 150 feet. It has a regulator and pressure gauge as well.

In addition, he carries a 120 of bottom gas clipped to his backpack harness under his right arm. Under his left arm is an 80-cubic-foot bottle of nitrox-32 for intermediate decompression stops. Both of these bottles have their own pressure gauge and regulator. Each of his regulators and pressure gauges has a tag marking it so that Packer doesn't grab the wrong gas at the wrong time and kill himself. Breathing the nitrox-32 or the air from his pony bottle at depth, for example, could quickly overload his body with too much oxygen, which could lead to oxygen toxicity, convulsions, and death.

Among the other necessities that he carries are a 15-cubic-foot bottle of argon hooked up as an inflator to his dry suit, a spare suit inflator, two handheld lights, a reel with 500 feet of nylon safety line, two lift bags, fins, a dry suit hood, gloves, mask, a "Jon line" to tie himself off to the anchor line at deco stops, the console with depth/time/pressure readouts, and a stopwatch to track decompression run time.

Four minutes into his slide down the anchor line, he's at 300 feet and starting to look around for the *Frankfurt*. The few divers who have been here before him have reported that the ship has two masts rising 100 feet above the wreck like spikes. Lots of nets. Plenty of sharks. Packer would rather not go crashing into those masts or the fishnets draping from them in this faint light, rather not get surprised by a shark. He would love to land on the deck and explore the massive gun turrets. But despite visibility that extends to the far reaches of his light beam, he sees nothing except the distant glow of Gentile's light below him as he continues to sink.

The trip down is beginning to feel endless when suddenly Gentile seems to be coming closer because he has stopped descending.

Holy shit, thinks Packer. *Gary's on the bottom. Finally!* The divers have taken 6 minutes to get here.

Packer expected it to be pitch-black down here, but as he levels off next to Gentile a few feet above the sand, the scene seems to glow a little. The water is so clear that ambient light is reaching all the way to the bottom. It's weird, unexpected, and a little mystical. Now he notices the light of a fourth diver. Jon Hulburt hovers overhead, unable to descend to the sand because of a suit inflator problem.

Hulburt's light casts around in several directions, searching for the lost ship as he keeps an eye on his friends in case there's a problem and someone needs him.

But if the *Frankfurt*'s down here somewhere with its spiky masts, fishnets, massive guns, and sharks, Packer can't see it. None of it. What he's seeing looks like images he has seen of the surface of the moon during a lunar landing. He feels like he has become a character in one of his favorite TV shows as a kid, *The Time Tunnel*, feels transported to a different time and a place far from Mother Earth. Looking at two tines of the *Miss Lindsey*'s grapnel snagged precariously under a piece of rusted steel plate in the *Frankfurt*'s debris field, Packer has a dark epiphany. He realizes that if the grapnel lets go and he can't catch hold of the line, there's only a slim chance that he can make it back to the surface alive. Even for a diver with his massive experience, managing a free ascent from 415 feet would be exceedingly challenging.

This is not a truth that he would like to admit to his wife, Kim, a nurse, or his nine- and ten-year-old daughters Kelli and Jennifer. He tells them that he would not make a dive if he thought it were unsafe. It's true, but right now the margin of safety is pretty damn thin. Still, all of Packer's life up to this point has been preparing him for this mission. Born in 1959 in the small town of Maple Shade, New Jersey, he learned early the virtues of hard work, mental focus, physical fitness, and grace under pressure from his father, playing high school football and running long distances.

After doing his first ocean dive in 1980 and meeting his dive buddy Steve Gatto soon after, Packer and Gatto began following veterans such as Gentile and Hulburt on deeper dives and discovered that they, like their mentors, had an exceptional tolerance for nitrogen narcosis. When many divers started to grow dysfunctional breathing air below 100 feet, Packer could dive into the bowels of the *Andrea Doria* at more than 200 feet to help recover one of the ship's bells or a dead diver lost in the wreck. During the eighties and early nineties, when sport scuba divers were still using only air, Packer's and Gatto's unusual ability to tolerate heavy loads of nitrogen made them favorite choices to be mates on dive boats seeking deep wrecks and afforded them thousands of hours of deep-wreck experience. After growing up in the family heating and air-conditioning business as a sheet metal worker, Packer has found that over time his diving, which started as a hobby, has become a way of life, a thing he's really good at—a passion that borders on obsession.

It's exactly this expertise and experience that Packer, Gatto, and Gentile rely on down here at 415 feet. Knowing that nearly certain death awaits if they lose the anchor line, each diver keeps an eye on the line and drifts close to his buddies downcurrent from the line so that if the grapnel pulls out of the debris, they have a chance of catching it as it drifts toward them . . . and a chance of catching each other. If they are upcurrent of the anchor line, there will be no chance to swim after it if it breaks loose. Thinking about that anchor line and seeing no artifacts of interest in the moon glow of the divers' lights are making Packer itchy to get the hell out of here. He feels like Chevy Chase at the Grand Canyon in National Lampoon's *Vacation* movie, when Chase takes one look at the canyon and nods before he bails. *Been there, done that.*

Is he scared? Not really. He just would feel really stupid if he died on what seems like the dark side of the moon.

One of the divers taps his wrist for his buddies to see. Time to go, dudes. Fifteen minutes of bottom time gone.

Packer shoots two thumbs up.

On his first deco stop, at 350 feet, he starts to let his mind drift a little. It occurs to him that he's still 100 feet below the sand level of the *Doria*. There are tons of water and more than two hours of deco between him and the land of the living. Mixed gases are a huge boon to scuba, but it would take something really compelling to get Tom Packer to go this deep again.

Something like the shades of the German submariners Johann

Rauh, Friedrich Torge, and Klaus Hänert. Packer knows that when and if a man comes back from such depths, he is forever changed. It's not that there is no more music, as was the case aboard U-*550* after its guitarist died and the U-boat crash-dived south of Iceland. But the music is different. For some divers returning to the surface brings a quiet sense of self-satisfaction. Borrowing a sentiment from his partner Steve Gatto, Packer thinks, "It's like I'm in my truck loaded with diving gear, heading home after a trip way offshore and after a deep, deep dive. I look around at all these other people in their cars. It's kind of weird. They have no clue how far from this world I've just been."

For many divers there's an adrenaline rush that hits them during decompression stops on the way up to the surface. They find themselves fist-bumping each other as they hang on the anchor line beneath the dive boat, waiting for nitrogen overloads to leave their systems. Once the emotions that the divers held in check during the deep, dangerous dive are out in the air and the sunlight again, some divers feel intense highs. For others—the ones who retreat to a corner of the dive boat and watch replay after replay of the video they shot at depth on their cameras—the music in their lives has clearly taken on a bluesy tone. So it is for Packer after diving to the remains of SMS *Frankfurt*. So it was for the mythical harpist Orpheus returning from the underworld, where he briefly found his long lost lover Eurydice . . . only to lose her again when he resurfaced.

29

Trapped

Mid-1990s

The diver hears a clunk, clunk. The sound jolts from the darkness overhead. He looks up through the shadowy water. The 50-watt halogen lamp clipped to his chest catches the silhouette of a tank, a big fella. A high-pressure reserve air tank sags from the ceiling of a sunken submarine named the USS *Bass* . . . then falls in slow motion. He raises his hands to break its fall to deflect it, but the momentum of the falling tank knocks him off balance.

The next thing diver Eric Takakjian knows is that he's lying on his back in 150 pounds of scuba gear, with a tank that seems the size of a sumo wrestler pinning him to the inside deck of this dead submarine. He's the only diver on this wreck, 80 feet inside the bones of a World War II antique scuttled by the navy, 160 feet beneath Rhode Island Sound. Half his air is already gone. The falling tank has stirred up so much sediment that all he can see is a black haze. He thinks maybe this is what it would be like to swim in an ocean of coffee with the grinds swirling all around. There's a good chance that his wife, Lori, waiting topside in their dive boat, *Grey Eagle*, will never know what has taken him out. Takakjian will be just another diver lost in a sunken ship. Now you see him, now you don't. Gone.

But Takakjian isn't going down without a fight. Fit, fine-featured, and with neatly trimmed sandy hair, he looks boyish except for his mustache and those intense eyes that show his exceptional attention to detail. He's the captain of a seagoing tugboat that moves oil barges as big as the *Pan Pennsylvania* up and down the Atlantic coast of the United States. Often he's towing bulk cargo into and out of New York Harbor over the same route followed by World War II convoys. It's a job that demands constant and exacting focus to avoid a collision, a grounding, or an oil spill.

The diver trapped in the *Bass* loves his job. He has been obsessed with seafaring since his youth, growing up with sailboats in the 1970s on the banks of the Hudson River at Piermont, New York. For just about as long as he can remember, he has been fascinated with submarines, especially the underwater boats of the world wars. Even before he was an adult, he was devouring World War II history and naval history like Brad Sheard. Now he has a library of hundreds of books on the subject, more than twenty books on U-boats and American submarines.

His reading has fueled his urge to dive the wrecks of subs. That's why he's out here today diving the *Bass*, carrying ten other divers aboard the dive boat *Grey Eagle* that he and Lori run when he isn't on a tug. The *Bass* is one of his favorite wrecks. He has always wanted to see the interior of the sub's control room. Today, for the first time, he has entered the broken hull at the forward end of the engine room, passed through the galley of this big sub, and slithered through a partially opened hatch into the control room. Just a minute ago he was looking around him at the chart table, the periscope, the dive plane controls, the gyrocompass, and the big brass gauges and thinking, "This is just freaking awesome." But then a little tapping on a gauge (that might make a cool artifact to take home) with his hammer and chisel set off vibrations that brought this damn tank down on top of him.

All the books and reading in the world aren't going to bail this trapped diver out of the mess he's in as he lies here on the floor of the *Bass* in a thick cushion of silt. What might save him are his experience and training.

"Stop, breathe, think, act." This is the mantra that every diver learns in his or her first scuba course. Takakjian committed it to memory before the first scuba dive of his life, on July 4, 1975. He had been snorkeling since age eight or nine, but his plunge into a quarry at Hamburg, New Jersey, with dive instructor Joe Mercurio was no joke. Divers die in quarries with nearly full tanks on their back because something spooks them and they panic. But Takakjian isn't going to panic. Not in a quarry. Not here trapped in the control room of the *Bass* surrounded by seawater as dark as coffee.

For a minute he's going to forget about running out of air. Forget about being blind in zero visibility. Forget about the search for artifacts that lured him deeper into this sunken sub than almost any diver has ever dared. Forget about the narrow hatch he has to find and wriggle through to get out of the control room. Forget about the mild July day and the sandwiches that the other ten sport divers are enjoying topside aboard *Grey Eagle* after having completed their dives. Forget that in an hour his wife will start to worry. Forget that he will most likely be dead by then. He's going to simply stop, breathe, think . . . then act.

After a pause and several deep breaths to slow his heart rate and push fear from his mind, he takes stock. His immediate problem is this tank on top of him. Exactly how trapped is he? A couple of shoves against the tank with both hands barely budges it. Pushing it off him is not an option. What's Plan B? What about wiggling? He's lying in 18 inches of silt. It spreads away from his arms when he moves them. Perhaps by *carefully* pushing some of the silt out of the way with his arms and legs, he can wiggle and burrow his way through the silt and eventually slither out from under the tank.

And so he starts to act—to scoop and burrow and wiggle. Until he feels the end of the tank, once under his chin, now resting on his chest. After more scooping, burrowing, and wiggling, the end of the tank is on his waist . . . then between his legs. He's free and back on his feet. He just can't see a bloody thing. He's still swimming in coffee.

Stop. Breathe, think. He can feel the sub's gyrocompass with his hand, knows that if he puts it at his back and falls forward he will have the partially open hatch to the galley right in front of him.

Act. He rises onto the tips of his fins, then lets himself fall forward with outstretched hands. When he is almost prone in his fall, his hands hit the hatch door. The exit—and life—lie straight ahead. But to get through the partially open hatch into the galley, he must shed the extra gear that he carries on his harness, just as he did on his way into the control room. He disconnects his light, his tool bag, his reel of safety line, and pushes them through the hatch ahead of him. Then he starts sliding through the small oval hatch on his side with his face against the open rim, his back and tanks against the partially closed hatch door. When he's halfway through the hatch, something grabs him by the harness from behind. Even with the light shining beneath him, the visibility remains black as night.

Stop. Breathe. Think.

His harness has come afoul of something. If he backs into the control room again, maybe he can free the harness. It's a good move. He's free. But he still can't see a thing. When he tries to slide through the hatch again, he's snagged once more.

Maybe he's a little narked because it almost seems to him that the wreck is saying, "Hey, asshole, you're not out of this yet."

Stop. Breathe. Think. He tells himself not to worry about how much air he has left, but he knows he's within a minute or two of his maximum bottom time. He reaches back with his hand to feel for whatever is grabbing his harness. This time he feels one of the steel dogs on the hatch, used to screw down on the door to make it water-tight. The dog is catching his harness like a claw. He backs up until his harness is free. Again his hand finds the dog. He moves forward through the hatch once more, but this time when he feels his harness about to hang up on the dog, he eases the harness clear with his fingers and bellies into the galley. The visibility sucks where he has disturbed the silt on the floor, but he can make out shadows of the sub's interior once he gets his light aiming ahead. After he has collected the gear that he pushed through the hatch ahead of him, he rises off his knees. He sees a collapsed air-conditioning vent before him, knows that it leads to the engine room and then out at the point where the bow of the *Bass* has broken away from the rest of the hull. Once again he tells himself not to worry about how much air he has left, tells himself to swim forward with just the slightest flexing of his fins so as not to wreck the visibility even more.

There's a faint glow ahead. It must be coming in through the hatch that will lead him out of the broken wreck. He's in the engine room now, swimming between massive diesel engines, reaching out for that glow. Suddenly his knuckles jam against a steel bulkhead. His hands feel for the frame of the rectangular hatch.

And then he has it. Hard and cold . . . like a lever that he can use to pull him back to the world of the living.

Outside the fractured sub, the visibility improves to 40 feet. He checks his timer. He has used up his full 25 minutes on the bottom . . . but not more. Everything is going to be all right, especially since he has left a small backup pony bottle of air on the deck of the sub in case he runs short on his deco stops.

During his long deco hangs, he doesn't freak himself out by reliving the chaos of the past 12 minutes. He thinks that maybe it's time to put the *Bass* behind him. If he's going to risk his life, why not get really familiar with mixed gases and go for something mythic, an Olympus among wrecks, not this foothill? Why not go looking for what some divers call "the last U-boat"? They mean the last unfound

U-boat lost off America's East Coast in diveable waters. For decades stories of U-*550* have nagged at him.

When he gets out of the water today, he will go home and write to the government. He wants to start gathering combat action reports, collecting everything he can find at the Naval History Center and the National Archives that relates to this missing U-boat. To him it's like a lost piece of history. When he dives among the bones of a ship, he imagines it and its crew in their glory and in their hour of need. And sometimes, his wife, Lori, will tell you, it is as if he lives underwater. Lives with the ghosts of forgotten battles and lost ships. If ever there were a lost ship with secrets to tell, U-*550* would be that vessel.

30

Playing Hurt

2007–2009

Joe Mazraani is nose-to-nose in the emerald-green water with a couple of black sea bass big enough to feed him and five dive buddies. He takes a sip of air from the regulator in his mouth, feels it surge into his lungs and thinks, "Holy shit. How great is this? Like somebody please pinch me and tell me I'm back."

He is 6 miles east of Barnegat Light, New Jersey, on a cloudy afternoon. The seas are 2 to 4 feet. Not a perfect day for scuba diving, but Mazraani will take it. He's drifting beneath 75 feet of water just above the bones of a nineteenth-century passenger liner called the SS *Vizcaya*. Wearing somebody else's dry suit, tanks, fins, and mask, he's feeling a little like some sort of Rip Van Winkle, like he has just woken from one helluva nightmare.

He has.

Born in 1978 as the son of a Christian family in Beirut, Lebanon, he lived through the sectarian violence in that city. After RPGs and sniper fire began whizzing through windows of the family apartment during that long civil war, Mazraani's family knew they had to get out, and young Joe finished the last two years of high school in the United States while teaching himself English.

He had begun free-diving off the beach in Lebanon, but he got really hooked on scuba while a student at the College of Staten Island after joining a dive club and diving for lobsters. In spite of suffering from seasickness, he couldn't get enough of the sport, especially wreck diving and bringing home artifacts from sunken ships. Like a lot of the divers at the time, he became drawn to the diving adventures and nautical history in Gary Gentile's books about the wrecks off the northeastern coast of the United States. Soon he was crewing on dive boats. By 2001 he was hanging around with much more experienced divers, absorbing everything they could teach him. This was the year that he first dove SS *Andrea Doria* and entered law school. He picked a career in law not because he loved it, but because he thought it could pay for his diving.

Mazraani's dark handsomeness, sparkling eyes, impish smile, and easy laugh attracted women, but with diving filling most of his weekends, more than one relationship foundered as the young diver submerged himself in books on nautical history, networked with his dive buddies, and quested for virgin wrecks. By the spring of 2003 he had befriended Tom Packer, Steve Gatto, and Brad Sheard, divers who just a year or two before had seemed unapproachable titans out of the pages of Gentile's books. And his reading of nautical history, especially the Battle of the Atlantic, had begun to intrigue him with the idea of finding legendary lost wrecks. He had read and reread the story of U-550 in Sheard's book *Beyond Sport Diving*.

On May 12, 2004, Mazraani finished near the top of his class in law school. He was feeling on top of the world with a lucrative career looming and a summer of challenging dive adventures ahead. But the next day everything changed. It was a fine day for diving—calm, cloudless, and warm. Mazraani was working as the mate aboard Captain Tom Napolitano's dive boat *Dina Dee* out of Point Pleasant, New Jersey, and they were diving the low-lying wreck of a schooner known as the Spike Wreck just 16 miles offshore in 165 feet of water.

As the mate, Mazraani had the job of being the first diver into the water and tying the anchor line into the wreck. The wreck is in an area known as the Mudhole, a trench cut in the sea bottom by the outflow of the Hudson River. Visibility in the Mudhole usually is a miserable 5 to 10 feet, but today Mazraani could see 30 feet, and this promised to be a spectacular day for artifact hunting. Because of the usually poor visibility, the wrecks in the Mudhole are not visited by many divers and therefore are rife with the nautical treasures that wreck divers love. Mazraani pictured collecting hundred-year-old deadeyes and rigging blocks from the wreck of the tall ship, and he felt his adrenaline start to spike.

But on his way down the anchor line to tie in, he felt something else, a little squeak in his right ear. It was an odd noise, but he squeezed his nose, cleared his sinuses and ears, and went on with the tie-in and the dive. He had two spectacular dives on the wreck, but after his second dive he began to feel nauseated. Aboard *Dina Dee* he lay down on the engine box, closed his eyes, and told himself that his nausea would pass. It must have been the grilled Italian sausages he had eaten for lunch aboard the boat before the dive.

When the boat arrived back at the dock, Mazraani felt even worse. He lay down on the dock and couldn't move, couldn't stand up. A friend had to load his gear in his pickup, and on the drive back home to his father's house in North Brunswick, Mazraani had to pull over every 15 minutes and close his eyes to ward off dizziness.

He felt better the next day except for a clogged right ear. He imagined that he had a case of swimmer's ear, but after over-the-counter medicines failed to relieve the problem, he checked in with a doctor, who administered a hearing test. The news was bad. Mazraani had lost most of his high-frequency hearing in his right ear.

Fearing that he had suffered a decompression hit in his ear, the diver headed for a doctor specializing in dive decompression injuries at the University of Pennsylvania in Philadelphia. The physician put him in a hyperbaric chamber for six hours and tried to use increased pressure and oxygen to reduce potential nitrogen bubbles in the tissues of Mazraani's ear. But his "chamber ride" did not clear up the problem.

By this point Mazraani was asking every physician who tried to treat him when he could dive again. The answer was uniformly the same. Forget diving. It's too risky. You could go deaf. Unwilling to accept this news, the diver sought out a highly regarded ear specialist who told him that he had suffered irreversible damage to his inner ear. When the doctor told him he should not try to dive again, Mazraani began to flood with emotions. "This is how I define myself. Diving is my life."

"I'm afraid you will have to find a new hobby, Mr. Mazraani."

"This isn't a fucking hobby!" Mazraani shouted.

But, with the counsel of family and friends, he took the doctors' advice to heart. He packed away most of his collection of artifacts, sold all of his dive gear at a flea market, broke up with his girlfriend, and "started eating like a pig." The only good news was that he and fellow attorney Joe Liguori quit their law firm and started a private partnership, with Mazraani specializing in criminal defense law.

He began to truly enjoy his work in front of juries, but in the back of his mind he never stopped hearing the call of the deep. And so it was that in the late spring of 2007, Mazraani stopped going to doctors. He told himself, "Fuck it. I'm going diving. Get back on that horse and ride." If he lost his hearing, he would deal. He just had to get down on a wreck again.

And here he is shaking off the feeling of having finally awakened from what seems like some other man's bad dream. It's his second dive today. The first one didn't go so well. Not because of his hearing, but because the dry suit that he borrowed had some annoying leaks and he felt uncoordinated as he tried to manage his buoyancy and swim.

But now he's wearing a different dry suit that's keeping him snug, and he's feeling as if a slow and steady grace is coming back to his swimming as he follows the two enormous black sea bass meandering between the four mammoth boilers of the *Vizcaya*. He's swimming with the sea bass among the boilers that rise more than 15 feet off the sea floor and stretch out 20 feet apiece, watching lobsters scuttling into and out of their lairs beneath fallen deck beams. He loves seeing the sea anemones waving in the light current. At one point he grabs some mussels, breaks them open, and feeds them to a school of bergalls. He barely checks the time on his wrist gauge. His mind's purring.

At one point the neon yellow stripes of a clutch of wrasses catch his eye. They are feeding on what looks like a metal tower dotted with anemones. It's the ship's vertical steam engine. He has long been a fan of old-school steam propulsion in ships. Now he finds himself circling the tower of rods and pistons, relishing the fact that they are still here, intact, despite being buffeted by more than a century of storms. Little by little, he feeds air to his suit and rises ever so slowly, spiraling up around the towering engine.

At the top, he stops, looks down on the engine and the boilers. They look so solid and permanent in the half light filtering down from the surface, as if they might withstand another century of North Atlantic gales. He's not sure why, but the scene comforts him. Part of him wants to shout, "I'm back! I'm really freaking back!"

But the moment seems to call for something less dramatic. So he spreads out his arms and just hovers, halfway between the land of the living and the land of the dead. He thinks about the souls of the sixty-eight people who perished here on the night that the *Vizcaya* collided with the coal schooner *Cornelius Hargrave*. His mind drifts. He thinks about so many souls lost beneath the sea, each soul and each ship with its own story. Hearing injuries be damned. Maybe he can be more than a spectator down here. Maybe he can be a discoverer. Maybe he can find a long-lost wreck and tell its story. That sub that Brad Sheard mentioned in his book might be the very thing. What if he could find U-*550*?

Fast-forward to August 2008. On a return trip from diving the wreck of the passenger liner *North American* south of Cape Cod, Eric Takakjian anchors his dive boat over a substantial lump that he can see on the screen of his depth sounder. The lump's rising above the ocean floor off Nantucket. Two hours later, he and the team of divers aboard—including Steve Gatto and Joe Mazraani—have dived the lump.

"Holy shit, Eric." Joe Mazraani snaps his face mask off after he climbs out of the water from his dive on the wreck. "We found it, didn't we?"

Takakjian, who's already out of his dive gear and back in shorts and T-shirt, nods. "Steel hull, vertical steam engine, cargo of antimony ingots. Only one wreck out here fits the bill."

It's the British freighter SS *Newcastle City*, which went aground on Nantucket Shoals in December 1887 . . . and it's a virgin wreck, a time capsule of its era. Untouched.

Mazraani feels the fever, the high of having found a virgin wreck, and it sends his mind flying back to a conversation he had earlier in the trip when he had asked Takakjian what he knew about a lost U-boat, the *550*. Takakjian had pulled out a chart and pointed to a symbol on the map very close to the edge of the continental shelf, a symbol labeled U-*550*. "That's in really deep water," said Takakjian, as if to raise a flag of caution.

"Doesn't scare me," thinks Mazraani. His mind can't let go of an image of a U-boat's sharp and shadowy bow rising above a sandy bottom. Mazraani wants that sub. The bigger the challenge, the greater the adventure. But where and how to start?

.   .   .

A year later he finds a moment to confess his growing obsession with U-*550* as he meets up with Takakjian at the Boston Sea Rovers dive clinic.

"How about we look for the *Five-fifty* one of these days, Eric?"

Takakjian cocks his head and gives a little smile. For more than twenty years he has been collecting "hang numbers" from commercial fishermen. Hang numbers are locations, measured by the Loran radio navigation system or GPS satellite navigation receivers, that fishermen have used to identify anomalies on the bottom of the ocean where they have snagged or lost fishing gear. These hang numbers mark spots to be avoided by offshore draggers, scallopers, and long-liners. Often the anomalies are wrecks, and for decades Takakjian has been on a quest to mate his hang numbers with known ships that have disappeared off Cape Cod in an area sometimes called the Graveyard of the Atlantic. By matching hang numbers with deep historical research, Takakjian has found more than seventy wrecks.

And as an aficionado of submarines, he has long been enthralled by the story of the U-*550*'s battle and loss. As far as he can tell, it's the last—and quite possibly the most intact—wreck of a World War II U-boat that remains undiscovered in potentially diveable waters off the Atlantic coast of America. It's a virgin wreck of the first magnitude, a wreck with more inherent history and drama than U-*869*, which lies off the New Jersey coast and is the subject of *Shadow Divers*. Takakjian has been gathering US Navy records on U-*550* for decades. He even has plots of related hang numbers and a search area for the wreck.

But in 2009 his hands are full with his work as a tugboat captain and exploring other virgin wrecks, such as the *North American* and the *Newcastle City*. Having met Mazraani through their mutual friends Gatto and Packer, Takakjian has been diving with the lawyer for a year. But now Takakjian senses something new about this young man bouncing back from a dive injury, senses the passion they both share to find the submarine. So it is that in the spring of 2009, Takakjian decides to open up his research on U-*550*. Eventually he shares a plot of hang numbers and a potential search area with Mazraani. It's a gift in the spirit of "There's so much to do and so little time, brother."

Maybe Mazraani can kick-start a search for the sub before someone else finds the wreck . . . if his damaged body is up to the challenge, if he has the guts to dive in really deep-ass water. He's going to need a team of committed, seasoned divers such as Sheard, Gatto, Packer, and Takakjian. He'll also want a dive buddy with state-of-the-art diving skills whom he can trust with his life. And two other details. He has to find a really rugged boat and a side-scan sonar operator to help with the search.

31

Lost and Found

Fall 2010

The limestone walls of the cave are pressing in on Anthony Tedeschi from all sides, pinching his shoulders, his belly, the knees in his dry suit, scraping against the frame of the rebreather pack on his back. The LED light in the hand of his outstretched left arm casts its light ahead like the headlamp of a train frozen in an endless tunnel. Just a minute ago he felt at total peace, an explorer of the sunken chambers of Neptune, a swimmer in a secret sea of crystal-clear fresh water nearly 100 feet below the surface of northern Florida. Now the twenty-five-year-old diver feels like a cork in a bottle.

With his friend he's taking a day off from working on his master's thesis project at Florida Tech. They have been swimming for more than a half hour into this cave at Ginnie Springs, north of Gaines-ville, exploring a network of caverns called the Devil's Eye, following their plan to circumnavigate the maze of chambers and tunnels known as the Sweet Surprise/Mainland circuit. Now that plan is most definitely starting to unravel. He tries to wiggle free from this bottleneck. But nothing's budging, and he's starting to feel dumb.

He tells himself that with a nearly completed master's degree in ocean engineering, ten years of serious diving, and virtually every scuba certification you can earn, he should be smarter than to get himself into a pickle like this. But here he is. And he can feel his adrenaline starting to spike. For him panic is not the first sign of his body going into survival mode, it's this self-abuse, this overthinking of the mistakes he's made. He needs to get back in the groove, stop beating himself up for things he can't change, and focus on the here and now.

For several seconds he concentrates on his breathing until he feels his heart rate slow. Then he consults the heads-up display glowing at the bottom of his mask. It tells him that his closed-circuit rebreather unit is delivering him the optimum amount of oxygen for this depth. He loves the rebreather in the aluminum frame on his back. It gives him the best breathing mix for each dive by offering him the option of mixing in helium and nitrogen (with the oxygen) at different proportions for dives to different depths. It also can last him more than four hours before he has to recharge it. In addition, he carries two bailout bottles of nitrox in case of a malfunction.

If Tedeschi were breathing from a conventional set of tanks and regulator known as an "open circuit" rig, as Eric Takakjian was when the fallen tank pinned him to the cabin sole of USS *Bass*, Tedeschi might be starting to worry about running out of air down here. But his heads-up display tells him that his equipment is functioning perfectly. The Kiss self-contained rebreather unit on his back absorbs the carbon dioxide that he exhales to allow the recycling of the substantial oxygen content of each breath. The unit then replenishes the amount of metabolized oxygen by the user, only about 4 to 5 percent of the oxygen inhaled, while chemically "scrubbing" toxic carbon dioxide from the exhaled gas.

Crude rebreathers have been around for two hundred years. They really caught on with military frogmen during World War II, but many governments blocked the release of this useful military apparatus until the collapse of the Soviet Union. With fears of attack by enemy divers diminished, Western governments stopped blocking civilian use of rebreather technology, and recreational diving rebreathers started to appear for sale.

For Tedeschi, purchasing his unit is $10,000 well spent. He has been leading his partner on the dive up to this point, and he knows from the glow of the man's light that he's still behind him. Divers usually communicate with hand gestures, but Tedeschi's in no position to shoot hand signals to the man behind him. Once again, he's loving that he has a rebreather. Open circuit divers breathing through a regulator can't do much more than grunt, growl, moan, or howl to another diver, but Tedeschi can kind of talk into his rebreather's mouthpiece. Now he's telling his buddy to tug on his legs.

With a few pulls from behind and a few pushes from his arms, Tedeschi feels himself skid out of the bottleneck. Then he tells his buddy to back up. When the beam from his partner's light grows dimmer, Tedeschi backs farther out of the bottleneck, folds himself into a ball, and rotates his body until he's facing out of this rocky tube. Problem solved. Just another day of exploring in a cave.

Sort of. Except now the divers have to find their way out of this maze of tunnels. The caves at Ginnie Springs are very popular with cave divers, and local volunteer cave divers have marked the caves with nylon lines that you can follow back to the cave entrance. Thicker gold line marks the main route. At regular intervals the line has been marked with arrows pointing the direction out and noting the distance. Side passages often have white ropes to guide divers. The white ropes are not connected to the main gold line. Sometimes they are marked by two arrows pointing to the closest exit.

When a diver wants to explore a side passage, he or she has to make a "jump" from the gold line to a white line that lies farther in the side passage. Cave-diving protocol dictates that when you make a jump, you tie a safety line (which you carry on a reel clipped to your gear) to the gold line and trail the safety line after you until you hit a white line. At the white line you drop the reel. Divers also use markers called "cookies," which snap onto the line. They should leave them at every "T" intersection where two lines meet so they know which way to turn on their return trips.

The problem is that Tedeschi didn't leave cookies at two Ts on the way in. Neither did he reel out his safety line to bridge the jump. He was planning on making a circuit and didn't want to have to return for the cookies or his safety reel. He had studied the cave map and knew the way. He had also kept track of which direction he turned at each T and the landmarks along the jump . . . just in case he had to return the way he came. But he's no longer leading, he's following, and he sees a problem. The tunnel's white line is caught on his partner's tanks. He feels the line go taut in his hand. It's tight to the point of breaking. Then it goes slack.

The good news is that the line is no longer pulling at his friend's breathing gear. The bad news is that somewhere up the line, it might have come adrift of its anchor or the rest of the line.

At the first T, his partner turns right. This feels wrong to Tesdeschi, but his partner seems so confident that he follows. The longer they swim, the stranger the cave looks. Nothing's familiar. No catfish or even snails to distract him. Nothing down here looks alive except the diver in front of him. Suddenly his partner stops. He's staring at the bitter end of the white line tied to a rock on the cave's floor. No gold line in sight. His eyes grow huge as adrenaline starts to jack his system, and he wonders, "Now what? Where are we?"

The partner signals for Tedeschi to station himself here at the end of the line, then swims deeper into the tunnel ahead. After the diver disappears beyond a sand berm on the cave floor, Tedeschi feels his mind starting to kick into self-abuse mode again. Ten times he calls himself a horse's ass. Tells himself that as the only son of a South Jersey nurse and ace auto mechanic/charter boat operator, he has learned to focus on safety practices from the first time he joined his father's fishing charters for bluefish and sharks off Atlantic City. A decade of diving, including working in dive shops and going as mate on dive boats, has imprinted his mind with the need to attend to the details of safety. Six years of undergrad and graduate school in ocean engineering at Florida Tech have made playing it safe a habit of mind. And during his past couple of summers, he has been invited to dive deep wrecks such as the *Doria* with Joe Mazraani, Steve Gatto, and Tom Packer. Men he has read about in diving books. Men who have seemed like legends to him. Men who would kick his ass if they knew that he got himself lost in this frickin' cave.

He's in the middle of thinking about all the stupid shit he did today when his partner reappears and beckons to him from the sand berm. As he swims over it, then under an outcropping of white limestone, he breaks into a larger chamber. Looking down, he sees the cloud of silt stirred up by the diver's fins. Beneath the cloud lies a straight, taut, gold line. He freezes. Notes which direction the cloud is drifting. Knows that downstream is the way out.

"Follow the flow, idiot," he tells himself. Then he signals the way out to his partner.

During the long swim out of the cave, his mind locks on two words: NEVER AGAIN. It's not just a promise to himself and his parents. It's also a promise to the men he will be diving with next summer when he gets back to New Jersey. Mazraani has started talking about mounting an expedition to find a lost German submarine called U-*550*. Finding the *550* would be a top-shelf adventure for Tedeschi, a once-in-a-lifetime opportunity, even though diving on the sub would be laced with danger. Mazraani says that the sub is so deep it might be safer to dive it on rebreathers. Tedeschi could bring some of the veteran divers on the *550* discovery team up to speed with this technology.

"You can count on me," Tedeschi says. When he gets out of grad school next fall, he'll start work as an ocean engineer. True, men such as Gatto, Packer, Sheard, and Takakjian were diving the *Doria* before

Tedeschi was born. But unlike these other men, diving will be his vocation as well as his avocation. As an ocean engineer he'll be logging hours underwater almost every day, surveying, building, and rehabilitating waterfront structures. He can keep his finger on the pulse of all the technological advances in both commercial diving and sport diving.

In his spare time he'll continue wreck and cave diving. Few divers could hope for such a high level of currency in the field. If he minds the rules of prudent practices, he should have something to offer a seasoned team in the way of safer equipment and protocols. Still, he's the new kid on the block, and sometimes he feels like he has something to prove. But he clicks with Joe Mazraani. They share a passion for underwater adventure, and they work well together in the deep. Maz won't be sorry to have him as a dive buddy or on the team. That's a promise.

32

Tenacious

The pitch of Joe Mazraani's voice jumps an octave every time he tells the story of the February day when he took possession of his dive boat. The words come in a staccato blast: "It was one of the worst moments of my life. We almost lost the boat . . . on the freaking maiden voyage."

And with these words he's right back in the moment. A winter day on the North Atlantic just a few miles off the New Jersey coast. Sunny. A mild southwest wind. Seas just 1 to 2 feet. Cold—the temp right around freezing. It's afternoon aboard the 45-foot Novi-built scalloper that her fishermen owners called *Atlantic Breeze* when it fished out of Ocean City, Maryland. Mazraani and two friends are ferrying the boat 130 miles from Maryland to its new home in Point Pleasant, New Jersey.

Only seven years old, the boat shows the wear of constant fishing. Since sealing the deal, taking possession of the vessel, and steaming out of Ocean City Inlet this morning, Mazraani and dive buddies Luis Jimenez and Bart Malone have discovered that half the electronics don't work. The bow thruster's inoperable. And despite the wash of deck hoses and boarding seas, grime has settled into the nooks and crannies of the pilothouse, forecastle berths, and expansive work deck that take up the back half of this 15-ton boat. Mazraani is a guy who likes to be in control, a man who likes everything spic and span and doing its job on a boat. But after five hours at the helm of the boat, looking at the grime, and fighting with the autopilot, which phases into and out of operation, the new captain needs a break.

He hands over the helm to his shipmates and goes below into the forecastle to curl up inside a sleeping bag on one of the V-berths stacked over each other in the bows. As he listens to the satisfying purr of the turbo-charged Cummins diesel and the swish of the bow wake against the hull, he tells himself that despite the grime and the problems with electronics and hydraulics, he did not make a mistake in buying this boat. The fiberglass construction and running gear have gotten top marks from Eric Takakjian's meticulous survey. The work deck will be perfect to accommodate a long bench on each side, where as many as four divers can suit up at the same time and still leave room for everyone's tanks and gear. Two fishholds beneath the work deck sole are big enough to store a large gas grill for cooking as well as all manner of tools and dive gear. The forecastle can be reconfigured to hold six berths in tiers. The galley table has space for computers and monitors for sonar searches while hunting virgin wrecks. The heavy stainless steel gallows frame mounted over the stern will be great for mounting a winch to retrieve a dinghy or lifting aboard artifacts. One such treasure is the 6.5-foot helm from the freighter *Ayuruoca*, which Mazraani has been trying to salvage for three years.

Best of all, Mazraani's new boat is large enough and fast enough (cruising at 10 to 12 knots) to carry divers safely to the most remote wrecks on the very edge of the continental shelf. These are the elements he began looking for when he decided months ago that he needed his own boat if he and his dive buddies aimed to mount a serious expedition to find Klaus Hänert's lost U-boat. It's time—like now or never—before someone else beats them to the wreck. This is what he wanted when he took $40,000 from a settlement that he and his law partner had won and borrowed $60,000 from his mother to buy the boat. Here's the project that Mazraani's dive buddies such as Luis Jimenez, Paul McNair, and John Butler signed onto with hopes of creating one of the most efficient and capable dive platforms on the mid-Atlantic coast. A man can almost snooze easily—even on the North Atlantic in February—when he knows that he has good friends volunteering their time and talents to make a dream become a reality.

Mazraani is drifting into and out of sleep, musing over the total improbability that he would actually possess his own dive boat at age thirty-two. He's wrestling with choices of a new name for the boat—kicking around the idea of calling it *Notorious*—when he suddenly finds himself snapped awake, bolt upright in his berth, by an instinct more than a thought telling him that he needs to get his ass on deck. Like fucking fast.

Leaping the stairs to the pilothouse, he sees Malone in the helmsman's seat, gnawing on a snack and steering the boat on the course that Mazraani set before heading below to nap.

"Something's wrong," says the captain.

"What?" asks the crew.

"I don't know." Mazraani looks out the portside windows of the pilothouse. "I don't know."

But then he does. He sees the familiar silhouette of Long Beach Island off to the left, knows where he is. The waves have a different shape than they had when he went below. They are still small, but steep-sided and close together. The boat's running onto shoals that stretch far offshore here. Checking the depth sounder, which is actually working, thank God, Mazraani sees that the boat has only 2 to 3 feet of water beneath the keel. He pounces in front of Malone, grabs the wheel, and cranks the boat into a sharp, 90-degree turn to starboard.

"What the hell?" Jimenez and Malone reach for anything to keep themselves from falling. They look at Mazraani as if he has gone crazy.

"Yeah, what the hell?" he says as the boat swings out of the turn and scoots into deeper water. "We almost wrecked the boat."

"But we didn't," says one of the crew.

"Good point," thinks Mazraani. Something had warned him about the shoals in the nick of time. When he's feeling in a superstitious mood, he will tell people that the boat talked to him. The boat didn't want to die on those shoals. This boat has a soul. A tough soul. A soul that doesn't give up when adventure is at hand. A soul like his own. Tenacious. Yeah, tenacious, not "notorious." *Tenacious* was telling him its name. Telling him that if he listens to this boat, it will take him far, take him right to U-*550*'s secret grave.

In the months and years to come, Mazraani will lavish a lot of his disposable income on giving *Tenacious* all the best bells and whistles a hardworking dive boat can have. His friends Jimenez, Butler, and McNair will devote hundreds of hours in helping its owner turn his Cinderella into a princess. After every dive trip, Mazraani will require that the crew clean the boat until every inch glistens, and woe to anyone who spills his peanuts or cracker crumbs on the pilothouse floor. Ever.

"She's my vice, my mistress," the captain will admit when his crew teases him about the fastidiousness that he brings to his care of *Tenacious*. And the divers who voyage in the boat will know that Mazraani isn't exaggerating. Not long after he gets *Tenacious* home to New Jersey, his then-girlfriend will come aboard and start complaining about how much time he's spending on the boat, and how she might be a little more tolerant of *Tenacious* if it looked more like a yacht and less like a work boat. Mazraani will get the message, and he'll make a choice. *Tenacious* will stay in his life. The girlfriend won't.

This diver and this boat have places to go, most importantly a German submarine missing 70 miles south of Nantucket.

33

The Finder

March 2011

Garry Kozak scans the hotel restaurant to make sure that the coast is clear, so to speak. In his early sixties with gray hair and riveting eyes, Kozak has the tightly packed body of a World War II fighter pilot. There's something about the catlike way that he moves that exudes both self-assurance and skepticism. He's not paranoid. But he would rather not be seen meeting Joe Mazraani here. Folks who know him and his reputation tend to get suspicious when they see him in a private conversation with a wreck diver, especially one as dynamic as Mazraani.

It's the first day of the annual Boston Sea Rovers divers' clinic at a hotel off I-95 north of the city. Thousands of sport divers have gathered at this hotel to learn about the recent technological developments in equipment and listen to presentations about some of the thrilling diving expeditions of the past year. Kozak has agreed to use the convention as an opportunity to discuss Mazraani's secret plan to search for U-550. A former commercial diver and one of North America's most highly regarded side-scan sonar operators, Kozak is a man whom some people call "The Finder" because he has discovered hundreds of shipwrecks and crashed aircraft underwater with his sonar systems. His résumé includes recovery operations on downed airliners such as Swissair 111 and Egypt Air 990 as well as decades of shipwreck searches around the globe with legendary scientists such as Dr. Robert Ballard of *Titanic* discovery fame and author Clive Cussler. Treasure hunters, collectors, and wreck divers are constantly trying to enlist Kozak in highly speculative searches for booty on the ocean floor.

Sometimes individuals and teams compete for his services as they try to beat another expedition to a perceived holy grail. Sometimes they snoop around to see if he's on a mission that they might shadow for their own purposes. He knows that two other groups of divers are searching, or hoping to search, for the *550* and interested in consulting with him or hiring him for their projects. He also knows that treasure searches and shipwreck hunting can attract a pretty crazy group. As he looks around this restaurant, he worries about dreamers, snoops, and sleazebags.

He doesn't think that Joe Mazraani falls into any of these categories. That's why he has agreed to this encounter. But he hasn't actually met the man, only talked with him by phone and email, and meetings like the one that he's about to have with Mazraani have led to some pretty sketchy moments. He remembers a series of expeditions in Alaska to a remote outpost called Twin Lakes, 150 miles west of Anchorage.

The year was 2001, and one June morning Kozak found himself sitting up in bed praying that he was still dreaming . . . because if he was awake, then he was face-to-face with a 500-pound grizzly. He had been recruited to be the sonar operator in a team of explorers who flew into Twin Lakes aboard a Beaver floatplane just a day before in search of an extremely rare Sikorsky S-39 flying boat that had been lost at the bottom of the lakes since 1958. The team was staying in a log hunting cabin as they set up for their search, and Kozak had been sleeping in a bed beneath a cabin window. Now, even with the pane of glass between him and the grizzly, his mind could smell the chilly, enduring odor of bear. He could imagine that at any second the animal, with its front paws on the sill inches from his face, might squint its black beady eyes and launch itself through the window at him with a snapping jaw and an unearthly roar. But as suddenly as the bear appeared, it vanished, leaving Kozak wondering why he had not brought a gun on this expedition. Wondering what new madness lay ahead, wondering if this adventure might actually get him killed.

He came close to realizing this fear on a second trip to Twin Lakes with more gear and personnel to recover the rare Sikorsky that he had located under 200 feet of water. To reach Twin Lakes bush pilots have to fly through Merrill Pass, a long, narrow, zigzagging valley between mountains of the Alaska Range. Named after a legendary Alaska bush pilot who disappeared without a trace in 1929, the pass is home to the wrecks of more than twenty aircraft that came to grief amid the bad weather, soaring crags, and box canyons. And on the day when Kozak was returning to Twin Lakes, the weather sucked for flying through the pass. Wind, rain, sleet, and a layer of churning clouds about 10,000 feet thick filled the pass.

The good news was that the expedition had chartered a single-engine, turboprop Cessna Caravan on floats with a pressurized cabin, making the plane capable of flying above the peaks. The bad news was that the descent from altitude had to be made with no visibility through a miasma of storm clouds while spiraling down between the unforgiving mountains that ring Twin Lakes. A safe arrival depended on the pilot's experience, instincts, and the coordinates he programmed into his GPS, a navigation system that was still in its infancy for aircraft at the time.

The flight above the weather went well enough, but the descent proved to be a different story. Kozak had grown up in Canada and learned early the speed with which travel conditions can change when warm and cold weather systems collide in the north country. He had also logged a lot of time flying into the backwaters of the world aboard light planes. So when he boarded the Caravan for the flight to Twin Lakes, he tried to ready himself for the inevitable bumps and sudden G forces that beset aircraft flying in thin air over windy mountain ridges.

But he was not prepared for what happened a couple of minutes after the Caravan started its descent through the warm, moist soup of clouds. As the plane screwed toward the earth in a steep bank, and the wind howled around the fuselage, nature threw a temperature switch. The plane flew into a layer of supercooled air. In what seemed like the snap of fingers, ice froze over the windshield, inside and out. The plane seemed locked in a cocoon of opaque and heavy crystal. The pilot seemed too freaked to speak as the aircraft nosed farther over and raced toward the ground while the altimeter unwound with alarming speed.

"This is it," thought Kozak. "The sleigh ride to hell." The plane had become a stone.

But just when the screaming of the wind over the skin of the Caravan could get no louder, the shadows in the cabin could get no darker, light flashed through the windows. The plane broke out of the cloud deck. Kozak's ears popped.

The ice was melting, streaming off the windshield and wings in a thousand rivulets. Below lay the cobalt-looking waters of Twin Lakes . . . and the Caravan's wings began to support its weight once again.

After the floatplane landed on the lake and began taxiing toward the shore and the base camp, the pilot turned to Kozak and said, "I guess we should have been wearing diapers."

In the end, after several expeditions to Twin Lakes, Kozak and his colleagues were unable to free the Sikorsky from the mud on the bottom. So to this day there the aircraft sits, too difficult for divers to recover.

As Kozak stands waiting for Mazraani at the hotel restaurant, he's thinking about that Sikorsky and how much he and the recovery team risked for that rare aircraft just to get no payoff. He has to warn Mazraani that's what his team is up against in their search for U-550. Kozak's got to be out front with the passionate diver. Given enough time and money, Kozak is all but certain that he and his side-scan sonar can find the U-boat with the help of Mazraani, his team, and *Tenacious*. But then what? The submarine may be too deep, too shrouded in poor visibility, and too current-swept to dive safely. The first two divers who approached Kozak about this project more than a year ago are dead. True, they didn't die actually chasing the shadow of the *550*, but they died in diving accidents. And any shipwreck known to be in the vicinity of SS *Andrea Doria* will definitely be a risky dive. It's the wild edge of the North Atlantic out there.

"I'm thinking of getting a life insurance policy on you right now," says Kozak once Mazraani appears and leads him to a secluded table.

The young criminal defense attorney flashes The Finder a big grin. "Naw, man, don't worry about it," he says. "Let's just do this thing, Garry. Let's find this sub."

Kozak leans back in his chair and sizes up the diver. At age thirty-three Mazraani could easily be Kozak's son. But the thick-shouldered diver with the heavy black beard presents more like a man in his midforties. It's not just Mazraani's flecks of gray hair that make him seem mature. It's the supreme ease in the way he talks, his intense eye contact, and the lightning bolts of energy that burst from his smile. He exudes the confidence of a man who has the integrity of a straight shooter . . . and a long track record of getting what he wants. A great combination for a criminal defense attorney. Kozak likes what he sees. It takes a Pied Piper to pull off a search like the hunt for U-550, and Mazraani seems to have the bravura, the skill, the team, the boat, and the money to fit the bill. But will his passion blind him to the risks?

After an hour spent picking over forgettable food—and poring over unforgettable charts when Gatto, Packer, and Takakjian join the table—Mazraani makes his pitch. "So what do you say, Garry? Are you in? Do we sign a confidentiality agreement?"

Kozak feels something surging beneath his skin; maybe it's anticipation for the hunt. But then he considers the potential risks to these divers. A trip more than a hundred miles from the US mainland in a small boat is not without its challenges. This is not like tracking down and diving a wreck in the Mudhole. This is an expedition potentially as challenging as trying to recover an antique Sikorsky from the Alaskan wilderness.

Kozak tries to temper his excitement. "We'll have to take this search one step at a time."

"And keep it to ourselves." Mazraani winks.

34

On the Hunt

July 27, 2011

You're usually going to find the wreck during the first hour of the search . . . or the last. Garry Kozak's words are echoing in the heads of Joe Mazraani, Steve Gatto, and Tom Packer. No question, the divers are primed for Lady Luck or Neptune to throw them a bone. It's approaching midnight on the third night of their three-day search for U-550, and so far the team has been striking out. Only one last lane of the search grid lies ahead to be surveyed, and there's no chance of jimmying together a new search plan.

"If the wreck doesn't appear on this leg," says Mazraani, "we gotta go." There's weather coming, and the Graveyard of the Atlantic 70 miles south of Nantucket is no place to get caught in a 45-foot dive boat when the wind starts to howl. The currents out here can conspire with storm winds to build wicked cross seas. For _Tenacious_ it's more than a ten-hour steam back to port at Montauk, on the eastern end of Long Island.

Six divers gather in the pilothouse of Mazraani's dive boat. Several peer over Kozak's shoulder at a laptop computer screen and hope to see something besides grainy images of an underwater desert. The autopilot steers *Tenacious* while the laptop displays images being sent to the surface from a 6-foot-long, torpedo-shaped echo sounder. Kozak's "fish" is trailing from a wire 440 yards behind the boat, 250 feet below the surface of the Atlantic, and scanning 400 yards to both sides for any bottom anomaly that might be *U-550*. Early in the search it spotted a lot of debris around a collection of Eric Takakjian's hang numbers—probably sunken fishing boats, according to Kozak. But none of the targets looked remotely like a sub. And the fish has seen virtually nothing at all for hours.

Kozak's services, hundreds of gallons of diesel fuel, and food/drink for seven men for three days don't come cheap. Most of the divers aboard have ponied up $1,500 apiece for the chance to be on this search trip. Mazraani's into the expedition for more than three times that amount. Anthony Tedeschi paid, but had to bail on the trip because of his work schedule. Eric Takakjian has been too locked into work and other diving projects to commit. Brad Sheard demurred, saying he was uncertain about diving on a wreck in more than 300 feet of water. At the last minute Mazraani has recruited dive buddies Harold Moyers, John Butler, and John Moyer to join the search, help with handling the side-scan sonar gear, and stand watches.

But despite the expense, the time commitment, and the hassles in trying to pull this search together amid bad weather and everyone's other commitments, Mazraani is feeling good. Tired but good. One reason has nothing to do with how this search is going. Just before leaving on this trip, Mazraani broke up with his long-term girlfriend, and he can't believe the relief he has been feeling since *Tenacious* left the dock. Being out here 100 miles from nowhere with a bunch of dive buddies can't be beat. The calm seas, sunny days, starry nights, the grilled steaks, the banter among shipmates, the sea stories. Good times. It's one hell of a better vacation, to Mazraani's way of thinking, than the week in a rental house at the beach that his ex had planned.

And except for an offshore lobster boat that has been hauling gear nearby, *Tenacious* has had the ocean to itself. There has been no sign of rival groups' search expeditions for *550*. And no word of a discovery in the dive community. This means that no one has found U-*550* and probably no one knows that *Tenacious* is out here looking. For Steve Gatto nothing has been lost but a little time and a little money. He's used to search trips going like this, has been on a lot during thirty years of diving. You get on the boat with all your gear, knowing that there's a good chance you may never find the wreck you are looking for. You know that you may never get in the water. The hunt is the thing.

A licensed captain, Gatto enjoys the seafaring almost as much as the diving. He also enjoys the planning of a search as well as the planning of a wreck dive. And today he thinks that the team, led by Takakjian's years of research, has done an exceedingly professional job in executing the search. During the months leading up to this expedition, emails and phone calls have been flying between the divers and Kozak as they brainstormed the best way to look for the *550*.

In the end, the team has built their search grid around the combat action reports and deck logs of USS *Joyce*, USS *Gandy*, and USS *Peterson*. Those documents gathered by Takakjian and others from the National Archives and Naval Historical Center in Washington gave the plotted positions of the DEs at 0800 hours and noon on the day of their battle with U-*550*. The warships also reported an approximate position for the sunken submarine (the one Takakjian showed Mazraani on the chart) and bracketed the depth at the site of the battle at 52 to 55 fathoms (312 to 330 feet). Using these data and Takakjian's hang numbers, the divers have crafted a search grid 6 miles long by 5 miles wide.

Gatto thinks that one of the most professional elements in planning the search was the choice to avoid going right to Takakjian's hang numbers or the reported position of U-*550* and scanning the bottom. This approach is common among divers searching for wrecks, and sometimes it turns up a lost vessel, as with Takakjian's discovery of the *Newcastle City*. But early in the planning Kozak convinced the divers that hang numbers were only one piece of the puzzle and that they needed a more systematic and scientific approach to find Klaus Hänert's U-boat.

"You have to mow the lawn," Kozak told the divers. "It's the only way to make sure you don't miss your sub." He said that in his experience sunken ships and airplanes are rarely where they have been reported to be. Furthermore, the general area where the U-boat sank is littered with shipwrecks. "It would be easy to get distracted by all that junk."

The divers agreed.

So now they have been mowing the lawn for two days, towing Kozak's fish back and forth across the search grid in lanes that are about 650 yards apart. The side-scan fish is a relatively modern creation. Following World War II, a German scientist named Dr. Julius Hagemann came to the United States and shared his echo-sounding research with the US Navy, but the technology and resulting scanners remained classified for Cold War military use, such as finding an atomic bomb that the US Air Force lost at sea and exploring a sunken Soviet missile submarine.

Among the innovators in the development of side scan were Dr. Harold Edgerton at MIT and his protégé Marty Klein, whom many people consider to be the "father" of the commercial side-scan sonars that became available after the US government declassified the technology in the 1960s. For much of his career as a side-scan operator, Garry Kozak has worked for one or the other of these two pioneers.

Towed by *Tenacious*, his fish broadcasts fan-shaped pulses toward the seafloor and listens for acoustic echoes, which render an image of the sea bottom within the swath of the pulses. Early side scans reproduced their images on rolls of coated paper, but modern devices create computer files that can be viewed in real time on a laptop screen.

Side-scan fish usually broadcast their echoes at frequencies of 100 to 1000 kilohertz. Higher frequencies produce images with better resolution, but the higher the fish's frequency, the less the range. When you are searching for a needle at the bottom of the ocean such as U-*550*, a low-frequency fish is what you want because it has a large field of vision. For this search, Kozak has brought two fish, a rare 50-kilohertz machine for broad searching and a 100-kilohertz unit for a closer look if a promising target appears.

But none has emerged. The 50-kilohertz unit is doing all the looking. And looking is just fine for Tom Packer tonight. He's not sure he's ready, at this stage in his career, to dive into more than 300 feet of water to see if Kozak's fish has actually found the wreck of the *550*. He has done similar and much deeper dives (to the Billy Mitchell wrecks) earlier in his career—at a much younger age. Not only is the bottom of the ocean out here deep, dark, and cold, but also this search is in an area where the currents are sometimes so strong they can sweep an unwary diver off into oblivion in a heartbeat.

None of the divers hunting for U-*550* carries more ghosts than Packer. He finds it hard to talk about some of them, especially the father-and-son deep-wreck dive team of Chris and Chrissy Rouse. Both Packer and Steve Gatto were on the dive trip during the fall of 1992, when the Rouses died. There's so much about the day the Rouses died that Packer would rather forget. He would rather forget how he bent on his knees with many of the other crew on the dive boat performing chest compressions, trying to keep Chris Rouse alive. He would rather forget crying after the coast guard rescue chopper airlifted the stricken father and son off the dive boat. He still gets choked up about that day, even after nearly twenty years.

And now aboard *Tenacious* as it searches for the *550*, Packer particularly doesn't like remembering that Chris and Chrissy Rouse died after a penetration dive into a German submarine, U-*869*. Any wreck can be a death trap, but subs, U-boats? They can be the worst of the worst. They are so simple and uninteresting on the outside that they beg curious divers to enter them, where the space is confining and debris reach out to snare you the way Eric Takakjian got caught in the *Bass*. In a sub it is beyond easy to get trapped the way Chrissy Rouse did to the point that he was short of air when he got free, to the point that he bolted for the surface without coming close to fully decompressing.

The *869* lies in 230 feet of water. The *550* is probably 80 feet or more deeper. *Shit*. That's what Packer thinks as he watches the images from Kozak's fish beaming up images to the laptop monitor aboard *Tenacious*. He must have told Mazraani and Gatto ten times to count him out on this mission, but here he is. His dive buddy Gatto asked him to help them with the planning. Next thing he knows, he's more than 100 miles east of Montauk looking for the skeleton of a U-boat at the bottom of the sea . . . with his dry suit, tanks, mask, and fins ready to go. *Damn*. If they find this wreck, does he really want to dive a wreck so deep again, another iron coffin?

That's the question swimming around in Packer's mind when Mazraani's voice echoes through the pilothouse. "It's not here, boys. Let's go home." The time is 0030 hours on the morning of July 28, and *Tenacious* has finished mowing the lawn of the search grid, no sub sighted. Maybe on another trip Packer will feel more like diving beneath 300 feet of the North Atlantic to see if their dive team has found their obsession, but for now Packer's happy to be heading home to his wife and two daughters. A lot of guys died out here on an April day in 1944, and sometimes, in the middle of a dark night like this, they seem too close for comfort.

"The DEs got the position wrong," says somebody.

"It was a war. Men were dying all around them. They thought that they might be next, what do you expect?"

"We'll be back," says Mazraani. "Slow and steady win the race."

PART FOUR

Discovery

35

Regrouping

Maybe Steve Gatto should be feeling a little low after coming up empty on this search trip, but he's not. He always gets a good vibe when he spots the lighthouse on Montauk Point at the extreme eastern tip of Long Island, New York. The lighthouse was the first public works project authorized by the new United States of America, in 1792. Standing on Turtle Hill, the Montauk Light rises 110.5 feet above the earth beneath. It's an immense red and white candy-striped obelisk, flashing a white light 18 nautical miles to sea to warn mariners that they are approaching shoal water and the fierce currents that surge between the end of Long Island and Block Island to the east.

But it's not the history of the lighthouse that endears the light to Gatto. For him the lighthouse is usually the first sign of a landfall when the dive boat that he's aboard is homeward bound after days at sea at the wreck of the *Andrea Doria* or some other ship sunk east of Montauk. These landfalls for Gatto always carry with them a sense

of accomplishment. For days he and his dive buddies have been literally immersed in a world of dead ships and dead humans. And on this
morning of July 28, 2011, Montauk Light has risen above the western
horizon winking a welcome home message out to Gatto and the
other men aboard *Tenacious*.

Even though the sun has been up for hours as the dive boat bashes
toward shelter through a building southwest wind and rolling seas,
in the morning haze Gatto pictures bonfires of beachcombers on the
shores of the state park that surrounds the lighthouse. He imagines
eggs and diced potatoes cooking over open flames and smells the
wood smoke while he takes a sip from his coffee mug and braces
himself on the bench seat at the dinette table. *Tenacious* pitches and
rolls toward its slip at the Star Island Yacht Club in Montauk Harbor,
tucked on the north side of the point.

Maybe he can already smell the scents of fried fish and clams, too,
cooking in the restaurants ashore because suddenly he's feeling hungry for the first time since dinner last night 110 miles at sea when
Tenacious was mowing the lawn during the fruitless search for U-*550*.
He's looking forward to tying up the boat, unloading his gear, and
heading down the road to John's Drive-In for an immense chocolate
shake. Maybe he and his buddies didn't find a lost German U-boat,
but it has been a good trip. For the past few hours the men aboard
Tenacious have been chattering up a storm, telling each other that
they have definitely ruled out a whole lot of ocean bottom where the
sub isn't. This certainty is a good thing to Gatto's way of thinking
because the last thing you want after one of these search trips is to
be left with a feeling of doubt. At this moment the crew of the dive
boat is sure of two things: U-*550* is not where the navy placed it on
the chart almost seventy years ago, and basing the position of the
battle site on the attack logs of the DEs *Joyce, Gandy,* and *Peterson* has
been an erroneous assumption.

All morning the guys have been bouncing around theories about
constructing a new search grid.

"What now, Garry?" one of the divers asks sonar man Kozak.

"We move east next time," he says. "We can find this thing."

"But how far east?" asks someone.

"We've got to go to the [National] Archives," say several voices at once. To define a new search area they need the deck logs of all the ships involved in the *Pan Penn*'s convoy CU-21. They need the convoy's route instructions. They need the deck logs of the rescue and salvage ships sent to the burning *Pan Penn*. They need radio traffic logs.

Gatto feels himself, Packer, Mazraani, and the rest of the crew getting amped as they hone in on a plan of action and *Tenacious* starts the turn toward the breakwaters at the entrance to Montauk Harbor.

"I'm telling you guys, we gotta start at the beginning. Plot the course of the convoy from the moment they left New York right to the site of the battle." Joe Mazraani's words come fast, loud. This is the voice of a self-assured criminal litigator, a dogged researcher. "We leave no stone unturned."

Others agree. The guys are refining their list of everything they need to ferret out at the National Archives when Mazraani's phone rings.

He listens for a second. "We didn't find it. We gotta hit the Archives, pal," he says into the phone, listens a few seconds longer, then clicks off. "That was Brad."

"So?" asks Packer.

"He's in." Mazraani smiles. "He wants to meet us at the Archives." After all of Sheard's waffling over joining the search for the wreck that has long intrigued him, he has finally committed to the *550* project.

The news brings a smile to Gatto's face, too, as he thinks about Sheard's insatiable curiosity. The man can't pass up a deepening mystery like the hunt for *550*, and along with Gatto, who has made scores of trips to the Archives over more than two decades, Sheard knows his way around the new NARA (National Archives and Records Administration) facility in College Park, Maryland.

"I'm good to go anytime," says Gatto. It's an impulsive commitment. He'd rather stalk evidence at the National Archives any day than work another union electrician's gig.

"Let's do it," Mazraani says to Gatto.

Brad Sheard feels like shouting, "Holy shit. Eureka." But he doesn't want to disturb the woman in the seat next to him at the long table where a half dozen other researchers like him are poring through records. It's a little after 1400 hours on August 9, 2011, at the huge four-story steel, concrete, and glass complex of NARA near the University of Maryland in College Park. He's in a second-floor research room at NARA with Gatto and Mazraani. A staffer has recently brought him a box that he requested from her 1:30 p.m. "pull" of documents from the building's record archives. The cardboard box, about the size of a case of wine, bears the label "DECLASSIFIED. BUREAU OF NAVAL PERSONNEL. DECK LOGS. SC-*1338*."

SC-*1338* was a 110-foot sub chaser with a crew of twenty-seven men sent from New York Harbor after the attacks on the *Pan Penn* and the *550* to assist in rescue and recovery. It was the first vessel on the scene of the burning tanker, arriving shortly after midnight on April 17, just sixteen hours after the battle, twelve hours after convoy CU-*21* and the destroyer escorts had left the scene to continue on to Londonderry, Northern Ireland. In the log for the night of April 16, the officer of the deck recorded a position from a star sight made with a sextant just a few hours before reaching the burning hulk of the *Pan Penn*. This is an extremely accurate position fix, much more accurate than the dead-reckoning fixes from the DEs *Joyce*, *Gandy*, and *Peterson* that the navy and the divers had been using to pinpoint the location of the battle and the sunken U-*550*.

"Damn," thinks Sheard, "SC-*1338* always had an excellent idea where she was."

In the log entries the sub chaser gives a series of position reports for the drifting wreck of the *Pan Penn*, which is floating upside down, with 10 feet of the bow and 100 feet of the bottom out of the water. The rear of the tanker is submerged, but oil is rising from somewhere near the stern and is burning.

Sheard sees one possible way to solve the puzzle of the missing submarine. He knows the exact location of the *Pan Penn* wreck; he dived to its bow in the 1990s. If he can plot all the relevant positions recorded by SC-*1338* he can plot the course and drift of the burning tanker back to its location sixteen hours after the torpedo attack. Once he knows the direction and rate of drift of the *Pan Penn*, he will be able to backtrack from the tanker's position when it was reached by SC-*1338* to come up with an approximate location of the attack.

He can't wait to go home and mark all of these positions on tracing paper overlaid on an offshore chart of the ocean about 100 miles east of Montauk and 70 miles south of Nantucket. True, the log of SC-*1338* is only one of half a dozen logs of the rescue ships that the divers need to research, along with the logs of all six DEs in CU-*21*'s escort group and the log of the *Pan Penn*, but finally here's some solid data.

He nudges Mazraani and Gatto with excitement. "Can you believe this?"

Mazraani's more than a little psyched at this discovery, but he's also zooming in on the position of the lead DE, USS *Poole*, at the time of the torpedo attack (0803 hours, April 16, 1944) and the position recorded by Captain Leidy of SS *Pan Pennsylvania*.

"The question, gentlemen," he says to Sheard and Gatto as they leave the Archives to head to the nearest Kinko's to photocopy a ream of research papers gathered from the Archives, "is how accurate are the dead-reckoned positions of the *Poole* and the *Pan Penn*?"

"Right," says Gatto. "They had been running in the fog all night after leaving New York . . . and the destroyer, for sure, wasn't steaming in a straight line. Their dead reckoning positions could be way off."

All three of the men remember that the 0800 positions recorded by the *Joyce*, *Gandy*, and *Peterson* vary nearly 20 miles from each other.

"But the *Pan Penn was* steaming due east for the whole night. His position could be solid," says Sheard.

"We won't know until we plot the convoy's track from New York to the battle site. This is like a math class I took. We replot speed, time, and course for the convoy from the minute the convoy leaves New York." Mazraani's voice has settled into its insistent tone. "We see if the *Pan Penn* and *Poole*'s DR plots lead us to the same place as hind-casting from the *1338*'s position."

Sheard cocks his head. This sounds good in theory. "But where did they turn east after leaving New York?"

"The outer end of the swept channel through the minefield protecting New York," says Gatto.

"And where is that?" asks Sheard.

"It's called Point Zebra," says Mazraani, who has unearthed CU-*21*'s convoy route instructions.

"How do we find Point Zebra?" Gatto's not being pissy. He's just thinking aloud.

"I don't have a clue," says Mazraani, "but I think I know who does."

"And that would be?"

"Eric."

"Good point." Sheard pictures Eric Takakjian. The guy has spent years—decades, actually—running a tug into and out of New York Harbor.

It's a day or two after the Archives trip. Eric Takakjian has cycled off his tugboat for two weeks. Now he's home and giving the mystery of *550*'s location his full attention. On hearing the news that the first search expedition came up empty, he was initially surprised. He thought the first search grid looked promising. But after a flurry of emails and cell phone calls with the other divers, he has come to see where the first trip went wrong.

The sun's setting as he sits at a chart table in his office. It's part of a large garage next to his house in Fairhaven, Massachusetts. Takakjian has divided the garage into a shop for the maintenance of his diving gear/dive boat and this office. The office is meticulous, has the look of an old-school shipping office with its drawers of charts and gleaming brass nautical artifacts like a ship's bridge telegraph. At the moment Takakjian is sipping a hot cup of Constant Comment tea as he leans over chart 12326, Approaches to New York, Fire Island Light to Sea Girt. The mid-August air of southern Massachusetts fumes with dog-days heat, only slightly mitigated by the ceiling fan spinning overhead.

In his right hand Takakjian holds navigators' brass dividers for measuring distance on a chart. His left hand holds a printout of CU-21's route instructions for departing New York Harbor on the night of April 15, 1944. Mazraani has sent him a copy of this long-classified record from the Third Naval District. The instructions give the ship captains in CU-21 headings and sometimes distances between more than a score of buoys, waypoints that guide the ships in the convoy from their anchorage out of New York Harbor to the critical Point Zebra.

The problem with reconciling any of these buoys in the route instructions with buoys on Takakjian's contemporary chart is that many of these buoys no longer exist. They were put in place during World War II to mark the clear passage, the swept channel, through the minefields protecting New York Harbor. After the war the mines and many of the buoys were removed. Probably they were never marked on any commercially available nautical chart. Who knows if any of them remain on Takakjian's contemporary chart? In addition, unlike peacetime lighted buoys, which use red, green, or white lights flashing at different intervals to clearly identify individual buoys, the wartime buoys all flashed white lights to confuse the enemy, especially

U-boats on the prowl. So Takakjian cannot use the light characteristics to identify the wartime buoys.

He reads the route instructions over and over, almost saying aloud each leg of the trip through the swept channel, picturing it in his mind. Picturing, too, how he would leave New York Harbor with a tug and barge today. There has to be a point where at least one of these wartime buoys corresponds to a contemporary buoy. There has to be a Rosetta Stone, a key to this puzzle.

And there it is. *Damn*. The answer has been right in front of his face all along. He absolutely knows the location of one of the wartime buoys. It has a corresponding buoy on his contemporary chart.

"No shit." He laughs to himself.

Then he sets down the route instructions, reaches for a set of navigators' parallel rulers and a pencil to mark the course as specified in the instructions from the known buoy to the next . . . and then the one after that. Before he turns out the light and fan in his office and heads back into the house to curl up with his wife, Lori, he has plotted the convoy's route to Point Zebra. Tomorrow he's going to triple-check his plotting, but he's a careful mariner and navigator. He's pretty sure he's got the location of Point Zebra squared away. Like totally nailed it to the point where plotting the convoy's trip to the battle site will be a piece of cake from here. Wait till he tells the guys. He can't contain what he knows is a shit-eating grin blooming on his face. *Sweet*.

36

Crunch Time

May–June 2012

"Life is good." That's what Joe Mazraani is thinking as he walks his new puppy Pirate around the quiet, middle-class neighborhood of James Street in suburban South River, New Jersey, just a few miles from Raritan Bay and New York Harbor. It's a warm May evening. There's a golden glow in the sky and Pirate, a ten-week-old Portuguese water dog that arrived from a private breeder in Louisiana just two weeks ago, is getting the hang of walking on a leash. Mazraani is feeling Pirate's gusto for life, daydreaming a little about the summer's expedition to finally find U-550.

"Yeah, things are cool." *Tenacious* is ready to go with a new hydraulic-powered, breathing-air compressor. The divers are refining the search grid south of Nantucket, and the boat slip is rented in Montauk Harbor for July. To Mazraani's way of thinking, the beauty of this summer's search expedition is that no one outside the regular crew on *Tenacious* knows anything about the team's plans to search for the sub. Scuttlebutt circulating among the wreck diving community claims that other groups are gearing up to look for the sub, too. While the competing groups are talking the talk of a search for *U-550* or shining the spotlight on their plans with Internet posts, the crew of *Tenacious* aims to slip away into the North Atlantic and find Klaus Hänert's lost U-boat. They want to be the first to dive the wreck. They want to swim with the ghosts of the lost crew and plumb the truth about what really happened on April 16, 1944.

This is the sunny scenario swimming around in Mazraani's mind when his cell phone rings. It's sonar man Garry Kozak, The Finder, and he's got a problem. He's not sure that he can do the search trip this summer.

If Mazraani could make a coherent sound with his mouth, the usually loquacious attorney would unleash a barrage of salty diver's oaths, starting with "You must be shitting me!" He pictures dreams of discovery, plans for summer adventure, and the secret mission going up in smoke. He feels so blindsided, so dumbstruck, that all he can do is lower the tailgate of his pickup in the driveway, lift his puppy into the bed of the truck, and nuzzle Pirate's soft and kinky black hair. After all the work the divers have put into this research, this can't be happening.

Garry Kozak takes no pleasure in delivering the bad news to Mazraani, but he's in a bind. Fed up with a company that he believes treats its workers poorly, he just lost his patience, made a split-second decision, and walked out on his employer one day in early May. True, The Finder has scored a new job within twenty-four hours. He has gone to work for his former employer's rival EdgeTech, a leading side-scan sonar manufacturer (among other things). But landing the new gig hasn't done much to quell the knot in his stomach. He's not sure how he will fit in with his new company and colleagues, not sure he can ask for time off to go looking for a German submarine that sank sixty-eight years ago. And really not sure that he can cope with the stress of his former employers launching a team of high-profile corporate lawyers at him and EdgeTech, threatening lawsuits if he gives away any company secrets.

Almost two weeks after telling Mazraani the bad news, Kozak hunkers down with a dog, too. Ross is a Pitt-Weimaraner mix, and he loves to curl at his master's feet when Kozak brews up a cup of Starbucks roast and retreats into his office after dinner with his wife, Kathy. In the basement office of his home in southern New Hampshire, Kozak tries to uncoil the knots in his stomach by slipping away from his worries about lawsuits and letting down the crew of *Tenacious*. He tries to escape into his computer, but he's not on it long before he finds himself exploring charts of the North Atlantic, poring over all the positions of the ships involved with the sinking and recovery of SS *Pan Pennsylvania* and its German nemesis.

The way he sees it, the *Tenacious* team has done an excellent job of researching and plotting the likely location of U-*550*. They are so close to the sub, he can almost smell it. And tracking a scent is an urge he can rarely contain. He starts looking at the constellation of ship positions and hang numbers pulled together by the divers. Then he starts to calculate how much ocean the dive boat can cover during three days on location. He thinks that *Tenacious* might be able to survey about 80 square miles of ocean towing his low-frequency fish. Given this limitation, how would he design a search area? Before he knows it, he's starting to lay out a grid on the chart, starting to imagine days of mowing the lawn north to south.

Kozak has spent a lifetime searching for and finding lost stuff underwater, but there's something about this submarine that claws at him in the middle of the night. It's not like the wreck is a lost treasure that will make him and the divers rich. Nor is it a rare artifact sought after by a collector. But this submarine calls to The Finder. Possibly finding this wreck will rewrite the story of the lives of all those American and German young men who came face-to-face with each other, their worst nightmares, and their soul-searing fear on April 16, 1944. Something about the search for U-550 feels rife with lessons about endeavoring against great odds. About loyalty, persistence, brotherhood, youth, courage, teamwork, and—strangely—family. A man doesn't often get an opportunity like this to look so deeply into the things that make us human, and Kozak would like that privilege. He wishes there were still some way that he could avoid letting such an opportunity slip through his fingers, a way that he can stand by his commitment to the divers. A way to satisfy his curiosity. A way to show that he is both a seeker and a man of principles.

"Meanwhile, I'm pulling my hair out," Mazraani will tell friends later when remembering the first weeks of June 2012. "I thought the mission was going down the tubes."

Days with no news from Kozak are flying by. It's already mid-June, but Mazraani still has no clue as to whether he has a side-scan sonar operator for the U-550 mission. And he's getting news through the divers' grapevine that a highly publicized search for the sub by a group of New England divers has put to sea to dive a wreck.

"To say that I was biting my nails is an understatement," remembers Mazraani.

After all the time and effort in investigating and planning the search trip that his diver buddies have been doing, he can't tell them that they might have to scrub the mission because Kozak is out. He just can't. He hints at the problem to Takakjian and Sheard but not the others. He feels like his credibility is on the line with guys such as Packer and Gatto, who have been spending untold hours planning how to make a safe dive to the sub if they find it. Going more than 300 feet deep in the potentially murky and current-swept waters south of Nantucket will require several blends of gases and precise attention to deco times for divers to avoid getting hurt or killed.

"So I'm freaking out," recalls Mazraani. "I don't want to let the guys down. It's looking like I might have no play here and another team is already out there hoping to dive a target."

But then, a sliver of hope. Mazraani gets a search plot via email from Kozak. The mere fact that he has taken the time to plot a search grid means he has not given up on the project.

At about the same time, Anthony Tedeschi calls Mazraani. Tedeschi has heard that the New England team that went out to dive a wreck they thought was the *550* has returned disappointed. The wreck turned out to be a fishing boat.

"This thing isn't over till it's over," thinks Mazraani. He jumps on the phone to Kozak. "I know you want this, Garry. What can I do to make this happen?"

It's June 18. The search trip is planned for just a month away . . . if it goes.

Kozak takes a deep breath. "Let me have a talk with the CEO at EdgeTech."

Days pass. To keep himself from going crazy, Mazraani takes Pirate on long walks and works with Takakjian and Sheard to refine the search grid. They decide that while Kozak's rectangular grid looks pretty good, they would like to flip it on its side to extend the grid farther to the east and west to take a closer look at a bunch of fishermen's hang numbers that Takakjian has recorded.

On June 21 Mazraani gets a call. The Finder says he has the greatest boss in the world. The CEO of EdgeTech has told Kozak, "Do what you need to do."

"So you're in?" asks Mazraani.

"I can give you three days in the middle of July."

"The boys are ready."

37

The Second Search

July 21, 2012

The air around Joe Mazraani is filling with smoke. He's lumbering toward the eastern end of Long Island in his black Ford F-150 and trying to find his chill. Smoke fumes from a fat Cuban Montecristo No. 2 cigar that he has gotten via family in Lebanon. Mazraani's not a smoker—bad business for a deep-wreck diver who expects big things from his lungs—but the Montecristo is a guilty pleasure that he indulges from time to time to relax before an epic dive trip. Tucked in his crate behind the passenger's seat, Pirate has begun to stir and whimper. When he smells the cigar smoke, he knows something big is afoot.

All week Mazraani has had his doubts about whether the *550* search trip would come off in concert with the tight windows of availability for Garry Kozak and some of the divers on the team. For days Mazraani and Eric Takakjian have been going back and forth debating with themselves and each other if a series of cold fronts and high winds that have been battering the northeastern coast of the United States are going to let up enough for *Tenacious* to head to sea safely. The more Mazraani looked at the marine weather forecasts, the more discouraged he got. He has seen this scenario of a strong Bermuda high and approaching fronts raise hell before. But readiness is all . . . so he has been throwing himself into a string of eighteen-hour workdays. On vacation from the law office, he has been dividing his time between keeping in touch with the team about the weather situation, preparing eight or ten different bottles of gas for a deep dive, and doing massive provisioning.

He should be dragging after making a long trip to dive SS *Andrea Doria* last weekend. But he has been so pumped over the coming search trip and all it entails that he has barely been able to sleep. Preparing dive gear and provisioning a boat for a trip of three-plus days offshore with a crew of seven men is always a drill. Filling his breathing gas tanks has taken several days. He has had to mix, fill, cool, and top off each diving tank from storage tanks in his garage workshop. The price tag for all this gas is $700, even when he mixes it himself. The cost of helium is sky-high.

Since buying *Tenacious*, Mazraani has set a high standard for himself in regard to the food and drink he provides the boys during a dive trip. In the past three days he has spent $600 on provisions. His shopping spree began with a raid on Sam's Club for bulk items such as five cases of bottled water and three cases of Gatorade to keep the team hydrated because hydration can help ward off the bends. He hit a specialty grocer for the organic milk and Banana Nut Crunch cereal that the divers like, stopped by the farmers' market for fresh fruits and vegetables, visited the team's favorite Italian deli to buy cold cuts and exotic cheeses for the lunches, and finally stopped at a butcher's shop to buy steaks and chicken breasts to grill for three dinners at sea.

It wasn't until last night that Eric Takakjian, the team's weather guru, said a weather window was about to open long enough, *maybe*, for the three-day search. Now Garry Kozak (with his sonar fish) and divers

Tedeschi, Takakjian, Sheard, Gatto, and Packer are heading for the Star Island Marina in Montauk and *Tenacious*. The mission is on. "Come hell or high water," thinks Mazraani. He sure hopes that Takakjian is right about the weather settling down, but he's not sure at all. The last time he checked the weather app on his phone, the winds were still blowing 15 to 20 knots out of the southeast. This will be right on the dive boat's nose when it heads more than 100 miles offshore to the search area. The waves could make for a brutal boat ride and be too rough for towing the fish. But what's a guy going to do at this point?

In his crate Pirate has started sneezing.

"Yeah, yeah," he says to the dog. "I hear ya." He ashes the cigar and opens the windows to let out the smoke. "Let's go see if Eric can produce some good weather, Pirate."

As a pickup truck carrying Packer and Gatto crosses the Verrazano-Narrows Bridge over New York Harbor and heads east toward Montauk, Gatto finds himself thinking in detail about the wreck that he will soon be searching for and, he hopes, diving. This mental review is what he always does before a wreck dive. He and Packer have been going back and forth for months, refining their dive plan, their use of five different gas mixes, their strategies for carrying a little more than 300 pounds of gear down and back to a wreck that likely will be in more than 300 feet of water. Now Gatto's picturing the wreck itself. He has dived quite a few U-boats before. But each wreck has its peculiarities, and Gatto doesn't like surprises. So he does his homework. He loves to study the plans of a wreck he's about to dive . . . or visit a sister ship.

In this regard Gatto has paid three visits over the years to the fully restored U-*505*, now a war memorial at Chicago's Museum of Science and Industry. The *505* is a Type IXC, almost a clone of U-*550*, and one of only four preserved World War II U-boats in the world. There's one at the U-boat Memorial on the edge of Kiel Harbor in Germany, one on the Mersey River near Liverpool, one in Hamburg, and the *505* in Chicago. For Gatto touring the *505* is the best possible hands-on research he can do to understand every detail of Klaus Hänert's lost U-boat, understand the interior of a vessel that his team might try to penetrate before this week is out.

Every time the diver from South Jersey has toured the *505*, he imagines the battle that captured it. He loves World War II history, and the story of the capture of U-*505* is nothing short of thrilling. On June 4, 1944, the US Navy hunter-killer group TG-*22.3*, comprised of the escort carrier USS *Guadalcanal* and five DEs, was on the hunt for German submarines operating off Africa's Cape Verde when they made sonar contact with a submerged U-boat. USS *Chatelain* attacked with hedgehog mortars, then swung around for a second attack, with depth charges, while one of two Wildcat fighters from the *Guadalcanal* dove on the submerged U-boat and fired into the water to mark the sub's position. The *Chatelain* dumped a full pattern of depth charges around the U-boat. As geysers of spray erupted from the ocean, an oil slick spread on the water. The sub was hit. Just minutes later U-*505* broke the surface with its rudder jammed. The lights and electrical machinery were out. Water was pouring in.

The *Chatelain* opened fire on the stricken U-boat, as did USS *Pillsbury*, USS *Jenks*, and the two Wildcats. The German crew was so desperate to escape that they abandoned ship without setting off the scuttling charges meant to send the sub to the bottom before an enemy boarding party could seize the boat. The Germans also left the submarine's engines running and in gear.

As U-*505* circled to the right at a speed of 7 knots, the escorts ceased fire and launched a boarding party from the *Pillsbury*. While the *Chatelain* and the *Jenks* picked up survivors, the *Pillsbury*'s boarding party of eight men clambered onto the sub from their whaleboat. The boarders disconnected demolition charges, closed flooding seacocks, and plugged leaks. They also gathered charts, codebooks, and papers. Eventually TG-*22.3* got the U-boat pumped out and towed it 1,700 miles to Bermuda, where the navy hid its existence until the end of the war. The leader of the boarding party, Lieutenant (j.g.) Albert David, received the Medal of Honor for saving the sinking sub, its codebooks, and its Enigma machine. The captured sub and its contents gave the United States invaluable intelligence about U-boats and the Ubootwaffe.

Gatto can't help but think that TG-*22.3* owes some of its inspiration to the events surrounding U-*550*'s fatal encounter with USS *Joyce* and its sister DEs *Peterson* and *Gandy* two months before the American victory over U-*505* off Africa. What a hurricane of events loomed for the men on these four warships and the men aboard SS *Pan Pennsylvania* on Sunday morning, April 16, 1944. Gatto's blood hums to think that this year, this trip, might be the moment when he dives into that hurricane.

Brad Sheard's getting strange feelings. Almost twenty-five years after writing that U-*550* is an "untouched prize," he's driving east on the Sunrise Highway toward Montauk with his diving gear. Through the windshield he's seeing, for the first time in fifteen years, the area where he grew up. It looks so familiar, yet changed. Less wilderness, more buildings. Way more traffic. This feeling of things being the same yet different is a little disconcerting. A sort of twisted sense of déjà vu.

He thinks about how many years and how many dives have passed since he left from Montauk in the mid-1990s with a group of divers looking for the *Pan Penn* and *550*. He finds it beyond strange to think that he's actually on another hunt for the German sub . . . after all these years. He was a bold young diver back in the nineties. Now he's fifty-four years old, and this drive is making him feel the passage of time, feel his age. But what goes around comes around, it seems to him. And here he is again about to hunt for the ghosts of all those youths lost 70 miles south of Nantucket sixty-eight years ago.

There's a poem by Alfred, Lord Tennyson called "Ulysses." It's a monologue by the hero of the Trojan Wars, who is now a much older man than he was when he led the warriors of Ithaca against Troy and then home again. In the poem Ulysses urges his old friends, his veteran warriors and mariners, to rise once more for a great adventure. Near the end of his speech he declares:

> *There lies the port; the vessel puffs her sail:*
> *There gloom the dark, broad seas. My mariners,*
> *Come, my friends,*
> *'Tis not too late to seek a newer world . . .*
> *We are not now that strength which in old days*
> *Moved earth and heaven, that which we are, we are;*
> *One equal temper of heroic hearts,*
> *Made weak by time and fate, but strong in will*
> *To strive, to seek, to find, and not to yield.*

So it goes for Sheard. He's most definitely hearing a Ulysses-like call to adventure. When he told Mazraani that he was "all in" last August, he meant that he was "in" like a poker player pushing all his chips to the center of the table and saying, "Bring it on." But as pumped as he is to actually be on the cusp of a great adventure, a corner of his mind pictures those lost German and American boys who have been lurking at the edge of his consciousness for so long. Sometimes he imagines the Germans scrambling onto the deck from inside their sinking submarine. Sometimes he glimpses the lifeboat from the *Pan Penn* spilling all those fellows into the freezing water mere feet from the ship's churning propeller. There's danger out here, no question.

In 1994 Sheard and his fellow divers found and dove the wreck of the *Pan Penn* in 240 feet of water. Quite possibly they were the first divers to ever do so. They returned and dove it again in 1995. He remembers it as a massive wreck, lying mostly upside down on the seafloor. Remembers that he saw the bulb of the tanker's bow, a shadowy presence looming in the dark water. In 1994 the visibility was poor enough that he worried about getting lost if he strayed far from the anchor line. Later, the dive boat searched for six hours using its depth sounder to look for the *550*. The divers never found the sub, but Sheard remembers that heavy currents swirled around the dive boat while it was on the hunt.

So now, as he imagines this new search and a challenging technical dive to the wreck if they find it, he pictures marginal visibility and currents. He can't forget a dive to the SS *Andrea Doria* in similar conditions. The current was so swift it swept diver Billy Campbell off the anchor line during one of his deco stops. As sunset and fog started to settle over the water, divers manned an inflatable boat with an outboard and set off downcurrent in search of Campbell. After four hours of looking, they found him floating and alive, but the only way the crew of the inflatable could find their way back to the dive boat in the fog was because someone on the dive boat guided them home using radar and a VHF radio.

A happy ending for sure, but a lesson as well. Second chances are rare opportunities for deep-wreck divers in the North Atlantic.

"Be careful. Take care of yourself," said Sheard's girlfriend Theano before he left their home in Ellicott City, Maryland, this morning.

"I'm going to check and double-check everything before I ever get in the water," he tells himself. This wreck could be 50 feet deeper than the *Andrea Doria*. Can his body take the pressure and absorb five different mixes of gases the way it used to twenty years ago, when he dove the Billy Mitchell wrecks with Gatto and Packer? Who knows? But finding the wreck, diving it, photographing it with his Canon 5D Mark 2? This is the stuff of dreams. To strive, to seek, to find . . . and not to yield.

38

Mowing the Lawn

July 22, 2012

Standing in the stern of *Tenacious* in cargo shorts and a tank top, Anthony Tedeschi cocks his fishing rod over his shoulder, then casts his tuna lure beyond the foaming wake of *Tenacious*. Fishing always eases the wrinkles in his mind. It's something that has worked for him since he was a kid on his dad's fishing boat in Atlantic City.

Maybe if he weren't fishing he could be bothered that the search team has been mowing the lawn of the search grid with Kozak's 50-kilohertz fish since sunrise this morning and has nothing to show for the effort. After an eleven-hour bash for more than 100 miles into 3- to-4-foot seas to get out here, the dive boat has been crisscrossing the search area along east-to-west lanes, slowly working south from the northern edge of the grid for twelve hours already. But the team hasn't seen much of anything on the side-scan monitor.

If a guy sits around on a boat with nothing to do for long, he can think too much about this kind of thing. It can take him down, make him wonder whether he has bought into a wild goose chase for $1,500 just to hang with the big boys. But Tedeschi's not going to give in to the malaise that can settle over a crew after a day of searching the sea with nothing to show for their efforts.

He's with the greatest of friends, and he does some of his best day-dreaming while fishing. What a day this is for dreaming. Cloudless and sunny. Still warm and bright, even though the time is already after 1800 hours—early evening. The wind and the waves have dropped to mere whispers. The water is a deep blue, as clear as the water back at the Dutch Springs aqua park at the end of April. Tedeschi can picture it. The flooded limestone quarry in Bethlehem, Pennsylvania, is a 50-acre lake that has become a prime attraction to scuba divers. The lake is complete with sunken boats, excavating equipment, a school bus, and two airplanes. There are even wrecks of a trolley car and a large helicopter that divers can swim through. You can dive wrecks here without the expense of a dive boat, the unpredictability of getting blown out by bad weather, or the dangers inherent in open-ocean diving. Lots of divers come here to complete certification dives and practice for open water expeditions. Tedeschi met Brad Sheard, Tom Packer, Harold Moyers, and some other deep-wreck divers here in the spring to sort out their gear configurations for diving U-550.

His mind drifts back to that day at Dutch Springs. He and the other wreck divers had taken over the picnic table closest to the water, covered it with all manner of dive equipment, and surrounded it with a cache of extra tanks. Some of the other divers gathering at the quarry were looking like US Navy SEALs in the latest assemblage of top-shelf gear and dive fashions. The guys suiting up with Tedeschi must have appeared to divers outside their circle as a motley crew. He could feel the SEAL types watching his boys from afar, could imagine them snickering at his friends fumbling as they wrestled with the best way to carry two or three extra bottles of travel mix and bailout gas in addition to the tanks of bottom gas or the rebreather pack on their backs.

Unlike the school of divers known as DIR (Do It Right), in which all the divers on a team wear the same gear in the same configuration, Tedeschi's buddies have each been evolving their gear individually over decades and thousands upon thousands of deep-wreck dives. It makes him smile to think that on that day at Dutch Springs, he and his buddies must have appeared to the DIR divers like circus clowns performing a sausage-making gag. Little did those witnesses know that this clown routine of bantering, arguing, adjusting, and re-adjusting gear was helping each man arrive at just the right gear combination and setup that would let him dive with confidence and safety to a depth only a very few scuba divers will ever see. Little did they know that these supposed clowns—who sometimes looked unsure of how to mount a headlamp—were about to mount an expedition in search of one of scuba's holy grails. Tedeschi gets undeniable satisfaction in knowing that he travels with outliers, with men who dare to be different.

When he comes out of his memory of Dutch Springs, a ball-busting session's getting rolling aboard *Tenacious*. Mazraani has the gas grill set up on deck and has started cooking steaks and baked potatoes. The scent of sizzling, marinated meat fumes through the boat. Tom Packer's sitting at the dinette table. He looks up from reading Gary Gentile's book *Track of the Gray Wolf*, about U-boat warfare on the Eastern Seaboard in World War II, stops snacking on a handful of peanuts, and says, "Hey, Joe, I hope you don't mind that I dropped a peanut on the carpet. Don't worry, man, I just ground it in."

"Clean that shit up." Mazraani shakes a fist at Packer. When it comes to keeping *Tenacious* clean, Captain Joe has no sense of humor.

Several of the other guys are starting to laugh at the captain's frustration. His fastidiousness can be a nearly constant source of entertainment.

"Isn't that Pirate's job?" asks Packer.

"Fuck you."

Packer knows exactly how to press Mazraani's buttons. It's hard to tell which he can fawn over more, his dog or his boat. Then, of course, there's U-*550*.

The banter could go on for hours. These men are such good friends, and have logged so many dive trips together, that they may as well be brothers. And with the autopilot doing a flawless job of tracking *Tenacious* back and forth across the search grid, Mazraani doing the cooking and Kozak monitoring his sonar fish, the rest of the guys have time to snipe at each other. It's what brothers do when they are feeling a little cooped up, keyed up, and in need of stimulation. In need of finding a long-lost submarine. Sometimes a search trip on *Tenacious* can seem like one of those odysseys with a posse of wild boys in the back of a minivan.

Packer's feeling the opposite from the way he felt on last year's search trip. He has had a year of thinking about diving the sub if they find it, a year to familiarize himself with every aspect of a Type IXC/40 U-boat and the gear configuration that will keep him safe if he goes down to a virgin wreck in more than 300 feet of water. He also has a new scooter to tow him around the wreck so he can see a lot with his limited bottom time. Preparation is everything to Packer, and on this trip he's prepared and in a jovial mood. His brothers love this about him. His exceptional good humor can be a distraction from thoughts about a dark and deadly sea, a distraction, too, from worries about never finding Klaus Hänert's iron phantom.

Packer's wit can wave a red flag when he fears someone could take an unnecessary risk. It's like the moment on another dive trip when Mazraani told the guys that he intended going inside the *550*, and Packer said, "Okay, Joe, but just make sure you tell us before you go where you keep the keys to the boat."

Packer gets an A+ from his shipmates for resilience because they know some of the nightmares he has bounced back from. They've watched him rebound. One nightmare was a body recovery during an SS *Andrea Doria* dive trip back in the nineties. Sometimes Packer tells his dive buddies the story of how he almost botched the recovery. He tells the story to bring fellow divers out of their shadowy musings and to remind them to keep their shit together. The death of the diver is, of course, solemn business for Packer, and a body recovery is a dangerous and stressful operation. But Packer's mocking his own behavior during this particular recovery dive seems to help him and the others cope with the deadly side of deep-wreck diving and the tedium, as well as the latent anxiety, of a long, deep-ocean search.

As Packer's *Doria* story goes, back in the 1990s, too many divers began to think that because they now had mixed gases to help them cope with nitrogen narcosis, they could venture into deadly, deep-ocean wrecks such as the *Doria*. Sport divers began paying thousands of dollars for a chance to dive the *Doria*, and they started taking outrageous risks to come back with souvenirs. For experienced divers such as Gatto and Packer, watching untested divers descend into the ruins of the *Doria* spawned something like the anxiety and guilt that John Krakauer expressed in his book *Into Thin Air* after witnessing unprepared amateurs dying in an attempt to summit Mount Everest.

During one dive expedition to the *Doria*, when Packer and Gatto were the mates on a dive boat, another diver convulsed from oxygen toxicity and died while searching for a souvenir inside the wreck. Because Packer and Gatto knew the wreck so well, they went into the *Doria* in search of the dead man. They knew that on a previous dive he had gone looking for dishes in the second-class dining room two decks below where divers could enter the wreck. With that in mind they dropped into the wreck and headed for the cavernous dining room. Because the ship lies on its side, the stairwell leading from their entrance on the promenade deck down to the second-class dining room is like a dark, horizontal tunnel that must be navigated before reaching the doorway into the dining room. The dining room, which stretches from one side of the ship to the other, appears to a diver like a huge cavern dropping away 90 feet straight down. Most of the china, silver, and crystal have tumbled down to the bottom. This is where Packer and Gatto expected to recover the body.

According to their plan, Packer waited with a coil of rope at the top of the cavernous room. Meanwhile, Gatto descended to the bottom with one end of the rope to tie to the dead man's tank harness. Once the line was attached, Gatto and Packer would hoist up the body on the line. That was the plan. But all of this was happening in a creaking wreck 200 feet below the surface. The water was clear within the beam of Packer's dive light, but aside from that, the wreck was completely and utterly dark. As his light followed Gatto into the darkness below, the line uncoiled through Packer's hands. He felt it slipping over his fingers . . . and then he didn't.

"It was one of those 'oh, shit' moments," says Packer when he tells the story. "I went chasing down after that sinking line."

But it sank faster than he could swim, and he knew at that moment that it was paramount to stop his descent so he could mark the exit from this black cavern for his buddy.

Then, before Packer could make his way back to the stairwell, Gatto rose out of the darkness and slapped the line in his buddy's hand in a way that clearly asked, "Can we focus?"

Packer felt stupid. This is what he tells other divers listening to his story. Like heads-up, guys. Shit happens even when you think you're paying attention.

Listening to Packer teasing Mazraani and offering up wisdom through the stories he tells on himself are just what Eric Takakjian can use this evening. He has been fighting off bad vibes. Lying in his berth in the forecastle trying to catch a little rest before dinner and his evening watch, Takakjian has been worrying that the 50-kilohertz fish is not doing its job. He's pretty sure that there are geographical features and shipwrecks on the bottom, marked by his plotted hang numbers, that the sonar has not been seeing.

Kozak's fish was designed for finding the wreck of the British light cruiser HMS *Edinburgh*, which sank in the Barents Sea during World War II with a load of 465 ingots of gold bullion. Divers found the wreck in the early 1980s. The gold they recovered was worth more than $60 million and stands as the biggest bullion recovery in the history of wreck salvaging. But the *Edinburgh* was nearly three times as long and more than ten times larger in volume than U-*550*. In Takakjian's mind, it seems possible that the resolution of the sonar "eyes" in the 50-kilohertz fish, designed to find an enormous warship, might miss a submarine, just as they probably have been missing known geological features and wrecks within the search grid.

When he's not stewing about the performance of the fish, his thoughts drift to the sub down there somewhere. He wonders about the stories it can tell. Wonders if it holds unknown truths about the battle in which it was lost. He can imagine those boys on U-*550* as it hides on the bottom of the ocean from three American DEs. He can feel the stress of their waiting, can picture what it must have been like to sit in the dim light of a U-boat, hazy with uncertainty and testosterone. Waiting. Just waiting. It must be a bit like how it feels to be sitting at the helm of *Tenacious* during his watch sometimes, holloweyed and stiff from the lack of movement as the dive boat mows the lawn east, west, and east again, searching for some telltale sign from the fish that there is something down there on the bottom, something that looks like a lost submarine beneath the pale rim of the Atlantic. Waiting for some hope, some sense of renewal, to relieve this feeling of being forever stuck in a place between two worlds, stuck in limbo while the sun sets and the air smells and tastes like ash.

At such moments it really helps to have Tom Packer and his wit around. Or to have some new and immediate challenge emerge. Now it's Garry Kozak who comes to the rescue.

"Instead of anchoring up," he asks, "how do you guys feel about towing the fish through the night?"

"Let's do it," say all the guys at once. Persisting with the search is the inspiration they need to distract them from their worries and keep them motivated. Takakjian, Packer, and Gatto know how to run the sonar. They can spell Kozak so he can get some much-needed sleep. The divers know that at the rate they are going, they will never cover the whole search grid before they have to run for home unless they search all night. This is their window of good weather. Maybe, just maybe, the fish is working. Maybe they can find the *550* before the shit storm hits.

39

Target

July 23, 2012

The second blue morning at sea. *Tenacious* has surveyed the whole grid, has only one serious target to show after 80 square miles of searching. And finding that target was an accident. Last night, at about 2240 hours, Gatto and Packer were watching the side-scan monitor. Mazraani was on the helm. Everyone else was sleeping except Sheard, who had just gotten up because he was keen to watch the monitor when the fish passed over a cluster of hangs that Takakjian had plotted. For Sheard, seeing a wreck or a bottom anomaly on the side scan at the site of these hangs would be the proof to his skeptical mind that the 50-kilohertz sonar was not a dud. But when the fish went by the hang numbers? Nothing.

Now Sheard was really convinced that the sonar wasn't functioning. But just as he was working up to a rant, the screen froze on the sonar monitor. The crew woke Kozak. He told Mazraani to hold his course, to proceed outside the search grid until the monitor came back online. So . . . Mazraani was holding the course when one of the guys at the monitor shouted that it was working again, and "holy shit!"—they were going over something. Mazraani marked the spot on his navigation laptop while Gatto, Packer, and Kozak watched a strange blip creep across the monitor screen. It looked too large to be a submarine, but it sure as hell was something BIG.

"This is just about all we have," says Mazraani when he calls a crew meeting after breakfast. "A mystery blip . . . and a few other sets of hang numbers outside the grid on the other side."

All the men are tired, some a little disheartened. Takakjian has been listening to weather forecasts on the VHF radio and a satellite feed. Despite current calm and clear conditions, he's sure that rough weather will be moving in tonight. The divers take deep breaths and weigh the question of heading for home now to avoid the worst of the weather or to make one last attempt to find the lost submarine.

"What's our absolute drop dead time?" someone asks Takakjian.

He says that they better start for Montauk by about 1900 hours or be ready for a spanking from Mother Nature.

"That gives us ten hours to look, guys," says Kozak.

All the men nod. "It's not over till it's over," they tell each other.

They can't quit yet. It's just not in their DNA. Basing their last-ditch plan on hang numbers, they design two new and smaller search boxes, "fingers," trailing off the initial grid like the sides of a horse-shoe. In short order the navigation laptop is programmed to guide the autopilot over the new fingers.

"Don't forget that blip," says Mazraani. "We gotta go back there. I have a feeling about that."

His shipmates convince him that before they go back to the blip, they need to finish mowing the lawn in the new grids, need to rule out more swaths of ocean.

Mazraani shrugs, gives in to the will of the team. "Whatever. But I'm telling you, we're going to find that sub today."

"Of course," says Packer with a grin. "It stands to reason. Today's my birthday."

But by 1500 hours, the team on *Tenacious* has not found anything after mowing the lawn in the fingers.

"*Now* we go back to Joe's blip," says Kozak. "And let's take a closer look at it with the hundred-kilohertz fish."

"At last," thinks Takakjian, "a more precise tool."

"Now we're talking," says Sheard.

Mazraani puts Takakjian on the helm because the boat will not be running on autopilot and Takakjian, with decades as a professional tug captain and dive boat operator, has the most experience at the wheel. Meanwhile the team retrieves more than a half mile of sonar cable by hand, swaps out the low-resolution fish for the 100-kilohertz unit, and deploys it. Perhaps an hour passes before *Tenacious* is ready for this last-ditch search. Although nobody says it, many of the guys realize that they have perhaps two hours left for looking before they have to pack up and head for Montauk.

Paralleling the western edge of the search grid, *Tenacious* steams north towing the new fish at a speed of 3.5 knots and a depth of 250 feet. It can see about 200 yards to either side. As they approach the blip, everyone gathers around the sonar monitor except Takakjian, who's at the helm, and Mazraani, standing beside him watching the chart plotter and depth sounder carefully.

"Here it comes," he says as the boat tows the fish toward the mystery blip.

"There. There it is," says Kozak a minute later, when the fish catches up to the blip.

"That can't be a sub," says somebody. "It's huge."

"We don't know that yet," says Mazraani. "Maybe it has fishing nets all over it and the periscopes are up."

Kozak says he wants to measure the target and asks Takakjian to start making passes from various angles.

With each pass, Mazraani feels his hopes dimming a little. According to Kozak, this is definitely a wreck. It measures 180 feet long and is 80 feet high over almost its entire length. This is not the profile of a U-boat.

"What the hell is it?" asks someone.

"That's too damn big to be a fishing boat," says someone else.

"I don't know." One of the team points at the monitor. "But look at that."

"It looks like a rounded stern, a ship's fantail."

"I think I can see a companionway." Gatto points to the monitor.

"I bet that's the stern of the *Pan Penn*," says Kozak. He's smiling. This guy *really* likes finding things.

Steve Gatto pictures a World War II action photo shot from the USS *Joyce*. The *U-550* is sinking in the foreground, and the *Pan Penn* is spewing smoke and fire in the background, possibly a mile away. If this is the broken-off stern of the tanker, than perhaps the sub is very close . . . close, that is, if the tanker's stern separated from the rest of the ship shortly after taking the torpedo. But none of the ship reports retrieved from the National Archives makes any mention of the tanker breaking in two. They only describe it as floating upside down and submerged by the stern. Still, the stern might have broken away.

The team can feel darkness and bad weather coming. The wind is starting to stir, and a layer of high, thin clouds has begun to obscure the sun. Very soon the team will have to start home for Montauk before their little boat gets slammed by brutal winds and waves. Takakjian's still on the helm. Mazraani's standing next to him contemplating the possibility of heading home empty-handed, but then he sees a 15-foot spike rise above the seafloor on his depth sounder screen.

"Guys, guys, we're going over something."

Takakjian hits a key on the chart plotter to mark the spot.

About sixty seconds pass. Then, at 1856 hours, the fish picks up an image.

The crew can't believe their eyes.

"Oh, my God."

"Wow."

"Jesus."

The six divers gather around Kozak and his computer monitor on the galley table. Gatto makes a cell phone video as the men gape at the picture on the screen beaming up from the fish. One of the divers says the grainy, golden image looks like a metal cigar "with a tit on it."

Actually, it appears to be a glittering picture of a fully intact submarine.

Despite the need to head for home and safety in the face of the darkening skies and building wind and seas, the dive team spends more than an hour making passes over the wreck from different angles with the fish, but none of the images is as elucidating as that first golden picture of the cigar on the seafloor. Kozak measures the image. It's about 250 feet long, like a Type IXC/40 U-boat. But how can the team be certain it's U-550? There's a lot of debate.

At one point Anthony Tedeschi, holding a celebratory bottle of Magic Hat #9 beer in one hand, grabs his set of laminated dive tables with his free hand and waves them as a sign that he's willing to suit up.

"I'll go," says Mazraani. But he knows that with foul weather brewing, there's not enough time to make a dive into more than 300 feet of water and return without putting the boat and its crew at risk.

Steve Gatto has a better idea. Why not use his drop camera to get some pictures?

In short order the guys on *Tenacious* retrieve the fish and carry what looks like a large metal spider to the side of the dive boat. The camera of this J. W. Fisher instrument is like the body of the spider. There's a bright halogen light mounted on each of its legs. With Takakjian holding the boat over the wreck, the crew reels out the camera on its video/power cable until the instrument is almost on the bottom. The first things that the divers see on the monitor are a number of codfish and lots of krill, sure signs that a wreck is near. Then as Takakjian watches the outline of the wreck on the depth sounder's screen and inches the boat toward the target, the drop camera runs smack into a wall.

"Get it up! Get the camera up!" guys are shouting. "Jesus, we hit the hull!"

When a cloud of silt clears, the guys watching the camera monitor can see the steel frames of a narrow deck . . . then the unmistakable outline of what can only be the distinctive shape of a torpedo-loading hatch on a World War II German U-boat. All of these men have seen similar hatches and similar deck framing on other U-boats that they have dived. The boat erupts with shouts and cheers.

"Any doubts now?" asks one of the crew.

"Hell, no," says Tom Packer. "What a birthday!"

"Gentlemen, U-*five-five-zero* . . . has been located." Mazraani's voice rings with quiet, reverential emotion across the deck of the dive boat, out over the sea. The man who has pulled this exceptional team of wreck hunters and divers together exhales deeply.

The team begins slapping each other high fives. The discovery has come during the last day, last hour, last minutes of searching before the weather gods start hurling lightning bolts at *Tenacious*.

"Now the fun begins," says someone.

But there will be no diving the wreck tonight, no prying into history on this trip. No communing with ghosts yet. Instead, the crew hauls the drop camera, lights up the gas grill, throws chicken breasts on the fire, and settles down in the saloon aboard *Tenacious* to sip some Strega that Gatto has brought along for just such a moment. Not long after the celebration ends, the crew, except the man on watch, head for their berths. But nobody can sleep. The guys are still too jazzed. For the rest of their lives they will remember wedging themselves into their berths for dark hour after dark hour while the wind whistles and the dive boat pounds into a 3-foot chop. It builds to a 6-foot head sea before the team finds shelter the next morning at Montauk.

40

First Dives

July 26–30, 2012

Fearing that other divers will find the wreck before the *Tenacious* team can get back and dive the *550*, they issue a press release about their discovery. Just two days after the dive boat's long slog back to Montauk in slamming seas, the *New York Times*, the *Washington Post*, the *Boston Globe*, TV stations, and a host of Internet sites are announcing:

WORLD WAR II–ERA GERMAN U-BOAT FOUND
OFF COAST OF MASSACHUSETTS

International publications such as *Der Spiegel* in Germany pick up the story as well.

TV anchor Brian Williams interrupts NBC's network coverage of the Summer Olympic Games with an announcement of the *550*'s discovery. The news goes viral, but the divers aren't hanging around to bask in the glory. They have work to do.

On July 28, *Tenacious* heads to sea. This time it's heavily loaded with tanks and gear for multiple deep dives. Garry Kozak and Eric Takakjian have had to return to their jobs, but divers Paul McNair, Pat Rooney, and Mark Nix have joined the usual crew.

Rocketing toward the bottom of the sea behind his DPV (diver propulsion vehicle), which the divers call a "scooter," Joe Mazraani can't believe his good fortune. It's the morning of July 29, and the visibility is outstanding. He can see at least 50 feet into the indigo abyss below. He's the first diver in the water and so pumped on adrenaline that he doesn't even remember that he hardly slept during the long trip to the wreck, barely remembers hooking into the wreck with the grapnel on the first try. Barely remembers the debate on deck earlier this morning as some of the men, such as Steve Gatto, argued for a delay to the dives because there was a current running. After the team waited for a while for the current to slow, Mazraani said "to hell with the current," suited up, and leaped off the stern of *Tenacious*, carrying about 300 pounds of gear, including four different breathing gases in five tanks.

He's scootering down parallel to the anchor line, pausing from time to time to clear his ears carefully, hoping like hell this deep dive won't do more damage to his hearing. At 270 feet he stops and looks around. He thinks, "I've never gone deeper than this before. I'm already below the sand level of the *Doria*."

It's getting really dark, but he doesn't turn on his dive light. He wants to let his eyes adjust to the darkness, wants to see the wreck the way it looks to the fishes or maybe Neptune. He can't even picture what lies ahead. Is it a broken, collapsed pile of rubble, like so many wrecks he has visited? Is it a crumbling pressure hull with the exoskeleton of the outer steel hull rotted away, like some other subs he has dived? Has the carcass of this war machine broken open from its crash dive or from the raking and tearing of scallop dredges and fishing nets? He has no clue. All he knows is that his eyes belong to the first human to witness this grave. At this moment he's feeling a little like Egyptologist Howard Carter finding himself at the uncovered door to King Tut's tomb for the first time.

He slows his descent now as he reaches 300 feet. There's something shadowy looming ahead, something at eye level, something thick and spiky and a little bent. It's rising from below, almost like the barrel of a deck gun on a warship. But it can't be. Subs don't have guns of this size. He snaps on his dive light, flashes it toward the shadow.

He's face-to-face with a giant steel noodle. *The attack periscope.* It's bent with the top broken off, no doubt, after an encounter with a commercial fisherman's gear. Mazraani follows the anchor line lower as it arcs past the scope. Now he sees the ring of the radio direction finder's antenna, with sea grass trailing off it. At the base of the antenna is the conning tower. In the picture that Mazraani has seen of the last minutes of the *550* on the surface following the battle, this tower looked like Swiss cheese, pierced and dented by 20mm and 40mm shells from the *Gandy*, *Peterson*, and *Joyce*. But now the tower looks whole again and alive, wrapped tightly in fishnets and covered with a thick patina of bushy hydroids. It's the proverbial octopus's garden. The tines from *Tenacious*'s grapnel have snagged the deck of the U-boat just forward of the tower, made themselves fast in the steel framework that once supported the wooden treads of the foredeck. This steel framework appears robust, barely deteriorated. Little orange fishes are schooling over the deck.

"My God," thinks Mazraani, "the wreck is intact. After all these years."

He reaches out a hand and touches the sub, feels a deep sense of reverence, a solemnity so profound that he almost forgets to breathe. It takes a score of seconds for the elation to hit. But when it comes,

The discovery team explores their prize find, the first to
see the U-550 in nearly seventy years (July 2012).
COURTESY BRADLEY SHEARD

Mark Nix examines the upper-port torpedo tube, which is open to the sea with a deteriorating torpedo still in the tube.

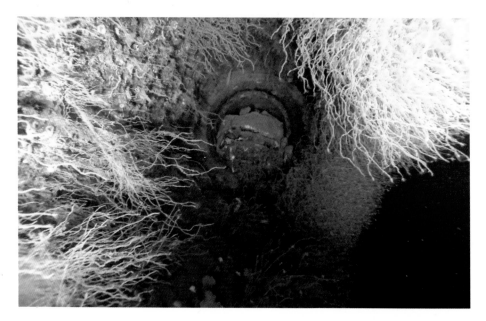

A closer look at the torpedo tube. The doors are open with the head of the moldering T5 torpedo just visible. This shows that the U-550 did not fire on the destroyer escorts, but the doors being open suggests that they were prepared to fire.

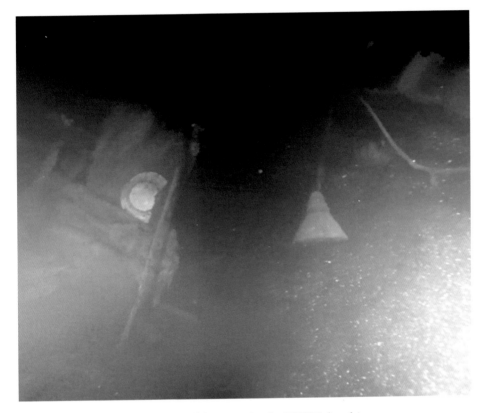

Light and shade still hanging in the NCO's berthing area.
COURTESY JOE MAZRAANI

Ammo boxes still filled with ammunition in the forward torpedo room.

Debris in forward torpedo room. The rails still hanging from
the overhead were used for moving torpedoes.

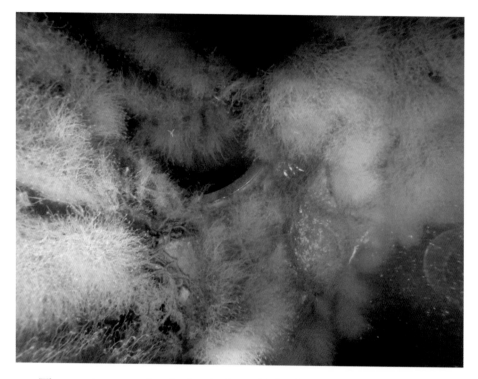
The conning tower hatch after Anthony Tedeschi cut away all the fishnets.

Mark Nix hovers over the conning tower looking aft.

Steve Gatto and Pat Rooney with an impromptu sign proclaiming the find;
Paul McNair in the background (August 2012).

it's not the fist-pumping, high-fiving that exploded aboard *Tenacious* after the discovery of the wreck a few days ago. It's a rare blend of feelings—accomplishment, humility, and wonder. Later Mazraani will describe this moment as something like the euphoria he had after winning a murder trial for one of his clients against all odds.

"There could be more than forty men in here," he thinks, remembering that only thirteen men made it onto USS *Joyce* alive. He kneels on the deck, makes the sign of the cross, touching his forehead, chest, and shoulders, and says in his native Arabic, *"Bismil Ab wa el eben wa Rouh el Kodos. Amin."* In the name of the Father, the Son, and the Holy Spirit. Amen.

By the time he ties in the anchor chain with loops of 3/8-inch nylon that he brought along for the purpose, Tom Packer has arrived with his own scooter. They shoot each other a thumbs-up signal as they look into each other's masks, search for their buddy's eyes, for his feelings. The message that each man gets from his friend is the same: "We're here. We did this. We're on top of Everest."

During the rest of his twenty minutes on the bottom, Mazraani circles the *550* counterclockwise, towed behind his scooter. He travels aft along the port side, notes that the sub is sitting almost upright on the bottom with just a slight list to port. The entire outer hull of the sub looks to be in one piece, albeit overgrown with a patina of brownish-green vegetation. Rounding the stern and heading up the starboard side, he sees the starboard propeller tucked down low. Then he notes that the after torpedo-loading hatch is firmly closed. No one escaped from back here. Passing the tower, he wonders where the 37mm gun and the two 20mm antiaircraft cannons are. Possibly fishing gear has carried the weapons away?

Perhaps one of the massive East German team trawlers that fished out here in the 1960s and '70s scooped up the guns before the Magnuson Act in 1976 extended US territorial waters out 200 miles from the coast and excluded foreign fishermen. Perhaps what was once German remains German. Just like this sub itself. Maritime laws unequivocally state that the wrecks of warships and combat aircraft lost at sea remain forever the property of their native government. U-550 will always be a German vessel, even though it lies in US territorial waters.

While Mazraani is circling the U-boat, Steve Gatto's nearing the wreck on his first dive. He doesn't have his video camera on this dive because he wants to get comfortable managing the extra gases he's carrying for this depth, get comfortable with the wreck itself, too. On the way down he's wondering if it will look like other U-boats he has dived . . . like the U-869 off New Jersey, U-853 off Block Island, U-117 off Virginia, or U-85 off Nags Head, North Carolina.

Sometimes when Gatto thinks about these U-boats, he feels disturbed by the story of the 85. On April 14, 1942, U-85 became the first U-boat loss of the German submarine offensive against America that U-boat Command called *Paukenschlag* ("Operation Drumbeat"), a coordinated attack that surprised the US Navy and claimed more than a hundred Allied ships off America's East Coast with the sinking of only seven U-boats during the first half of 1942.

As one of the unlucky ones, U-85 found herself caught at night on the surface and attacked by USS *Roper*, an American destroyer. After taking serious battle damage, the sub's skipper ordered his crew to abandon ship as the U-boat began to sink. The *Roper* continued to attack and dropped eleven depth charges, killing the men in the water with the concussions from the explosions. The next morning the bodies of twenty-nine Germans were recovered and taken to Hampton National Cemetery for a nighttime burial that was likely meant to be secret. Gatto doesn't think of those wasted lives as he observes this other U-boat from 30 feet above, before descending to the sub, but sometimes when he's not in the middle of a deep technical dive like this, thoughts about the unnecessary dead from U-85 make fleeting dashes across his consciousness.

He can see Packer's and Mazraani's lights playing back and forth, up and down over the conning tower and the foredeck. The lights illuminating the wreck add a certain Hollywood drama to the moment. He feels a thrill running through his body. Divers live for moments like this, transcendent moments. "Here's history staring me right in the face," he thinks. Hovering above the sub, watching the sweep of lights over the shadowy hull, Gatto finds his mind slipping back to the famous battle pictures of U-550 tacked on the bulletin board in *Tenacious*. Looking at the shadowy conning tower, he can almost see the silhouettes of the thirteen men waiting there for rescue on April 16, 1944.

Meanwhile, Tom Packer buzzes to the bow with his scooter. Like Mazraani, Packer's astonished that a wreck that has been on the bottom twelve years longer than the *Doria* has not started a full-scale collapse the way the liner has. At the front of the sub, he drops right down to sand level 25 feet in front of the bows, lets his scooter hang from its tether at his side, and stares up at the sharp, knife-like prow. From this vantage point, the *550* looks utterly majestic. It's hardly buried in the sand, and with its rakish cant to port, it seems like an immense shark veering toward its prey. Packer thinks the sub is in such good shape that it looks like it could rise off the bottom and set sail, so to speak, like some latter-day *Flying Dutchman*.

"Even if I never get back here again, I'll have this picture in my mind till the day I die," he thinks.

This is a *Das Boot* moment for Packer, with the shadowy bows of the sub looming overhead, as it does at an iconic moment in the film. He and the guys are going to watch the movie tonight after dinner. Mazraani has the DVD tucked in his seabag, Gatto has brought a 32-inch flat screen TV, and Tedeschi has packed aboard a small generator to drive the TV. Movie time . . . later.

Mazraani has almost used up his bottom time gaping at this iron monster. But as he drifts with the slight current aft from the bows toward the anchor line in preparation for his long ascent to the surface, he notices that the forward torpedo-loading hatch is open. He wonders how many men might have escaped this sinking hulk. Possibly more than the thirteen rescued by the *Joyce*. He kneels down on the deck and peers into the hatch. Something about the darkness inside calls to him. *Really* calls to him. Later he will tell his buddies that "it seemed like such an inviting place." With the right gear configuration, he believes he could swim into this sub.

"Maybe another time," he thinks as he peers into the dark core of *550*. Then his mind switches over to his high school German. *"Auf wiedersehen."* See you again. His voice murmurs into his regulator, echoes as if he's sending a coded message.

When Brad Sheard starts following the anchor line down along with Mazraani, Gatto, and Packer, he's not going to lie to himself. He's scared, even though he has practiced with this exact gear configuration at Dutch Springs and has three decades of deep-diving experience under his belt.

He doesn't like diving in a current, and he hasn't gone this deep since diving the Billy Mitchell wrecks almost twenty years ago. Now he's not sure his tissues can take all this stretching from the gases the way he once could. He's definitely not liking that it has taken him a full seven minutes to pull himself down the anchor line to the deck at 316 feet.

But damn. For a guy who loves to photograph wrecks, it doesn't get much cooler than this. Definitely the most complete U-boat wreck he has ever dived. He tries to shoot with two strobes. But only one is working, so he turns them both off, cranks up the film speed (ISO) on his Canon, and tries to capture the scene with just ambient light. It's dark down here for his eyes, like a starry night, but even darker for the camera, which struggles to get an image in the dim conditions.

Cautiously he swims to the forward torpedo-loading hatch. He's surprised to find it not only open, but also with the hatch cover nowhere in sight. This is a puzzle that clings to the back of his mind until he gets to the surface safely and has time to reflect on what he has seen. Later, back aboard *Tenacious*, he remembers the navy *Eastern Sea Frontier War Diary*'s speculation that men may have escaped from a forward hatch after the sinking. Weeks after the battle, the navy picked up three bodies of men that they identified as part of the *550*'s crew. He pictures the German boys rising out of that dark hole in the sub with small single tanks of gas and oxygen masks pressed to their faces.

He's thinking that the *War Diary* might well be right about these escapes until he remembers something else he saw on the wreck, a huge crack in the pressure hull. It's about 3 feet long and runs right into the welded rim of the forward torpedo-loading hatch. Sheard's an aeronautical engineer. It's his business to analyze stresses in metal, and one look at this fissure in the hull tells him that something dramatic happened here. Some tremendous force inside *550* ruptured the hull and blew the hatch off, flooding the sub and destroying any chance of anyone inside ever escaping. Something's wrong with the *War Diary*'s explanation of how those dead men from the sub turned up floating weeks later.

For Anthony Tedeschi, his first dive on *550* has a more serendipitous feel. Like Mazraani, Packer, and Gatto, he's pretty much blown away by the sub's amazing condition, but he's also stoked about this being his deepest dive ever. As he rises to his deco stops on the way up, he ticks off his previous deep dives. The *Doria* at 260 feet. The SS *Carolina* at 230 feet. The SS *Ayuruoca* at 175 feet. At one hang during his decompression he knows that both he and his dive partner, Pat Rooney, are feeling a little giddy about their adventure to 330 feet when he feels the sudden urge to sing along after Rooney starts humming the *Wizard of Oz* tune "If I Only Had a Brain."

.   .   .

During the next day's diving on the sub, after giving their tissues twenty-four hours to recover from the heavy gas loads of their first dive, the team pauses for a photo shoot. While Steve Gatto operates the camera and lights, Tom Packer and Joe Mazraani pose on the 550's deck in front of the conning tower and display a 3-by-5-foot, red, white, and blue Boston Sea Rovers expedition flag. It's a triumphant picture, no question. But behind the showmanship, the divers feel a nagging chill of suspicion.

With the open forward hatches over the torpedo room and galley, with that crack leading into the forward torpedo-loading hatch, U-550 does not look like a tomb. It looks like a wreck that the entire crew might have escaped from before it sank. What happened to them? Could the story of the three DEs' attack on the U-boat and the rescue of thirteen crewmen—the story promoted by the navy's *War Diary* and on the US Coast Guard website—be incomplete? Is there more to the story of what happened out here on April 16, 1944, than the world knows? The U-550 discovery team isn't sure. But they aim to find out. They have no more time for deep offshore exploration this year, and the hurricane season is coming. But make no mistake, the team will be back next summer.

PART FIVE

Looking for Answers

41

Out of the Blue

Fall–Winter 2012

By the time the divers return from the *550*, Joe Mazraani's email and voice mailbox have been slammed with messages.

Among the first to arrive is an email from Germany. The correspondent is Tilmann Kuhla. He's the twenty-eight-year-old grandson of Dr. Friedrich Torge, the physician aboard U-*550*. He has read about the sub's discovery in *Spiegel Online*. His grandfather died in 2009, but his family is very interested in the story of the discovery, eager to see pictures and to help in any way. A fast response by Mazraani yields an equally fast response from Kuhla. His family has pictures and stories to share. The Kuhlas would love to meet the divers if they ever come to Germany.

Among the other emails to arrive is one from Heather Bender Baker, whose grandfather "Grand John" Bender was the ASW officer aboard the *Joyce* who detected and helped to coordinate the depth-charge attack on the *550*. Grand John, she says, is alive at age ninety-two, but in frail health.

"Wow," thinks Mazraani, "an eyewitness to the battle and rescue."

And John Bender is not the only living American eyewitness. Another email leads the divers to John Hudock, a former crewman on the *Gandy* who lives in western Pennsylvania. There's also contact from Mort Raphelson, the chief radio officer of the *Pan Penn*. He's in his nineties, but in good health and living in nearby Cinnaminson, New Jersey. Clearly, Raphelson and Hudock offer the divers a chance to ask questions and get answers. In short order, the discovery team makes plans to visit the American vets and videotape their stories of what they remember about events prior to, during, and after April 16, 1944, aboard their ships.

On August 2, 2012, two more astonishing emails arrive. One is from Wolf Hänert, the son of the *550*'s skipper. The second is from John Rauh, son of Johann Rauh, who was a machinist aboard the *550*. Both the sub's captain and the machinist survived the battle. They have since passed, but the sons are deeply interested in the discovery of the lost U-boat, and both offer astonishing news. According to Rauh, his mother, Helga, knows of two survivors of the *550* who are still living near Frankfurt, Robert Ziemer and Albert Nitsche. Wolf Hänert says that U-*550*'s engineer, Hugo Renzmann, is also alive and living in Kiel, the very port from which *550* sortied almost seven decades ago. These are the last three German survivors still alive. More eyewitnesses.

Another blockbuster email arrives from Kim Joshi. She's the granddaughter of the captain of USS *Joyce*, Robert Wilcox. Her grandfather died in the mid-1990s, but as the keeper of the family archives, she has learned a little about the battle of April 16, 1944, and a lot about what happened after the war to these men. She says that, as surprising as it may seem, following the war Wilcox and some of the Germans whom he rescued became friends for life. She would like to send the divers letters from these men and photos from her grandfather's collection of memorabilia.

"Please," Mazraani writes to Joshi. He has the feeling that his reasons for being interested in this lost submarine are about to take a major turn.

A few days later a huge file lands in the divers' in-box from Joshi. Her attachments open a window on a most surprising, honest, and intimate friendship growing between former enemies, including three letters to Wilcox from POW camps.

21 December, 1946

Dear Sir,

Thank you for your kind letter, which I got some days ago. I have been very glad of your lines. Special thanks for the photographs. I had found a picture of our sinking sub in the New York Times while in prison-ship in the States. Till now I kept it like a relic. You know how a sailor cleaves together with his ship and therefore you will know my gladness about your photographs.

I would say many thanks if you could forward a photo of the conning-tower of our sub.

Sir, I beg your pardon if my letter does not show always a real English style, but my knowledge of your language is not so well to write excellent letters.

I am glad to hear that you got over the war in good health. I am glad too that the war is over. The lost war is naturally very hard for our country. It is an old law that the loser must pay off the debt. We are ready to do so but now things happen here that make great embittering.

Nobody except ourself can imagine the emergency of our country. No coal, hunger rations of food, destroyed towns, housing-problems, add to this millions of banished persons of the Polish and Russian controlled areas. And all that now in the bitter German winter.

Add to this there are personal things. Always I loved my father-land and always I have done my best to help my country. Like all my comrades I have this will even today. But everywhere we find difficulties in getting new jobs. You know the reason: former officer—militarist. And I have thought only to have done my duty like every professional soldier of any other country. Now, that is the result. You see it is not a pleasure now here to have been a soldier.

By chance now I am in training of a justice-official, a real desk job. Very different from being a technician and a sailor. My greatest wish going to sea again is unrealizable for long time, if not forever.

Also it is impossible to visit your country once more. But I should be very glad to see you here if you shall come once to Germany. Of course pre-war German beer doesn't exist previously.

The letter will reach you when Christmas is over. I shall hope that you and your family have had better days than we shall have. For your Christmas-greetings I say my best thanks.

I wish you and your family a happy New Year and wish you to have further good health and luck.

You will allow to enclose my picture taken in wartime, some weeks before going for my last trip.

Yours sincerely,
Hugo Renzmann

In a second letter Renzmann writes:

Dear Sir,

Many thanks for your letter from March 21, 1947, and the separate cover containing the copies of the conning tower of our sub. Conformably to your wish I have sent second copy to Kapitantleutnant Hänert. He commissioned me to say you his best thanks. But I believe he had written a letter to you himself.

He and our Doctor are always behind barbed wire in

*England. For the present it is no chance for him as former
submarine-captain coming home. In this occupation zone also I have
gotten news from former sub-captains and chief engineers, that they
must go for some days to English interrogations camps by order of the
Royal Navy. I do not know what the purpose. Some day I will get the
same order, I think, and then see the matter.*

*I have caused copies to be made of your pictures and have send them
to relations of our sub-crew. To this people this is the last remembering of
their sons and husbands, who fought and died for their fatherland.*

*Beg your pardon, that I answer you not till today. But in these
times I have much work in my kitchen—garden to have potatoes and
vegetables in wintertime. Yet we have always a great food shortage.
Therefore one must see how getting some additional things keeping
alive. With 200 grams of meat that we get rations per person within
one month no one can live.*

*In your letter you are anxious about me, that I may be involved in
plots against the occupying forces. I can make your mind easy. It is
possible that a few persons are trying resistance. But we know that
such things are thoughtless. Our people only will have calm
and peace. We will try to work to live in friendship with our
neighbors. But—I must say it too, the world let us do a very hard way.
I am not embittered toward the enemy, who fought as a soldier
against us. But now, two years after the end of the war, we have the
right of a living wage, I mean.*

*Always I hope that our former enemies examine one day that the
German people is the heart of Europe and that Europe cannot live
without this people.*

*I hope that the western allies and Russia will find a way to a
peaceful future. If not—only the United States have the might with
help of England and Germany to save western Europe from
Bolshevisms. We, in this country know the danger and I hope
America and England will see too.*

If this letter will reach you, eventually you will have gone to sea again. I am envious of your command, but I wish you luck and a happy course all time.

Joshi tells Mazraani that her grandfather sent CARE packages to his former enemies during the difficult years following World War II, while West Germany was rebuilding. And she also sends a copy of a handwritten letter dated March 16, 1948, and sent by Dr. Torge from an English POW camp to Wilcox.

Sir,

I learned a short time ago from Hugo Renzmann the engineer is still in touch with you. Therefore I am encouraged to forward to you this best letter from behind the barbed wire. After the repatriation of our captain Hänert on December 31, 1947, I shall be the last of our crew who is now going home after being prisoner nearly four years. This long time exceeded my expectations I had aboard your unforgotten ship. The return to Germany has for me a character of doubtful adventure. But my repatriation this week shall give us a little hope for a new start after the long P/W—journeys started in the Nantucket Lightship area—ended tomorrow aboard the hospitalship Oxfordshire, *via Southampton—Hamburg.*

If the new time of my life should be more successful in spite of the desolate situation in Europe and especially in Germany, I should like to write you another letter but this time without the seal of prisonership on the occasion of the fifth or tenth anniversary of our Atlantic meeting which was indeed my 2nd birthday [marking the date of his being given a new life on April 16, 1944].

I remain yours sincerely,
F. Torge

In addition to the letters, Joshi sends an article from the *New York Herald Tribune* about Wilcox and Renzmann meeting in 1960 in New York while Renzmann is training with the US Navy to take command of an American-built NATO destroyer. Along with the article are photos of the former enemies shaking hands, smiling, and talking over coffee.

Just looking at these pictures and reading the letters give the divers shivers. None of them expected that finding and diving a shipwreck would ever draw them into this extremely human story about combatants and their families reaching out to each other across space and time to try to heal themselves and each other after a terrible war.

"I feel honored," says Tom Packer. "We all do." He says that he and all the members of the discovery team feel as if Fate has selected them as catalysts for bringing closure to the veterans and their families who have never forgotten the traumatic events of April 16, 1944, never fully recovered from the Battle of the Atlantic.

The lingering pain of the vets and their families rings even louder when another email file of memorabilia arrives from Germany. This time the sender is Stefan Gardt whose uncle Karl Gardt was a seaman in *550*. He died after the attack on his sub by the *Joyce*, *Gandy*, and *Peterson*. Gardt's email includes a scanned copy of a brochure that Klaus Hänert printed and sent to the families of all *550*'s crew in memoriam of all their lost loved ones. But even more astonishing is a letter that Hänert wrote to the parents of Gardt's lost uncle. The letter is in Old German script, but eventually the divers find German scholars who can translate it to modern German and then English.

Dear Mr. Gardt,

A few weeks ago I returned home following my release from an English Prisoner of War camp. Comrades and I would like to take this opportunity to take up contact with the immediate family of my men, who shared joy and sorrow for so long with me on board. I'm not sure how much you

know about the loss of the U550 and therefore the death at sea of your
son Karl, so I am of course prepared to write you a report of the boat's last
battle, if you would like. We were such a good community on board that I
will never be able to forget a member of my crew. You can be assured that
your son did his duty with bravery and dignity until the end. He will live
on in my thoughts as a particularly level-headed and reliable soldier, who
was loved by all of his comrades.

> *With sincere regards*
> *Your loyal*
> *Klaus Hänert*

For the Swiss woman who translates Hänert's letter from Old German to modern German, the captain's prose drips with so much remorse that she finds herself moved to tears several times during her translation work. The divers, too, are touched by the pathos in the German skipper's words. This story is getting too close for comfort.

It's while the divers are mulling over their own strong emotional responses to the human stories that are beginning to surface that Mazraani receives an email from Anne Marie Incalicchio. She says that she knows who took the famous photos of 550's conning tower crammed with men just minutes before the U-boat's sinking, the photos that are tacked on the bulletin board aboard *Tenacious*, the images that crossed Steve Gatto's mind during his first descent to the 550, the picture that Renzmann claimed to have seen in the *New York Times*. According to Incalicchio one of these photos actually made it onto the cover of *Time* magazine in 1944. Incalicchio says that her father, Emmett Patrick O'Hara, was a chief petty officer in the US Coast Guard aboard the *Joyce* during the battle. "He took the pictures of the capture and sinking of the U-boat. He was never given credit for the photos, but we had them around the house for years until my mother had a flood in her basement."

What clues do the pictures offer to confirm or challenge the official navy and coast guard story of the sinking of U-*550* and the rescue of some of its crew? At one point the divers turn to the official US Coast Guard website, with its page about USS *Joyce* and its sinking of U-*550*. One of the alleged O'Hara photos shows at least a dozen men in the water off the port side of the sub, most in life vests but a couple in one-man rafts. In addition to these men, at least fifteen men remain on the tower. Most of these men in the tower were eventually rescued by the *Joyce* from the starboard side of the U-boat. Here's clear evidence that far more than the thirteen men that the *Joyce* rescued escaped the *550*. Looking carefully at the photo, the divers think that some of the men in the water appear to be swimming toward something just beyond the right edge of the picture. *What?*

In hopes of adding more pieces to their picture of what actually happened on April 16, 1944, the team visits Mort Raphelson from the *Pan Penn* in New Jersey and John Hudock from the *Gandy* in western Pennsylvania. Unfortunately, John Bender dies before the divers can meet with him. After hours of videotaping with Raphelson and Hudock, one takeaway is the tremendous pride that both the vets and their families have in their wartime service, in their doing their duty under excruciating circumstances during the Battle of the Atlantic. There's good reason why men such as Hudock and Raphelson are called part of the "Greatest Generation." The other takeaway from these meetings with the vets is that contrary to claims in the action reports from the DEs that the submarine fired on the American warships, Hudock and Raphelson say that they never saw, and do not believe, that U-*550* fired its deck guns at the DEs.

The official version of the surrender of the *550* seems to be developing holes in it. The divers feel that they have to look deeper for answers, for truths that can bring closure to the veterans and their families. This search is beginning to feel more like a moral obligation than an adventure. Did U-*550* ever fire on the Americans, and where are its missing men?

42

A Harder Look

Mid-July 2013

"Shit." Joe Mazraani feels a jolt of adrenaline rock his body as he squints through the midnight blue water at the dark wreck just ahead of and beneath him. He's the first diver to reach this wreck today, the first diver to reach this wreck ever. It's a virgin.

Towed by his scooter, he has followed the anchor line down 260 feet from _Tenacious_ to the top of this wreck that he and the U-_550_ discovery team have been calling the "mystery blip." This is the target that they found last summer with the side-scan fish while mowing the lawn for Klaus Hänert's lost submarine. The blip is massive, more than 180 feet long and rising 80 feet off the bottom. But it isn't the immensity that's rattling Mazraani. Nor is it his anticipation, after waiting a year to finally have a chance to confirm a suspicion that he shares with several of the other divers on the team.

What's setting the diver on edge is that he sees where the dive boat's grapnel anchor has hooked into the wreck. Or—actually—_not_ hooked into the wreck. The only thing that's preventing the dive boat from drifting away from Mazraani and, now, Tom Packer, who has arrived by scooter too, is one tine of the grapnel. It has not snagged the wreck at all. The tine has only hooked a fishnet draped over the wreck. And right now the weight of *Tenacious* tugging on the grapnel from above has lifted part of the fishnet 10 feet off the wreck until the net looks like a tent.

Mazraani needs to tie the grapnel into something sturdy on the wreck itself before the tine breaks free of the fishing net. He needs to do it fast. If the grapnel breaks loose, it could leave him, Packer, and Anthony Tedeschi (who is just arriving on the scene) stranded on this wreck with no clear, stable, or easy way to ascend to the dive boat and to manage their decompression stops.

Next to running out of air, losing the anchor is a lot of wreck divers' greatest nightmare. Case in point: Brad Sheard's story about how losing the anchor line sent diver Jerry Rosenberg into such a panic that he gulped down all the air in his tanks, fought a fellow diver over a single air supply, and died. The prospect of losing the anchor line in deep water like this is so daunting to some wreck divers that they swear that they would rather just sit on the bottom of the ocean until their air runs out than die of the bends after losing control during their decompression stops in a free ascent or while surfacing on a skinny little safety line attached to a lift bag.

Sensing that he only has minutes, if not mere seconds, to stop the grapnel from breaking free, Mazraani falls back on his training. He stops, breathes, thinks . . . acts. Quickly. Really quickly. He realizes that if he ties together the two 15-foot lengths of 3/8-inch nylon line he has brought with him to tie the anchor to the wreck, he will have enough line to span the distance from the anchor chain to a steel beam he has spotted on the shipwreck. Tedeschi sees what Mazraani's up to and joins the effort in tying the two lines together while Mazraani ties the lines into the wreck and the anchor chain. It all happens so fast that Tom Packer can't even join the drill.

The anchor line secured, the emergency is over. The only sign to Mazraani that anything out of the ordinary has occurred is the pounding of his heart. It's time to *really* stop, breathe, and think before he does what he came to do down here, what he and the rest of the team came more than 120 miles out to sea to do. They are on a mission to survey this wreck to see if it is a big chunk of Mort Raphelson's old tanker.

According to the US Navy, the tanker remained intact and drifted for two days before navy ships and planes sank the burning hulk to eliminate it as a hazard to navigation. But who knows if the tanker really stayed in one piece? The commander of the navy's armed guard on the ship reported that he saw the deck buckling on the tanker where the torpedo or torpedoes struck forward of the stern deckhouse. As the tanker drifted and burned, the stern remained shrouded in smoke. The navy rescue tugs reported that the stern was submerged, but it could well have totally broken away if the ship's backbone had been destroyed by the torpedo strike. The stern of the ship could have sunk within an hour or two after stray fire from the *Gandy* set the *Pan Penn* aflame. The divers have come here to settle the question. And what could be better than finding a second virgin wreck in two years?

The wreck lies on its port side. After a survey up and down its length Mazraani, Packer, and Tedeschi are certain that this is the stern of a World War II–era tanker. The size, the hull shape, and the construction of the deckhouse are like other tankers from the war that they have dived. Seventy years on the bottom of the ocean have wiped away the engine room funnel. A lot of the steel superstructure from the upper decks has collapsed to the seafloor, leaving what was likely the mess deck of the tanker looking like an 80-foot wall stretching from the top of the wreck to sand level. The remains of the superstructure's bulkheads stick out from the wall like jagged steel shelves. In the middle of this wall there's a huge hole where the funnel once stood.

Beyond that hole is an abyss that Tom Packer has penetrated for a look around. Even though the visibility has been good outside the wreck and the water temperature at 52 degrees is 10 degrees warmer than the divers expect on a wreck this deep, the steel cavern, which Tom Packer has entered, feels spooky. It's pitch-black beyond the beam of his dive light and there's a definite chill in the water. This reminds him of the danger zone on the *Doria* known as the second-class dining room, the place where he and Gatto made the difficult body recovery back in the nineties. But this wreck lies at least 80 feet deeper than the *Doria*. As soon as his light picks up images of engine room machinery to confirm where he is on the wreck, he turns around and heads for open water.

It's nearly time for him to start up to his first deco stop, and none too soon. He has had an uneasy feeling since the problem with the grapnel snagging the fishing net. In the divers' minds, they are convinced by the size, shape, construction, condition, and location of the wreck that this is the stern of Mort Raphelson's ship, but Packer would really love to find some hard evidence.

It's while these thoughts are tumbling through his head that his constantly searching eyes see something circular covered with silt lying on top of one of these shelf-like bits of bulkheads. Three decades of hunting for artifacts, often chinaware, on wrecks trigger an alert in his head: "plate." Carefully he clips off his scooter to his tank harness and scoops up the plate . . . then a bowl nearby. But he's out of time. He has to start up to his deco stops. Seeing what's going on, Tedeschi moves in and bags the china so that Packer can start up. Teamwork at its best. These pieces of china in Tedeschi's goody bag could be just the proof that the team has been looking for.

Back on the surface the guys examine the manufacturer's logo and the dates on the dishes. One says "Warwick. Made in U.S.A. 1942." The other says "1943."

"Hey," says Packer. "I think I just found Mort's breakfast plate."

He's right. This is the kind of china that American tankers carried in 1944, and only the *Pan Penn* sank anywhere near this location.

"We ought to clean it up and give it back to him," says Mazraani. Then he thinks, "Weird dive, but mission accomplished." Another mystery solved. The stern of SS *Pan Pennsylvania* has been identified and located. It's some 20 miles from the rest of the tanker.

Following a winter and spring of presenting the story of their U-boat find at prominent diving conferences, the team is eager to dive the *550* again. One of the big issues that the divers have been debating is whether it is too dangerous for a man to try to enter through the forward torpedo-loading hatch to see if the sub is a charnel house of bones, a massive war grave. The divers also want to learn if Klaus Hänert fired more than the initial three torpedoes at the *Pan Penn*. Did he launch one or more torpedoes at the DEs and antagonize them to attack the submarine with nearly relentless vigor?

The debate about trying to enter the sub still remains an open question when *Tenacious* anchors over the wreck on the morning after the divers dove and identified the stern of the *Pan Penn*. The group is divided because while entering the wreck is exceedingly dangerous, nothing—not a camera or an ROV (remote operated vehicle)—can catch the big picture like a set of human eyes.

The two youngest divers, Mazraani and Tedeschi, are keen to try to penetrate the wreck. Meanwhile, Sheard's pacing around the dive boat saying that penetration is a crazy idea. Takakjian has a faraway look in his eyes, as if he may be remembering being trapped in USS *Bass* and says, "Bad business."

Mazraani has a smirk on his face. "You think I'm not going to be careful?"

"Famous last words," says Packer.

Mazraani and Tedeschi are undeterred. They are in the water shortly after Gatto and Packer shoot down the anchor line and tie in the grapnel to the *550*'s deck aft of the conning tower. The visibility is astounding. Better than 60 feet, and the ambient light from the morning sun and sand bottom is so good that the divers barely need their lights. Once on the wreck Mazraani and Tedeschi head to the foredeck, on their mission to penetrate the U-550 through the forward torpedo-loading hatch. The plan is for Tedeschi to photograph Mazraani going in.

His shoulder still hurts a little from a suspected hit of the bends that he took yesterday during his deco after diving the *Pan Penn*. But Mazraani is undaunted, not deterred in the least by his first careful look at the narrow aperture that opens into the forward torpedo room. The pressure hull of a U-boat is built from a collection of short cylindrical sections, welded together. The flanged joints where the segments weld together act as reinforcing framing to give the hull its ability to withstand the extreme water pressures of deep submersion without rupturing. At places where there are hatches cut into the pressure hull that span the position of these frames, U-boats have heavy metal bars to act as trusses that can span the hatchway and carry the load of the missing frame. U-boat crews removed these truss bars when they needed to have the forward torpedo-loading hatch fully open to lower torpedoes into the torpedo room from deck storage or ashore.

Mazraani's inspection of the hatch shows that the two truss bars are still in place, limiting the space he has to enter to a rectangle that measures about 24 inches fore and aft and 26 inches side to side. It's going to be a hell of a squeeze with all this gear, especially the diving harness, with two big tanks on his back. And as good as the visibility is outside, on the deck, it stinks inside the boat. Flashing his light into the torpedo room, Mazraani can see only about 5 feet through a cloud of brown silt in suspension, possibly stirred up by fish. But what the hell. He's going for it.

If Mazraani had ever been a cave spelunker, he would know that the first rule of penetrating a narrow space is that you go in headfirst so you don't get stuck. But he decides that his best chance of entry is to try to drop, finsfirst, through the hole. And so he does. As Tedeschi watches and films, Mazraani, facing aft, wiggles and slithers deeper between a truss bar and the after edge of the hatch . . . until he is in up to his neck and feeling crunched by the truss bar against his tanks on his back and the after edge of the hatch against his chest.

He wiggles, pushes with his hands. Kicks with his fins. Nothing. At some point he realizes that his efforts are causing him to suck up his bottom gas faster than usual and that he's got to get out of here. Finally, with a jolt of his arms against the rim of the hatch, he launches himself upward and free.

He signals for Tedeschi, wearing a more compact side-mount rebreather (without tanks on his back), to try.

Tedeschi tries headfirst, but it's no go. His gear on this dive is not configured for a tight squeeze.

"Let's go," he mumbles into his mouthpiece and signals to Tedeschi.

On their way back aft to the anchor line, they pause atop the tower to cut away some of the fishnet wrapped over the wreck in search of the tower hatch and the sky periscope. During this cutting, Mazraani feels the vague pain in his shoulder from yesterday's hit during deco flare into a bolt of lightning.

"Here we go," he thinks. "I've really been zapped. I'm going to pay for this dive." He can already see that as soon as he gets topside he's going to start popping painkillers and retreat to his berth for the duration of this voyage. Maybe he's going to need a trip to Philly and a "ride" in the decompression chamber there. Well, at least, he chased his dream. He's not dead. And he'll be back to try again. Smarter. With better gear . . . and none of this freak jabbing in his shoulder. Just wait.

None of Mazraani's misadventure is known to divers Brad Sheard and Mark Nix, who are shooting photos up at the bow while Steve Gatto films a video while swimming over the deck. Meanwhile, Harold Moyers goes back aft to assess the damage to the sub from depth charges and the ramming by the *Gandy*.

As Eric Takakjian heads down the anchor line for his first dive on U-*550*, he's pretty much blown away by the amazing visibility and strong ambient light. For months he has been worrying about this dive, not in a terrified way, but in an informed way. In a way that any sane fifty-four-year-old diver should who has thousands upon thousands of wreck dives in his logbook and more than enough close calls. Naturally cautious, Takakjian puts great stock in preparations for a dive. He has spent untold weeks checking and double-checking his gear and all his calculations for the deco times and stops as well as the gases he will breathe during this adventure. He's never dived below 260 feet before, and he knows that most men who do this kind of extreme diving are in their twenties and thirties. How many times can the tissues in his body take the stress of these gas loads and decompression? Then, of course, at more than 300 feet you have very little time to sort out any gear malfunction or a problem like losing the anchor line. "I could be dead real fast" is a thought that has been flitting through his brain all too often.

But geez, it looks amazing down here. From 50 feet above the wreck he can see the outline of the hull and the tower coming into view. Stopping to clear his ears, he thinks, "Holy shit. This is unbelievable." Every iota of worry that he might have harbored before getting into the water is vanishing in a surge of joy. Twenty years of researching have led to this moment. He lets go of the anchor line and drifts over the tower, touches down on the foredeck by the open galley hatch. Kneels there.

As his hands and knees feel the sturdiness—the utter intactness of this wreck—supporting him, another blast of endorphins rocks him. He listens to the slow hiss of his regulator. He feels a warmth flowing through his body and just takes in the scene, doesn't even need his dive light to illuminate this secret world. The massiveness of the sub, the sweet blue light, the brilliance of the sand bottom contrasting with the dark hull of the U-boat, the schools of little orange-red fishes weaving around him and into and out of the wreck.

He has been on hundreds of legendary wrecks in lots of places around the world, but nothing like this. As a former coast guardsman like Bob Wilcox and the crew of the *Joyce* who rescued the men off *550*, and as a merchant mariner like Mort Raphelson and the crew of the *Pan Penn*, Takakjian feels an almost blood connection to this wreck and the history it evokes. If ever there were a ghost ship for him, this is the one.

Later, after spending fifteen minutes circling the central section of the U-boat and trying to locate things like the after gun mounts, the air induction vents, the hatches for the life rafts, and ammunition stowed between the outer hull and the pressure hull—and after an hour and a half of deco obligation—Takakjian surfaces wondering how he will tell his wife, Lori, about this dive. Will he say, "I have been to the dark side of the moon and lived to tell about it"?

43

A Disturbing Phone Call

Even after diving on U-*550* for a second summer, the divers remain baffled by the sub. Their surveys, videos, and photos of the wreck have not yet revealed whether it fired its deck guns, as the captains of the DEs reported. The interviews with eyewitnesses such as Mort Raphelson from the *Pan Penn* and John Hudock from the *Gandy* have cast doubts on the official story that the sub fired its guns. And diver Harold Moyers, a virtual almanac of U-boat technical details, has pointed out that in the pictures of U-*550* after the battle, the flak shields on the 37mm gun remain folded. The gun is rigged for traveling, not firing. Moyers has also noted that the two 20mm antiaircraft cannons on *550* are locked in their secured positions, pointing skyward, not horizontally, as they would be if the German crew had been firing on the Americans. And who knows whether the *550* fired one or more T5 torpedoes at the DEs? Even more importantly, U-*550* has not yet shown the divers if it is, in fact, the grave of more than forty of its men or whether those men escaped the submarine, only to die some other way.

To try to answer these questions, Joe Mazraani unearths the phone number of one of the 550's last three living survivors. With the help of translator Lisa Svec, Mazraani calls German veteran Robert Ziemer during early November 2013. Over the phone Ziemer sketches an astonishing tale. He says that it is too painful to go back to the memory of the final minutes aboard his submarine. It was too horrible. After the destroyers ceased firing on the U-boat, all living members of their crew—more than fifty men—scrambled out of the sinking U-boat. Most of the crew assembled on the foredeck. The last men out, Ziemer among them, came up through the tower hatch and remained on the tower's observation deck and Wintergarten. As the boat flooded beneath them, it started to wallow in the swells, began to teeter like a seesaw.

The U-boat's first officer led his men gathered on the foredeck into the water. He told them to swim to the nearest destroyer escort, which was not far off the port side of the 550. The men were in their white life vests with their escape lungs strapped to their chests. A couple of sailors had one-man life rafts. No living Germans had gone down with the ship, as the action reports of *Gandy*, *Joyce*, and *Peterson* implied. None had been trapped in the forward torpedo room, as the navy's *Eastern Sea Frontier War Diary* had speculated when trying to explain how the three dead sailors from U-550 turned up adrift on the North Atlantic weeks after the battle.

Ziemer watched more than forty of his shipmates swimming to a DE in freezing water, only to have the ship pull away from the swimmers. The men's calls for help echoed over the 40-degree water for a few minutes. Then there was silence. Ziemer's brothers were dead. He's sorry, he tells Mazraani and Svec, but with all due respect, he would not want to meet with the divers if they came to Germany to talk about his U-boat service. At age ninety-one he must put such memories behind him.

Ziemer's story strikes a raw nerve with the divers, particularly Brad

Sheard, who, since the team's first dives on the sub, has been bothered by the large crack in the *550*'s pressure hull on the edge of the forward torpedo-loading hatch. Sheard has begun asserting to his dive buddies that the crack meant that the forward torpedo room could not have been watertight after the sub sank. No men could have survived the flooded forward torpedo room during the sinking of the sub and escaped hours later after the destroyer escorts had left the scene. The navy's speculation in the *War Diary* seems just plain wrong.

After additional research the U-*550* discovery team turns up an interview conducted in 1984 between a US Coast Guard oral historian and a crewman from the *Peterson*, Radarman Second Class Collingwood Harris, who spoke about what he called the hysterical "euphoria" that pervaded his ship. "I know there was a lot of wanton shooting because there were some descriptions by some of our men about shooting guys in the water. I remember one fellow . . . said, 'Did you see that [guy]? I shot his head off!'"

These words leave the American divers shaken. Some can almost hear the 20mm cannons of the *Peterson* pounding away at those boys in the water. When the divers began their search for the *550*, they never imagined that it would bring them to such a face-to-face confrontation with the violence and cruelty of war. With each new dive to the *550*, each new revelation, this battle has become more personal. In a strange way the divers feel like their discovery of the wreck has made them custodians of its uneasy ghosts. Maybe the divers can't save lives here. Maybe they can't recover bodies either. But possibly they can help the families of the men involved finally achieve some understanding of events and rest in peace.

"We gotta go to Germany," Mazraani tells his dive buddies. "We gotta hear the other Germans' stories. We gotta find the truth."

44

Mission to Germany

November 22, 2013

"This is it," says Anthony Tedeschi. "Stop." He's riding shotgun in an Opel van, staring at the GPS map on the smartphone in the palm of his hand. The six men of the original U-*550* discovery team, along with diver Harold Moyers and translator Andreas Schalomon (recruited from the student body at Goerthe University in Frankfurt), lurch forward as the van brakes. It's a gray morning in Germany on November 22, 2013. The van has come to rest in front of a small, neat house in a subdivision of Hassloch, a town about an hour's drive south of Frankfurt.

"Let's not overwhelm this guy," says Mazraani, who has been driving. "He's had two or three strokes, and he sounds weak on the phone."

The divers nod, talk in soft tones as they exit the van. But their abrupt movements betray their excitement.

While Mazraani and Schalomon are led into the house by a

woman, the rest of the discovery team holds back to see how things will unfold. Steve Gatto snags his video camera and tripod from the back of the van. Others check over their digital cameras.

"This is a big deal," says Tom Packer. He's really talking to himself, not his buddies. It's his first time in Europe. He lost his job more than a year ago when the company that he worked for closed. Money has been tight. He did not think he could afford to make this trip, but at the last minute his wife, Kim, told him he should go. It would be a once-in-a-lifetime event. There would never be another chance to meet the men who survived the sinking of their U-boat, a chance to meet their families. Almost all of the surviving U-boat veterans have since passed away. One of the last living U-boat skippers, Reinhard Hardegen, is turning a hundred years old. Here's a rare chance to put faces and names and personal stories on a shadowy hulk lying more than 300 feet beneath the North Atlantic, a chance to soak in the courage and wisdom of men who have been to a deep, dark hell and come back.

Albert Nitsche is the man whom the divers have flown across the Atlantic to visit in hopes that he can set the record of the battle straight. He's one of the three survivors of U-550 still alive. A shipmate and longtime friend of the late Johann Rauh and his wife, Helga, Nitsche was for years the man who facilitated reunions of the 550 crew. With the help of Helga, Rauh, and her son Johnnie, Joe Mazraani has arranged this visit through a series of difficult phone calls in German, taxing his high school German to the max and requiring the aid of translator Lisa Svec. In the end Nitsche has agreed to meet with the divers if they come to Germany and tell them about life and death on U-550. They really want to hear his story. They hope that he can confirm or deny the disturbing story that Mazraani has heard from Robert Ziemer.

The third survivor of U-550 is Hugo Renzmann, the sub's engineering officer. He lives in Kiel with his wife. Several times he has turned down Mazraani's request for a meeting. The divers know that perhaps their only chance to hear a survivor's story and clear up contradictory information about the battle is here and now in Hass-loch.

While Mazraani and Schalomon are in the house, a short middle-aged man with a mustache and wearing a gray, pinstriped sport jacket and tie, beckons to the rest of the team from a gate in front of the Nitsche home. He turns out to be Albert Nitsche's son, and he has been waiting for the divers. He says his whole family has been wait-ing for the Americans, especially his father. As the divers file into the small house and gather around a long dining room table, they learn through their translator, Schalomon, that the man they came to see built this house, has built a number of houses. He's proud to have helped in the reconstruction of Germany after the devastating bombings of World War II. He has always been a man who finds joy in creativity. But right now he's nowhere to be seen.

It's an awkward moment for the divers. They aren't sure what to do next. The table, which fills almost all of the dining room, is set for a feast. It seems like every chair in the house has been commandeered for service at this table. Each chair has a place setting with utensils, napkin, and a water glass. The center of the table holds platters of cold cuts, cheeses, fresh bread, and salad. Bottles of mineral water, seltzer, and soda, along with pots of coffee and tea, flank the platters. The room is so jammed with people, furniture, and victuals that Steve Gatto has difficulty finding a place to locate the tripod for his video camera.

Several of the discovery team are trying to practice German greetings on Nitsche's son, when Mazraani and Schalomon appear on the steps leading from the second floor of the house. Then the clatter of a wooden cane on the steps grabs everyone's attention. A man hobbles into the dining room accompanied by his wife, Rosina. Despite his struggles with walking, Albert Nitsche has a strong pres-ence. He's a small man with slick, gray, thinning hair. His body looks trim and fit in a pressed checkered shirt beneath a brown cardigan. But what really arrests his guests are his rosy cheeks, broad grin, and twinkling eyes beaming out through wire-rim glasses. He welcomes his guests with warmth, vigor, and a cascade of German phrases. Then he invites them all to sit and tell him why they have come all the way from America to see him.

At first the conversation unfolds with pleasantries about the divers' trip to Germany. Translator Schalomon tells Nitsche the story about how the divers became enthralled with the idea of finding and diving his lost U-boat. With every sentence that Schalomon translates into German, Nitsche seems to grow a bit larger in his chair. His frame rises a bit more erect, and his smile broadens. It's clear to everyone here that Nitsche feels among kindred spirits. Nitsche's daughter-in-law, high-school-age grandson, and granddaughter join the festivities, and now all the Nitsche family and the divers are smiling, laughing, and helping themselves to the salad, the cheeses, and the cold cuts. The party has begun . . . and with it the sharing.

At one point the divers present a letter that they have volunteered to carry to Nitsche, Renzmann, and the families of U-550's crew. It's from Kim Joshi, Captain Robert Wilcox's granddaughter, the woman whose emails to Joe Mazraani first unfolded for the discovery team the story of how Wilcox became friends after the war with the survivors of U-550. Back in America, the discovery of the 550 has brought up a lot of deep emotions among the Wilcox family, and Joshi has sent this letter as an acknowledgment of those feelings and an uncommon bond that her family shares with these Germans and their families. It may well be her attempt to close an emotional circle that opened on April 16, 1944.

November 21, 2013

Dear Mr. Renzmann, Mr. Nitsche
and the Families of the U-550 Crew,

I am the granddaughter of Robert Wilcox and my memories of him are those typical of most relationships shared between a grandchild and grandparent. It is only after his death that I have learned who my grandfather was during his service to our country.

It is heartbreaking for me to wish that he was here today to witness the discovery of the U-550 and to share his story of that day. I can only piece together the story through the information he passed on to his family in photos and paperwork.

However, what is most important to me and what I believe he would wish for me to remember is what occurred after the war. This is evident in the letters from survivors of U-550 and photos of reunions with handshakes and smiles that he preserved. I wish you and your families a very prosperous future and calm waters.

Sincerely,
Kimberly Wilcox Joshi

As Schalomon translates the letter to Nitsche, waves of emotion pass over the face of the veteran. After the reading, he sits quietly for several seconds, seems to stare at invisible faces that hover in the air all around him. Then he takes off his glasses, sets them on the table, and wipes tears from his eyes.

"*Gut,*" he says at last. Good.

As well over an hour passes at the table, Nitsche tells the divers and his family the story of his naval service. At age seventeen he volunteered for the navy and left his home in Waldensburg, Sudetenland, to attend basic training before being transferred to U-550 and heading to battle as a seaman first class. He was the 37mm gunner and the officers' steward. He grows agitated as he recalls manning the 37mm gun during the air attack south of Iceland, recalls the gun jamming, recalls the loss of his shipmate. It was a dark day, and it was his twentieth birthday. He's on the edge of tears again as he talks about the loss of his fellow gunner, the guitarist, that day.

He grows animated as he talks about being allowed on deck the night before the attack on the *Pan Penn*. He tells Schalomon that he read later in a newspaper that his U-boat had been sunk far at sea, but on the night before the attack they were so close to New York, he could see the buildings. He had never seen buildings of such magnitude. Later that night, because of his work as the officers' steward, he heard Klaus Hänert discussing his plan to attack a convoy, but the captain did not tell the crew until he called them all to their battle stations the next morning.

All the side conversations at the dining room cease as Nitsche takes his listeners into the battle.

"Were you the only U-boat out there?" asks Mazraani. He wants clarification because the action reports of the DEs speculate that there was a second sub with the *550* and that the second sub actually fired on the DEs.

"Ja," says Nitsche. Yes. U-*550* was the only boat. "That was the bad thing. There was just us against the three destroyers."

Nitsche says that after the depth charges exploded around the U-boat there was flooding in the stern, and men charged out of the diesel engine room into the control room to escape, shutting the watertight door behind them.

"There was no order to attack, only to get out." No order to man the guns. No one manned the guns. Nitsche would know; he was the 37mm gunner. The only orders were to bring the U-boat to the surface and abandon ship. There was chaos in the boat. It was every man for himself.

Nitsche says that he saw Klaus Hänert climb into the tower with a white flag when the boat surfaced to surrender, but the firing from the destroyers wounded the captain and knocked him back down into the control room.

One of the divers asks whether Hänert fired a torpedo as the sub was surfacing.

"Nein." The only order was to get out of the boat, says Nitsche again.

The divers pass him the famous photo of U-*550* with men in the tower and afloat in the water. Nitsche points out a figure standing at the very after end of the Wintergarten. "That's me."

He says that the men in the water were swimming to a destroyer escort just out of the picture. Here's confirmation again of what Ziemer has said and the divers have suspected from looking at the battle photos from the *Joyce*.

The *Joyce* came along the starboard side and lowered a scramble net. By the time Nitsche reached the *Joyce* he was so cold he could not climb the net. He saw some men just push the net away and drown. A black American sailor came down the net and helped him out of the water. This was the first black man he had ever seen.

He raises his hands and shakes, shivers as if it were April 16, 1944, all over again. He says that once he was on the deck of the *Joyce* and wrapped in a blanket, Dr. Torge offered him schnapps to drink from a flask.

Someone asks the crucial question. Did all of the crew who were alive when the U-boat surfaced get out of the boat?

"Ja, ja." Everyone got out of the sinking U-boat. But many died in the water after the destroyer on the port side pulled away.

Did anyone alive go down with the boat?

"Nein." Nitsche is almost sure. He was one of the last men out of the *550*.

The meeting, which the divers had hoped might go for an hour, runs much longer. Hours pass. Family members come and go. Eventually Nitsche and his grandchildren invite the divers out for a late lunch at one of his favorite restaurants. Once the conversation moves beyond the details of the battle and Nitsche's escape from the sinking U-boat, the conversation broadens among the divers and the German family. Nitsche and his granddaughter both speak of their affection for the United States. He tells of a visit to Washington,

DC, to see the White House with a friend he made after the war who had served on the *Peterson* the day the *550* sank. That friend was Collingwood Harris. Nitsche also tells of spending two years in a POW camp in Mississippi picking cotton with black farm laborers.

"How was that?" asks one of the divers.

Nitsche seems to understand the question even before Schalomon translates it. The U-boat vet sprouts a mischievous grin, laughs, and says something to the effect of "I was the man."

Hours later, with the sun now low on the horizon, after all the conversation, after the banqueting at the Nitsches' home, after the feasting at the restaurant, the divers gather outside the Germans' home in Hassloch. The good-byes are difficult. Almost everyone has wet eyes. There is much shaking of hands and hugs. And then the divers climb reluctantly back into their van and prepare for a five-hour drive northeast, to Berlin. Their last image of Albert Nitsche is of him standing at the gate to his house in drizzling rain, leaning on his cane, his arm around Rosina. He's waving good-bye with tears on his cheeks.

"That was beyond anything I could have imagined," says Tom Packer.

"Albert rocks," says one of the other divers, as if he has known Nitsche all of his life.

"A miracle of resilience," says someone else.

What began as a fact-finding mission seems to be turning into something different. Something that in its own peculiar way feels like family to these American divers.

45

Berlin

November 23, 2013

"It was strange . . . the news of the discovery [of U-*550*]," says Karoline Kuhla, propping her elbows on the long dining table surrounded by divers. "It was like a boomerang coming back to my family after so many years." She nods her head as if to affirm her choice of the word "boomerang."

Kuhla is the twentysomething granddaughter of *550*'s physician, Friedrich Torge. She's the sister of Tilmann Kuhla, who originally emailed Mazraani shortly after the sub's discovery, and she is a journalist who has already authored features for online publications about her grandfather and his escape from the sinking U-*550*.

On behalf of her family, she has invited the dive team to meet her for lunch at a posh Turkish restaurant called Hasir, in the Wilmersdorf section of Berlin. The luncheon has two goals. Kuhla and her friend Sarah Levy are interviewing the divers for a story they intend to write about these Americans who have become obsessed with a long-lost German U-boat. She is also here representing her family and sharing their memories and memorabilia of their patriarch and his U-boat service. Dr. Torge died four years earlier after a long battle with Alzheimer's. In the end the only detail of his past that he remembered was the name of his skipper on the *550*, Klaus Hänert, the man whose life he saved.

She says that she found out about the divers' discovery of the wreck when she checked *Spiegel Online* before going to bed one night in late July 2012. But she did not recognize the number of the U-boat until one of her brothers called her the next morning to say that this was, indeed, *Grossvater's U-boot.*

"We all came together and talked about the U-boat. It never seemed real before." But now with her whole family talking about Grandfather's submarine and retelling each other all the stories they have heard, everything about the battle and Dr. Torge's survival seems so real and personal, she says. The discovery of *550* has been a time for the families of Torge's two daughters to remember the doctor and celebrate him. Kuhla tells the divers that Torge, a dermatologist after the war, remained a physician in the naval reserve throughout his life and was buried with military honors. Kuhla says that the discovery of the sub has made her family revisit the joy and good humor associated with her grandfather.

"He had such a big head," she says. "I mean, physically, a very large head." She raises her hands inches away from her ears to demonstrate and makes a silly face, giving the impression that she and her siblings found amusement in their grandfather. Not that they mocked him, but they saw him as larger than life. Having watched this mythic man fade away beneath the cloud of Alzheimer's was painful for Kuhla and her family. But now, thinking of him as a young navy doctor wearing his dress uniform and his Red Cross armband—big head and all—standing by the wounded Klaus Hänert as one of the last two men off the sub as it sank beneath them, has brought back visions of an exceptional young healer brimming with courage and a sense of duty.

Kuhla's English is good and so is the English of her friend and colleague Levy. The Turkish feast quickly deviates from any script or list of questions that either the journalists or the divers have for each other as the divers talk about their astonishment at seeing the remains of the Berlin Wall and the Cold War's Checkpoint Charlie earlier that morning. Kuhla and Levy are quick to laugh as diver Harold Moyers relates humorous anecdotes about Packer and Joe Mazraani at the wall.

Packer has daughters the same age as Kuhla and Levy, and as the meal and tales unfold, a fair amount of what feels like father-daughter teasing gets traded back and forth. At one point the young women ask the divers what their wives think about their obsessions with wreck diving and with the 550.

Quite a lot of clearing of throats follows as several men prompt Packer for a confession.

"Some things are better left unsaid." He grins. But after more prodding and teasing, he admits that one of his daughters was born while he was diving the SS *Andrea Doria*.

"You left your pregnant wife to go diving?" asks Kuhla. She's pretending to scold.

"No. The baby came two weeks early. I swear." Packer has his hands up in surrender.

Kuhla and Levy nod. It may well seem to them that submariners and deep-wreck divers share a certain penchant for life on the edge, that both submariners and deep-wreck divers are larger than life.

Recalling her grandfather's stories about his final minutes aboard 550, Kuhla says that he told her family a story similar to the one that the divers heard just a day ago from Albert Nitsche. There was never any attempt to retaliate against the destroyer escorts after the depth-charge attack. When the flooding U-550 was surfacing out of control and the captain was giving orders to abandon ship, the officers got pushed to the back of the queue as men scrambled to evacuate the submarine. This may well have saved the doctor's life because, according to him, the first forty or so men out of the U-boat swam to a destroyer that left them in the water to freeze.

"There it is," says one of the discovery team. "This is the third time we have heard that story."

"It doesn't seem like something the survivors would make up," says someone else.

Mazraani says that in his phone call with Robert Ziemer, the vet said he did not see any reason to revisit the DE's leaving of his ship-mates in the water. "He said, 'We are friends with the Americans now.' In other words, why reopen an old wound?"

Kuhla nods. She understands Ziemer's point of view.

Levy says that the divers have to understand that people in Ger-many, especially veterans, rarely if ever have talked about the war. It is an extraordinary gift that Albert Nitsche gave up his stories to the divers. The war was a national shame and a trauma. It has only been in recent years that veterans have been willing to talk at all about their experiences. Not even noncombatants like to revisit World War II, says Levy.

Thoughts of war and its trauma seem on the verge of dampening the spirit of this luncheon until someone proposes showing Kuhla and Levy the two videos of discovering and diving U-550 that the team has put together to show at dive conferences. With Sheard's laptop set at the center of the table, the Germans and the Americans crowd around as the screen shows images of divers drifting over the wreck.

Kuhla rests her elbows on the table, puts her chin in her hands, and leans in to the images. As the film unfolds, she seems to sink deeper and deeper into the peacefulness of the underwater world, as if she's gazing into an aquarium. Everyone else follows suit. What an antidote to stress. In the video U-550 seems to have found eternal rest. Whether the submarine is actually a war grave remains a ques-tion, but it is so clearly not a war memorial, such as its sister ship U-505, restored to near battle-ready condition at the Chicago Museum of Science and Industry. The wreck of the 550 is a garden of hydroids, a home for all manner of fish. And it most definitely can teach anyone who sees the sub in its watery grave something about the value of putting the nightmare of a world war behind us. It's in this spirit that Kuhla tells the divers that this feast is a gift of thanks from her family to the divers, a very personal peace offering. A gesture of closure like Kim Joshi's letter, which the divers have presented to Kuhla and her family.

Later in the day, the divers' van cruises north, toward Kiel. They intend to rendezvous with the son of Klaus Hänert and, possibly, with Hugo Renzmann. As the drive unfolds, the conversation turns back to the story of the American destroyer escort leaving many Germans in the water.

"It seems like this truly happened," says one of the divers. "One of the DEs left all those men to freeze in the water."

"It wasn't the *Joyce*," says Brad Sheard. "The pictures shot from her deck as the sub was sinking put the *Joyce* on the starboard side of the *550*. The swimmers are on the port."

"And it wasn't the *Gandy*," says someone else. Just before the shooting stopped, the *Gandy*, according to its action report, was proceeding at 15 knots, with guns firing "along the starboard side of the sub," with the *Joyce* coming in behind her. This maneuver would not have left the *Gandy* the time or the space to circle back, close with the port side of the U-boat, and stop in the vicinity of the German sailors who entered the water almost as soon as the DEs stopped firing. The *Gandy*'s action report shows that the captain "drew off" to assess damage to his ship. He was concerned because one of its diesel engines had failed shortly before the attack on the sub. The *Gandy*'s skipper was also concerned because his ship had damage from taking fire while circling the surfaced sub, because several men had shrapnel wounds, and because the bilges need to be checked for damage due to ramming U-*550*.

"What about the *Peterson*?" Gatto asks.

"Her action report is what you might call short and sweet," says Takakjian.

The description of the battle in the *Peterson*'s action report is far more concise than the narratives in the action reports of the *Gandy* or the *Joyce*. After noting that he fired depth charges from his K-gun launchers (at about 1004 hours), the skipper of the *Peterson*'s next sentence reads, "1420 [1020 hours local time] this ship and USS GANDY acting as screen while USS JOYCE engaged in picking up crew of submarine." The report leaves sixteen minutes of events unaccounted for. It was during this time that almost all of *550*'s crew of fifty-six men, except the men in the tower rescued by the *Joyce*, entered the freezing water and swam away from the port side of the sub, never to be rescued.

46

Kiel

"All of our families have scars," says the tall German in the blue Helly Hanson foul-weather jacket. The divers huddle around him in the control room of a restored U-boat.

His name is Wolf Hänert. He's sixty-one years old. He has chiseled good looks and the fit body of a much younger man. The son of the captain of U-550, a resident of Kiel, an accomplished sports medicine physician with a long career in the German Navy as well as with other government agencies, Hänert has joined the divers as they tour the National Naval Memorial at Laboe, across the harbor from Kiel. The showpiece of the memorial is the fully preserved Type VIIC/41 attack U-boat 995. On this brisk Sunday morning in late November, the divers have already spent more than an hour scrutinizing almost every detail of the last example of a Type VII similar to the U-boat featured in *Das Boot*. Along with U-505 in Chicago,

U-*995* is one of only four U-boat survivors from a fleet of submarines that once numbered more than eleven hundred.

Hänert's remark about families with scars comes after having just heard the stories of the divers' extraordinary visits with the Nitsches, Karoline Kuhla, and American vets John Hudock and Mort Raphelson. His use of the word "our" does not seem accidental. It betrays his sense of kinship with the Americans. Not only have the members of the *550* discovery team been drawn intimately into his father's world, the war stories, and the associated emotional wounds of the vets and their families, but also Dr. Hänert shares a passion with these men. He, too, is a diver. As a NATO officer, he trained as a deep diver with the US Navy in America. In fact, he specializes in the effects of deep diving and cold-water submersion on human physiology. All the men in this U-boat feel a sudden and uncanny bond with the German. For some, meeting Hänert this way in the control room of a U-boat is almost like stepping through a time warp and meeting the captain of U-*550* in his milieu, a little like being the Old Man's shipmates. It's an odd but not altogether disturbing feeling.

Dr. Hänert tells how his father grew up loving the water, sailing small boats in Flensburg, where the doctor's grandfather was a civilian instructor teaching engineering at the German Naval Academy. Not only was Klaus Hänert a sailor, but he was also an avid swimmer in the Baltic, a sport that he practiced all his life. As a graduate of the naval academy in 1936, he was a member of the so-called Olympic Crew, as were many of Germany's most famous U-boat skippers. After a world cruise on the battle cruiser *Emden*, Hänert served in destroyers until landing a post as an adjutant for the head of the navy, Grossadmiral Erich Raeder. Viewed as a young officer of promise, he nonetheless left his position on Raeder's staff and volunteered for combat in U-boats, serving in U-*68* for two successful cruises with ace commander Karl Friedrich Merten. But not even the glory of

serving with Merten or his post with Raeder could match the importance of U-*550* to Klaus Hänert.

"The sinking of the *550* was the event of my father's life," Dr.
Hänert tells the divers.

He says that as a boy, he heard people tell him about the *550* and
his father. One day he asked his father about it. "Did you fight back?
Were you a hero?"

His father said, "Listen. It wasn't like that. I did not fight the
destroyers. I told my men to abandon the ship."

The divers catch their buddies' eyes. Here's more testimony to add
to what Hudock, Raphelson, Nitsche, and Kuhla have already said.
The U-boat intended to surrender from the moment it started its
uncontrolled ascent toward the surface. It never engaged the destroyers. And according to Hänert, the DEs were taking friendly fire from
each other.

The son of the U-boat commander says that his father told him
that he and the doctor were the last two men to leave the boat. When
the Old Man entered the water, it was freezing. His life vest had been
shredded from the shrapnel that ripped open the side of his face, arm,
and leg. He believed that he would have drowned after he hit that
freezing water had he not been so used to swimming in the cold Baltic. The other thing that saved him was a rope tossed from USS *Joyce*.

"I wrapped myself in that rope. I made up my mind that if the
Americans wanted their rope back, they would have to pull me in
with it," Klaus Hänert told his son.

More than forty of the Old Man's shipmates were not so lucky. A
destroyer left them to freeze to death, says Dr. Hänert. He adds that
the story of all of those men freezing to death compelled him to
research and publish a scholarly article about the devastating effects
of cold-water emersion. Here's yet more corroboration of the story
of a destroyer leaving scores of Germans in the water.

The control room of U-*995* goes silent as the divers recall their own
dangerous run-ins with cold water, especially during body recoveries

such as the dives Gatto and Packer made to bring home the crew of the tugboat *Thomas Hebert*. It's as if all the men in this historic submarine can feel the cold winter waves of the Baltic pouring in on them.

"I remember going to see the film *Das Boot* with my father," says Hänert.

"What was that like?"

"He said the real experience was a lot more boring than in the movie. He said the heads of the bolts never exploded from the pressure during deep dives. But the comradeship of men in the boat was as it was in the film. It was something my father would never forget." He says that his father loved attending reunions of the survivors in his later years and hearing his old shipmates call him *"der Alte,"* the Old Man.

Wolf Hänert says that his father believed strongly in the brotherhood of mariners. No matter their nationality, they shared the struggle against the sea and the weather. "When I first went to sea, he told me, 'You must take care of your men.' I think that's why he could never understand why the Americans did not pick up all of his crew."

"We can't either," says one of the divers.

After the divers take Hänert to lunch at a seaside restaurant, he leads them back into Kiel to the navy base at the historic Tirpitz Pier, where *U-550* said good-bye to its homeland nearly seventy years ago. On this cold November night, the pier seems a dark and lonely place. A jumping-off place for so many young men and U-boats who sailed into oblivion.

Back at the divers' hotel that evening, Wolf Hänert shows the divers some of his father's memorabilia, including photo albums. Some have pictures of his patrols with Merten in *U-68*, haunting snapshots of freighters on fire and breaking up after a torpedo strike.

While the divers are poring over the photo albums, Hänert tells them that he will be taking tomorrow off from work. Reporter Andreas Schmidt of the NDR television network has gotten Hugo Renzmann to agree to an interview with NDR and the divers.

"I should come along to translate," says Hänert. "Hugo is in poor health. He has known me since I was a boy. I think he will be more comfortable to talk with me, ja?"

Flanked by his wife and seated in a lounge chair in a private room of a nursing home, the former chief engineer of U-550 welcomes the divers. He's bald and pale with a thick neck and slouching body beneath his gray plaid shirt. His eyes dart back and forth. It's obvious that the presence of all these people makes him, and especially his wife, nervous. For a minute or two there is a muffled conversation between the Renzmanns and TV reporter Schmidt. The divers get the distinct impression that the veteran and his wife are having second thoughts and that the interview may be off. But eventually Schmidt tells the divers that Renzmann is willing to talk to Wolf Hänert, Joe Mazraani, and Schmidt. The other divers take seats out in the hallway. Steve Gatto, carrying his video camera and tripod, sneaks into the room with the cameraman from the TV station.

As the interview unfolds, Renzmann unpacks his memories of his final moments aboard U-550 to Wolf Hänert, Mazraani, and Schmidt, who sit with him almost knees-to-knees. He says that as the engineer it was his job to be the last man out of the boat, to scuttle it so that the Americans could not seize the boat for intel. He raises two fingers beneath his nose and says the water was this deep in parts of the sub when he made his final pass through. Water was pouring in now from below *and* above. He feared that he would drown, so he blew the last of the compressed air into the ballast tanks to keep the U-boat afloat for just a few more minutes so he could escape.

Memory starts to overwhelm him, and he begins speaking rapidly. His eyes widen. He waves his left hand in the air, pointing at Schmidt as if to make his case, as if to say, "Do you understand? I thought I was going to drown in that icy water." He had opened the vents to flood the boat. There was no time to fire scuttling charges, just enough time to leave the sinking *550*. When he was out and getting into the water, he saw the doctor and Klaus Hänert standing on the sub's bow.

Like Nitsche two days earlier, Renzmann grows animated. His back stiffens, he braces his shoulders a bit as his body gathers itself in the chair, no longer slouching. The old warrior is coming alive again. He asks if the divers found any bones in the U-boat.

"We don't think anybody died in the sub," says Mazraani, "except the men killed in the tower."

"Did you find any bones?"

"No. Nein."

Renzmann nods slowly as if he's certain, like that was his job to make sure everybody got out of the boat.

When Mazraani hands him the famous photo from the *New York Herald Tribune* of him and Robert Wilcox meeting in New York in 1960, a smile spreads across Renzmann's face.

"Wilcox," he says with vigor and delight. "Wilcox."

He seems very excited, ready to talk about anything now, but his wife has begun sending signals to Schmidt that she's worried about her husband. He's getting too agitated. It isn't good for his health.

"I think we have to end this soon," Schmidt whispers to Mazraani and Hänert.

At this point Mazraani presents Kim Joshi's letter from the Wilcox family to Renzmann, and Wolf Hänert translates it.

When the translation is over, Renzmann seems to sink back into his slouch. A peaceful smile crosses his face. "Wilcox." His voice is just a whisper.

Mazraani asks if he would like to see pictures of the *550* at the bottom of the sea.

Renzmann shakes his head "no," pushes the pictures away.

Later, Mazraani will say that he got the feeling that Renzmann was telling him that he was finally finished with U-*550*.

"The man was at peace," says Mazraani. "I think we brought him some peace."

Later, Mazraani gets a call from Wolf Hänert. The divers had given him a copy of the letter in Old German from his father to the Gardt family offering his condolences on the death of their son.

"I asked my mother-in-law to help translate the Old German. She's crying. She says she never knew such a tender side of my father. My family thanks you."

One night in Kiel, the divers go out for beers at a lively *Brauhaus* complete with a disc jockey spinning songs for a crowd that's in the mood to sing along. Hearing that the divers who discovered the wreck of *U-550* are in the beer hall, the disc jockey plays the song "It's a Long Way to Tipperary" in their honor. The song is the one that the crew of the U-boat in *Das Boot* sings. It's a nostalgic World War I song from England, a favorite among warriors of many nations, especially for U-boat crews in World War II. The song in the context of the German film gives voice to the men's brotherhood and their sense of a common fate, bound as they are to a lonely underwater boat. To say that the divers at this moment know the feeling would be an understatement. And for a few seconds the youthful faces that the divers have seen in photos of Klaus Hänert, Hugo Renzmann, Albert Nitsche, Johann Rauh, Robert Wilcox, Mort Raphelson, and John Hudock seem to float in the steamy air with the shades of all their shipmates from the Greatest Generation.

So . . . the divers rise from their seats, hoist their glasses, and sing. Everyone in the beer hall does.

> *It's a long way to Tipperary,*
> *It's a long way to go.*
> *It's a long way to Tipperary*
> *To the sweetest girl I know . . .*

47

A New Season

Almost seventy years to the day when SS *Pan Pennsylvania* shuddered from the concussion of the torpedo launched by Klaus Hänert's U-boat, the *550* discovery team surrounds Mort Raphelson in the living room of his suburban New Jersey home. There is a news team here covering the event, and Steve Gatto is shooting video as the divers present the former chief radio officer of the tanker with a large plaque. It contains a photo of the *Pan Penn* and the fully restored plate that Tom Packer recovered from the wreck of the tanker's stern.

"We want to give you back your long-lost breakfast plate," says one of the divers.

"And we want to recognize your heroic service as a merchant mariner in the war," says another. Like his fellow divers who have descended on the wrecks of dozens of merchant ships sunk by U-boats that are war graves, this diver is glad for the chance to celebrate the largely unacknowledged courage of the merchant marine vets.

Raphelson sits in his armchair. Ever unflappable, he beams out a wry smile at the surrounding group of family, friends, divers, and media.

"I figured you guys were going to bring me a dish," he says. "But where's the biscuit?"

A laugh bursts from the assembled group. The laugh is a recognition of both Raphelson's wit and a sense that some things are lost forever. But life goes on.

A month later, on an early Saturday morning in June, Joe Mazraani and Anthony Tedeschi are prowling deep into a U-boat's forward torpedo room. Not the torpedo room of the *550*, but the torpedo room of its restored sister ship U-*505*. The sub is the centerpiece of the massive collection at Chicago's Museum of Science and Industry on the shores of Lake Michigan, and the divers are here to celebrate the seventieth anniversary of the day when US Navy personnel seized the U-boat off the coast of Africa in 1944. The capture was one of America's great intelligence coups during World War II.

The museum took possession of the *505* as a donation from the US government in 1954, established it as a war memorial, and restored it. For years it sat outside the museum's main galleries, but in 2004 the museum moved the sub into an underground bunker to protect this priceless artifact from the weather. Now tens of thousands of museum guests each year visit the U-boat in what looks like one of the U-boat pens that protected the German sea wolves at their bases such as La Rochelle in occupied France.

Mazraani and Tedeschi have come to Chicago to make a presentation at the museum about finding the *550*. In exchange, they have been given private access to the *505*, and the divers are hard at work shooting pictures of every detail that may guide them if they penetrate the wreck this coming summer. At one moment Mazraani pauses from his photographing and measuring and just looks around as he stands in the narrow corridor with the tiny radio rooms to port and the captain's cabin to starboard. The wood veneer lining the hull above the skipper's berth glistens like new. The Enigma coding machine on the Funker's desk looks like an old-fashioned mechanical typewriter. In 2014 it is hard for Mazraani to imagine that the Allied quest to capture one of these antique-looking machines had been like the search for the pot of gold at the end of the rainbow back in 1944.

"This is how it was," he says to Tedeschi.

The other man nods, knows that for a few moments Mazraani is seeing that wrecked submarine that lies beneath the North Atlantic seventy miles south of Nantucket as it once was moments before USS *Joyce* pummeled it with depth charges.

Mazraani can imagine the lanky frame of Klaus Hänert lying on his back atop the gray woolen blanket in this berth, hands behind his head, eyes closed, modeling for his crew grace under pressure as his U-boat hides on the bottom . . . while the *Pan Penn* begins to disintegrate overhead and the relentless pinging of the DEs' sonars rings through the hull.

"I know some people who would pay a lot of money to know where you found the *550*," says a member of the museum's curatorial staff who is accompanying the divers.

"Huh?" Mazraani's cheeks twitch, as if waking from a dream.

"The Russians are desperate to have a U-boat. Money is no object."

Mazraani gets the picture. England has a U-boat, the United States has the *505*, Germany has the Type VII in Kiel and a Type XXI in Hamburg. The Russians are the only major combatants in the Battle of the Atlantic who do not have a trophy of the U-boat war.

"Technically U-*550* belongs to the German government," he says, recalling admiralty law.

He considers Russia's current agitation in Crimea and eastern Ukraine, imagines how unlikely, given today's political climate, the

Germans would be to let the Russians salvage the wreck. Then he thinks that the *550* is a monument to the lives of more than forty German sailors as well as the twenty-five men lost from the *Pan Penn*.

The pressure seems to build inside this submarine. He can hear a drumming in his ears, as if he's on the bottom in the twilight, somewhere in the wreck. The lost boys are singing about Tipperary.

"Actually . . . she belongs to the ages," he says. He'll never give up the position of the sub. If the Russians or anyone else wants to find it, they can strap on dive gear and go out there and look for themselves.

On the morning of July 18, 2014, *Tenacious* arrives over U-*550* for a third summer of diving on the wreck. But things are not going well. The team has been in a twitchy mood since yesterday, when they were tied into another wreck and a single-engine plane appeared out of nowhere and buzzed them. Small, private aircraft rarely venture so far out to sea, and the only conclusion that the discovery team can draw is that the plane has been sent by rival divers to spy on them and find the location of the *550*. Their only solace is that they were not at the wreck of the sub when the plane appeared. The GPS fix noted by the spy plane will not lead claim jumpers to U-*550*. Still, after all the team's hard work and expense, just the thought of claim jumpers sets their teeth on edge.

And so do deteriorating conditions. There's a perceptible current running on the surface, and a 12-to-15-knot breeze has begun stirring up surface chop. It takes the team seventeen tries before they hook into the wreck. According to the dive plan developed by the team, Gatto and Packer will be the first two men down to do the tie-in. But they are concerned that the current might be worse deeper in the water or that the growing chop could suddenly dislodge the anchor, leaving divers to make a challenging, possibly dangerous, free ascent with no anchor line to help them maintain consistent depths at their deco stops. Driven by the wind through the water, an unanchored boat can create drag on a diver hanging on the anchor line and bring him to the surface rapidly. Gatto and Packer remember that a situation like this killed a very experienced diver named Dave Bright in 2006 on the *Doria*.

They elect to wait topside and see if the wind and current abate. So do three of the other five divers. But by ten thirty Mazraani and Tedeschi, eager to try penetrating the wreck at the forward torpedo-loading hatch, say to hell with waiting. They are going down to the wreck. They will do the tie-in. They will also take Brad Sheard's GoPro camera mounted on a pole with lights. If conditions on the bottom seem safe, they will release a Styrofoam cup to the surface as a sign for the other divers to suit up. If conditions are too challenging, they will not release the cup, nor will they try to penetrate the wreck. Instead, Tedeschi will crawl as far as he dares through the forward torpedo-loading hatch and take photos with Sheard's pole camera rig. Mazraani will spot for Tedeschi in case anything goes awry.

Unlike the previous two seasons of great visibility and ambient light on the wreck, today is different. The visibility is probably less than 30 feet. Descending below about 200 feet on their scooters, the divers need their dive lights to stay oriented. It's pitch-black when they reach the chain and grapnel at the bottom of the anchor line. To add to the eerie vibes that Mazraani's getting from the darkness and limited visibility, a current of more than a half knot is sweeping at an angle over the wreck. Without the help of a scooter, a diver could get carried away from the wreck or the anchor line and never get back. Furthermore, the grapnel has snagged the wreck right on the knife edge of the sub's bow, and there's no easy place to tie in the anchor line. This part of the U-boat is a smooth, steel shell. The set of the current and its pull on *Tenacious* are the only things holding the grapnel in place. If the current changes, the anchor may well let go of the wreck, leaving any divers on the wreck with a difficult free ascent to the dive boat. Tedeschi and Mazraani do not release the foam cup to the surface.

The two men shoot each other looks through their masks. "Do we stay or do we go?"

They tug on the grapnel. For the moment its tines are clawing the bow of the sub with vigor, and they spot a small cap on the sub's bull nose to tie in the anchor chain to the wreck with nylon rope. If they are fast and careful, they might still at least make a quick inspection of the forward torpedo room using Sheard's camera, looking for any evidence of human remains and signs that 550 fired a torpedo from tube number two at the DEs as it surfaced. Ever the criminal defense attorney, Mazraani is nothing if he is not a man committed to digging for evidence and finding the truth. Tedeschi is fearless, known in professional circles as an ocean engineer who gets the job done no matter how challenging. He will give the pole camera a shot while Mazraani stands watch beside him to make sure he doesn't get himself fouled in the wreck or the camera gear.

They let the current carry them aft from the bow to the open forward torpedo-loading hatch. The visibility has dwindled to a sketchy 15 to 20 feet. For perhaps 10 minutes Tedeschi is on his knees over the hatch, probing the innards of the submarine with the camera as it records a new image every few seconds. If he stops to think about it for a moment, he might well consider that he is staring into the maw of a death trap. But that kind of reflection has no place in the mind of a man on a mission. So he focuses on the job at hand. He tries to judge how deep the silt is in the torpedo room, surveys what looks like the metal frames of the pipe berths where the crew once slept. Tries to see if there are still live torpedoes on the cabin sole or if the crew reloaded all the tubes. He also looks for the gray edges of human bones.

He's so deep into the search that he's losing track of time when Mazraani signals that they gotta go. It's spooky down here, and time's up. They need to start their deco. All the divers can do now is be glad they are safe . . . and hope for a chance to come back.

48

Jackpot Dives

August 8–11, 2014

Spectacular. The word echoes through the mouthpiece and gas tubes of Brad Sheard's rebreather as he stares up at the bow of U-*550* from the floor of the ocean. The visibility this morning could not be better on the wreck. Sixty feet or more. The water has that cobalt tinge of a Gulf Stream eddy. Bathed in a glow of ambient light from the surface, the sub looks like a movie set from an adventure film. Work ashore has prevented Tom Packer and Eric Takakjian from making the trip, but divers Mark Nix and Harold Moyers have joined Sheard and the rest of the *550* discovery team aboard *Tenacious.*

Sheard's thinking that the bow of the sub looks like a fresh wreck that has been on the bottom only a few years, as his eyes catch on something halfway down the port side of the bow. A rectangular dark spot. He has been looking for this, thought that he saw it on a dive the previous year. Slowly he scooters up to it, sees it is the slotted exit of a torpedo tube.

After his first dive today Joe Mazraani reported that he had peeked into this torpedo tube and thought that he saw a torpedo rotting away inside. Sheard and his dive partner Nix are here to confirm and document Mazraani's claim with Sheard's trusty Canon 5D, Mark 3, camera. If this is tube number two, then it's the tube that Klaus Hänert claimed he loaded with a T5, antidestroyer torpedo. He told British interrogators in the POW camp that he intended to fire as he surfaced to meet the American DEs . . . but could not fire because the tube doors were jammed. But back in Germany he told German naval authorities that he ordered the T5 in tube two to be fired manually. If Hänert fired this tube at the Americans, then he provided the catalyst to turn what might have been a peaceful surrender into a deadly battle.

While Nix illuminates the torpedo tube with his bright cave-diving light and brushes back 6-inch-thick hydroid growth on the outside of the hull with his hand, Sheard sets up to take pictures. He sees that the sheet-metal outer door of the torpedo tube is missing or has been pulled back into the hull, as if the tube were ready to fire. He has seen exactly this situation in bow pictures of other U-boats, such as the 505 in Chicago. Looking deeper, he sees that the inner pressure door to the tube is open as well. "Damn. This could not have been an accident," he thinks. The U-boat's crew had prepared to fire from this tube. Might have fired. If ever Sheard has witnessed what appears to be a smoking gun this is surely it . . . unless the bullet is still in the chamber. He feels his heart starting to pound, knows that he is beginning to inhale faster than usual. Tells himself to be glad that he's wearing a rebreather with hours of gas at his disposal. On open-circuit gear he would be sucking through his gas at a dangerous rate.

Out of habit, he stops, breathes, thinks . . . until his respiration moderates. Then he lets his scooter dangle from the clip at his waist and looks deep into the number-two tube. Nix's light illuminates the crumbling head of a torpedo stuffing the launch tube. "Holy shit. It's still here . . . just as Mazraani said," he thinks. Sheard points his camera, clicks away at the rusting and decomposing nose of a sixty-year-old ship-killer. Whether Hänert gave the order to fire the T5 in this tube or not, it never happened. Sheard has photographic evidence. It does not seem that U-550 came up to meet its enemies fighting. Although the open doors suggest that the intention may well have been there, here's irrefutable proof that the U-boat had bared its teeth, but it does not seem that it had bitten . . . at least not with this tube.

Like so many instances of extraordinary fortune related to the story of the sinking and rediscovery of this U-boat, torpedo tube number two being open for investigation and documentation seems almost unbelievable to Sheard. It's as if the 550 has been waiting to tell its story, waiting to help the divers correct seventy years of ambiguity and misunderstanding related to what really happened here on April 16, 1944. The diver feels his skin prickle with adrenaline. U-550 has shared a secret with him that the team can unfold for the world.

Anthony Tedeschi can't help himself. He's suddenly squealing with delight. For the past few minutes he has been hovering near the top of the conning tower, hacking away with his dive knife at the heavy fishnet caught over the tower. But with the last rip of his knife, the net has peeled back, exposing a 22-inch-wide bronze hatch combing that marks the entrance to the tower beneath. And not only is the bronze of the hatch combing still gleaming after all these years, it is also wide open. It's too narrow for a diver to penetrate, but wide enough to look through for a good view of the compartment that contains the battle helm, the compartment where Klaus Hänert sat on the bicycle seat of the attack periscope and tracked the *Pan Penn* and possibly the DEs.

The visibility is so good that when Tedeschi shines his dive light down the hatch, his eyes can follow the aluminum ladder all the way to the floor of the tower. He can see a collection of gauges and instruments mounted and dangling from the walls, but what really catches his interest is the bicycle seat of the attack periscope. In all of his imaginings about the last minutes of U-*550*, he has pictured the sub surfacing while its skipper was seated at the attack periscope with his eyes glued on what lies ahead of him. But the position of the bicycle seat shows that the last place that the scope was looking before the crew abandoned the tower was aft. The bicycle seat is pointed aft. Why was the sub's captain looking back there?

Harold Moyers thinks he may find the answer during his dive on the wreck. Since he first dove on the *550* back in 2013, he has been trying to figure out what happened to the stern of the U-boat. The stern bustle, about 20 feet of sculpted sheet steel that gives the sub a long, pointed tail above its two rudders, is missing. The back of the sub seems to be cut off right above the rudders. Now Moyers, diving without a partner, has scootered back to the stern to absolutely confirm his theory that when the *Gandy* rammed the *550*, it broke off the stern bustle.

Moyers also wants to see if he can find the stern torpedo tubes, number five and number six. The tube doors should be hidden beneath the hydroid growth above the twin rudders. These are the tubes that Hänert said were loaded, like tube number two in the bow, with T5 antidestroyer torpedoes. These are the tubes that Hänert claimed were damaged from the depth charge attack. He testified to both British and German interrogators that his crew could not open the torpedo doors or fire the torpedoes.

"So how bad was the damage back here?" Moyers wonders as he surveys the ocean floor around the stern. There are some small pieces of debris but no stern bustle. He concludes that the *Gandy*'s ramming of the sub cut off the stern bustle and that it lies some distance from the wreck.

Swimming close to what looks like a vertical wall above the rudders, he sees that the wall is actually the blunt end of the U-boat's pressure hull. The torpedo tube doors should be here, looking like the side-by-side barrels of a shotgun. He's brushing away the hydroids, looking for the tubes, while the GoPro on his head tries to record his search when his eyes spot a deep recess in the steel wall. It seems to be a torpedo tube. And it's open. There's no jammed door. There's no outer door or inner door. The tube is wide open to the sea. He shines his dive light inside, can see at least 7 feet into the tube. He expects to see the corpse of an ancient T5 torpedo staring out at him. But there is nothing in his line of vision, zilch. The tube appears empty. "Jesus," he thinks, "did they fire a torpedo?"

Back on the surface aboard *Tenacious* hours later, he remembers the words of his wreck-diving mentor Jon Hulburt, "You haven't really done the dive until you have watched the video of your dive twice." Moyers reruns his GoPro video yet again. Now he sees that what he thought was the port stern torpedo tube actually seems to be the starboard torpedo tube, number six.

"You still want a smoking gun?" he asks his dive buddies. "This is it. The tube is empty and the attack periscope is looking pretty much in the direction tube number six would have fired. I think Hänert let one fly at the DEs."

Not all of the divers agree. The housing on Moyers's GoPro collapsed from the extreme pressure and destroyed the camera before it could give visual confirmation of the empty tube. No other diver has seen the empty tube.

"This one's still up for grabs," says Mazraani, with his criminal defense attorney's skepticism, "until we get more confirmation."

The night before his second dive to the wreck on this trip, Joe Mazraani tossed and turned in his berth. He couldn't sleep. He kept thinking about his plan to penetrate the sub on his coming dive, and he kept hearing Eric Takakjian say to him in a phone call right before *Tenacious* left Montauk, "If you can't get out, you are going to die. Leave while you have a chance."

Now he's hearing those words again as he wiggles into the forward torpedo-loading hatch up to his waist as he had a year ago when he got stuck. But this time he has shed himself of all his auxiliary gear and bailout bottles, leaving all the extras on the deck of *550*. Still, he has to admit he's scared. But not scared enough to turn back. He didn't name his dive boat *Tenacious* for nothing. Hasn't invested years of time and buckets of money to stop without seeing the belly of the beast. So . . . he raises one arm over his head to reduce the breadth of his shoulders, feels the weight of his dive gear dragging him deeper. Then, suddenly, he drops, slips like a greased watermelon through the hatch into the torpedo room.

When he lands, he's facing aft and looking through the open pressure hatch in the bulkhead at the after end of the torpedo room. As Anthony Tedeschi perches at the outside edge of the hatch and spots for him, he flashes his dive light into the compartment. Before him lie the moldering pipe berths of the NCOs' quarters and a pantry. The galley is at the after end of this compartment. He sees two lamps, complete with shades, still hanging by their cords above him. The lights look almost ready to be lit again, and he has the odd feeling that he is drifting back in time.

Ducking through the open hatchway, he emerges in the berthing area and faces off with a jumble of unidentifiable debris—thick cables, pipes, and vent conduit that has come loose and is hanging down. Before he takes in the sights, he looks around for what could be a hazard and what he needs to avoid. He does this almost instantaneously because a slow snowstorm of minute rust particles has started to follow him in from the entrance. Everything he touches billows up a cloud of rust and silt, so he must be on his guard before he starts to move.

A few feet in front of him lies a pile of crumbling wooden cabinetry, like the cabinets of the pantry and galley that look so glossy in the *505*. Just beyond the dark bulkhead at the distant end of this compartment is the wardroom where Albert Nitsche served meals to Klaus Hänert, Hugo Renzmann, and the other officers. Here, in this very section of the U-boat, men gathered to sing before their guitarist died in the air attack by the Canso.

For more than a few seconds Mazraani hangs weightless in the still, dark core of the wreck and takes in the scene. He can almost hear the crew singing "It's a long way to Tipperary . . ." A chill passes through him, and Takakjian's warning nags at him. "If you can't get out, you will die. Leave while you have a chance."

He spins, kicks up a plume of silt with his fins, and reenters the torpedo room. Flashing his dive light forward from right to left, he sees that the ceiling-mounted rails and chain falls that the crew used for loading torpedoes have fallen and blocked deeper penetration. What appears to be a spare torpedo and the yellow skin of an unused life raft lie amid the debris on the cabin sole. He can almost hear the water starting to flood the room, can imagine the crew clambering to escape from this iron coffin before it sinks. Fears start to tighten his back, his neck, his arms into knotted cables. He thinks, "Time to go. Find the hatch. Swim. Now."

He's on the move, as eager to get out as he had been to get in. But an instant after his head rises above the rim of the forward torpedo-loading hatch, he hears the clink of metal on metal, feels the shock as the back of his rebreather jams against the iron truss spanning the forward half of the hatch. The air rushes out of his chest. Takakjian's warning burns through his consciousness. "If you can't get out, you will die."

He pictures Takakjian stuck in the *Bass* twenty years ago. But unlike Takakjian, Mazraani's not alone, and his dive partner Tedeschi has already spotted the problem. He grabs at the top bar of Mazraani's rebreather frame.

He feels a crushing in his chest as he's forced forward hard against the hatch combing. Then there's a strong, fluid tug on his harness.

And he's rising. He's out.

He's not going to die in there. He thinks, "Holy shit. Thank God for Anthony being here and knowing exactly what to do." Years ago, when he joined the U-*550* discovery team, Tedeschi promised himself and his dive buddies that one day he would prove his worth to them. In truth, he has done it already a hundredfold, but right now, in Joe Mazraani's mind, Tedeschi is not just the best of dive buddies. He's also life.

A score of seconds passes. Free and lingering like a fat codfish above the swirl of silt boiling from the forward torpedo-loading hatch, Mazraani doesn't move. He soaks up the moment, feeling more than a little glad that he has seen no sign of bones in the sub. He has traveled deep into the land of the dead and heard the songs of ghosts. The wreck's last supper lies half buried in the silt beneath the hanging lampshades that sway in the current and the darkness. U-*550* seems as at peace as it does in the video that the divers shared with Karoline Kuhla. And so—after all these years of relentless searching and dangerous, deep dives—is this diver.

49

Final Thoughts

Fall 2014

After hearing the American veterans Raphelson and Hudock say that they did not see, nor did they think, the Germans ever returned gunfire on the Americans, the divers were confused about the official coast guard and navy portrayals of events. The DEs' action reports claim the Germans opened fire. But after saying that U-*550* came to the surface firing, Bob Wilcox admitted in a videotaped interview that he never saw men at the U-boat's guns. Did anyone? Or did Wilcox only *think* that the sub was firing because USS *Gandy* reported it to him over the TBS? The three DEs were peppering the air with ordnance during their attacks. All the Germans interviewed tell the same story: after the depth charges caused terminal damage to U-*550*; the only thing on anyone's mind in the submarine was getting it to the surface and escaping.

But what about the battle damage from shells that the *Gandy* suffered, and what about four of her crew who were mildly wounded?

Did these wounds, the battle damage, and the firing that the *Gandy* attributed to the sub actually come from friendly fire originating from the *Peterson* or the *Joyce* as all three DEs attacked the U-boat from different sides and directions? According to Wilcox, the destroyers had the sub caught in a crossfire. That crossfire might have been mistaken as firing from the sub.

The testimony of Americans Hudock and Raphelson, the German survivors, Wilcox's statement about a dangerous crossfire, and the final photos of the *550* with its deck guns in their traveling positions build a strong case for the Germans never firing their guns at the DEs, a strong case that in the heat of their attacks the destroyer escorts mistook friendly fire for the enemy's armed defense. Collingwood Harris from the *Peterson* has gone on record with US Coast Guard oral historians talking about the wild firing frenzy. Furthermore, the DEs admitted that stray fire from the *Gandy* is what accidentally lit the spilling gasoline from the *Pan Penn* on fire. The *Gandy* had never seen action before. John Hudock told the divers that the battle with the sub came on the first day of the *Gandy*'s first convoy. It had never seen the enemy or combat before. No doubt some of its crew were more than a little rattled by the attack on the *Pan Penn* and the sudden appearance of a surfacing U-boat. In such a situation gunfire might easily miss its intended target.

A second nagging question for the divers asks if *550* fired torpedoes at the destroyers when it was rising to the surface mortally wounded. Once again the surviving German vets and stories told to their families deny any torpedo launch. But at various times during the first hour and a half following the attack on the *Pan Penn*, the *Gandy* reported that its lookouts had seen suspected wakes of torpedoes in the water. The problem with this claim is that by all accounts U-*550* was hiding on the bottom at this time and in no position to launch torpedoes.

What confuses this question for the divers is that after the war Hänert reported to the new German government that he intended to fire his three T5 torpedoes on the DEs as he surfaced. He says that the outer doors on tubes five and six jammed, but he ordered the eel in tube number two to be fired manually. But in his interrogation with British intelligence during his POW internment, Hänert says nothing about firing the T5 in tube two. He only mentions that he could not fire the eels in stern tubes five and six.

What is the truth? Did Hänert fire the eel in tube two? Did he claim to his German interrogators after the war that he fired it to make it sound like he put up a fight to the very end? Or did he not mention firing tube two to the British for fear of a reprisal for his belligerence or to mask the fact that the torpedo failed to strike a DE?

It was with these questions in mind that divers such as Brad Sheard, Mark Nix, and Joe Mazraani did their best during their dives to the 550 in the summer of 2014 to ascertain whether the torpedo in tube number two had been fired. Their discovery that a torpedo still sits in tube number two puts an end to Klaus Hänert's contradictory claims about firing or not firing the T5 in that tube. But the documented certainty that both the inner and outer doors on tube number two are open seems like clear indication that 550 surfaced ready to do battle if need be and not just surrender.

Of course, Anthony Tedeschi's discovery that the attack periscope seat is pointed toward the stern, and Harold Moyers's contention that stern torpedo tube number six is open and empty leave more than a little room for speculation about whether, despite the German skipper's consistent testimony to the contrary, he actually fired a defensive torpedo from a stern tube. The world may never know. As Joe Mazraani has said, "This one's still up for grabs." The eel in tube number six may have been launched. But it may have slipped from the battle-damaged tube when 550 made its uncontrolled steep ascent to the surface . . . or when it went bow high for the last time and sank beneath the North Atlantic.

.   .   .

The darkest question that the divers asked during their investigation of the battle and the sinking of U-*550* is, without a doubt, what happened to more than forty of its men. Did they sink with their boat as it took on water following the depth charge attack and the ramming by the *Gandy* . . . or could they have been saved? Did some of them escape later after being trapped in the forward torpedo room?

The divers' discovery of the crack in the pressure hull at the rim of the forward torpedo-loading hatch, a crack most likely caused by a combination of the expanding air in the sub as it sank and an explosion (known to have happened on other U-boats) when salt water hit the batteries, dispels any possibility that men could have survived in the forward torpedo room when the sub sank. With that crack, the forward torpedo room could not have been watertight. The divers' inspection of the torpedo room with a camera on a pole, as well as penetration dives by Mazraani and Tedeschi, have showed no sign of human remains. Furthermore, the testimony of Ziemer, Nitsche, and Renzmann, along with the stories told to the families of Dr. Torge and Klaus Hänert, are absolutely consistent: all the crew escaped the U-boat except possibly two men killed by the shelling in the tower. Collingwood Harris's testimony about men on the *Peterson* firing at Germans in the water adds to this picture. The O'Hara photo of U-*550* minutes before it sank, flanked on its port side with at least a dozen men in the water, tells the same story. To the divers' way of thinking, the official narrative about the sinking on the US Coast Guard website, and the story widely echoed over the Internet, is inaccurate and based on combat action reports from the *Peterson*, *Gandy*, and *Joyce* that avoid the issue of what happened to the rest of the Germans.

Almost any combat commander you ask will tell you that the less said in an action report, the better. Former navy skippers from World War II interviewed anonymously for this book have said that under no circumstances were American warship captains expected to pick up enemy combatants in combat situations. In fact, some of the US fleets' top commanders discouraged captains from this practice.

Stopping a ship during combat to pick up men in the water is dangerous. The men on the *Peterson* and the *Joyce* only had to remember what they witnessed a month earlier for an illustration of that danger. While stopping to pick up survivors from the USS *Leopold*, the crew of the *Joyce* claimed that they were the targets of at least two German torpedoes.

"You have to consider what had happened on the previous trip and nobody was taking any chances," *Peterson* vet Harris has said for the record. "It was not apparent that Germany had not won the war, and our perception was that the sea was alive with submarines."

Video interviews with *Peterson* vets in the 1990s show them saying the same thing as Harris. Their skipper believed that other U-boats were prowling in the area, and he was not going to sit still and make a target of his ship, not for the sake of picking up a crew of men who had torpedoed one of the largest American tankers and who were responsible for twenty-five American dead tankermen in the water. In addition, the escort group's commander on USS *Poole* was urging *Peterson*, *Gandy*, and *Joyce* to put an end to the U-boat and return to the convoy, which was getting away from them to the east with only three DEs to defend it.

Given the situation, the captains of the *Peterson* and the *Gandy* were acting according to orders and priorities set by their group commander on the *Poole*, as well as in accord with established protocols for US Navy skippers in battle conditions. Leaving living men to die in freezing water probably did not rest easily on the consciences of the captains of the *Gandy* and the *Peterson*, but there was a war going on around them. One of the largest tankers in the American fleet was afire and sinking. The DEs had a convoy to protect, and stopping to pick up more than forty enemy combatants in the water was an unnecessary risk if there was another U-boat there waiting for a chance to attack another American ship. Bottom line: as inhumane as it may seem to some critics seventy years later, the skippers of the *Gandy* and the *Peterson* did their jobs. They followed orders.

The man who exceeded his orders was skipper Robert Wilcox on the *Joyce*.

"If you exceed your orders and everything turns out well, you're a hero," one naval commander told the discovery team. "But if things go south, there'll be hell to pay."

Lucky for Robert Wilcox and his career, things went his way. He made a split-second decision—based on his own private agenda—to save lives where he could. Surely his guilt over not rescuing more of the *Leopold*'s men must have nagged at him. He had gone to sea as the son of a US Coast Guard officer who thought that the coast guard's most important mission is to save lives at sea. Wilcox had joined the service with a firm belief in his father and the service's ideals. When it comes to saving lives at sea, coasties tell each other, "You have to go out . . . but you don't have to come back." For Klaus Hänert, Hugo Renzmann, Albert Nitsche, Robert Ziemer, Johann Rauh, and the other seven survivors of U-*550*, Robert Wilcox was exactly the right man in the right place. If the wreck of that phantom sub 70 miles south of Nantucket has guardian angels, one of them is named Captain Robert Wilcox.

SOURCES AND ACKNOWLEDGMENTS

The six deep-wreck divers at the heart of this book welcomed me to their band of brothers ten months after their discovery of U-*550*. As the idea for this book took shape, I joined Joe Mazraani, Steve Gatto, Tom Packer, Eric Takakjian, Brad Sheard, and Anthony Tedeschi on numerous dive trips to remote deep wrecks near the edge of the continental shelf off New York, New Jersey, and New England. We stood watches together aboard Mazraani's dive boat *Tenacious*. We endured long trips in bone-jarring seas. We navigated through the fog and ship traffic. We held our breath together one day 65 miles offshore when we had two divers down on the wreck of the freighter *Bidevind* and a monster, 20-foot great white got way too curious about our dive boat.

Little by little the guys have shared the secrets of their fraternity with me. The blending of gas combinations of oxygen, helium, and nitrogen that they use for diving to places that were considered impossible to reach just a few years ago. The rituals of suiting up. The careful checking of gear. The rigging of the boat for diving. The watching and waiting for the men who are down on the wreck or pausing at decompression hangs on the way back to the surface. The sharing of discovery stories once everybody is back aboard after a deep dive.

I was in the email loops and the onboard conversations as the divers bantered about weather and dive strategies related to research and exploring *U-550* and other wrecks. I was there when lift bags popped to the surface carrying artifacts such as zinc bars and brass portholes from wrecks. There one day when Brad Sheard and Anthony Tedeschi both suffered potential deadly issues related to their rebreathers in 230 feet of water. There when Tom Packer cut his bottom time and deco time short to race back to the surface because he was worried that he had lost sight of Mazraani on the bottom. As it turned out Joe had surfaced early because of a problem with a gas mix. Everything was okay . . . this time.

And I was also aboard *Tenacious* for less intense moments. Aboard when we dragged out the gas grill and Joe Mazraani cooked up steak tips, baked potatoes, and asparagus. Aboard while Anthony Tedeschi had wrestling matches with Joe's dog, Pirate. Aboard for Tom Packer's good-humored ball-busting sessions, especially as they related to the fastidiousness of our captain Mazraani ("Don't let Joe catch you eating cookies over his carpet, dude"). Aboard for the sea stories and the sharing of videos. Aboard for the midnight watch when the boat was anchored over a wreck 70 miles at sea and the guys in the six forecastle berths were snoring like a pride of lions. The divers simply made me feel part of the crew. "We're a team," Mazraani would say regularly. "Where we go one, we go all." In this regard we were like the crews of *U-550*, the *Pan Penn*, and the destroyer escorts. Words can hardly describe how honored I feel to have shared such brotherhood. Never has researching for a book or a magazine article been more personally rewarding. These men endured tens of thousands of questions from me during the hundreds of hours we spent together.

In addition to the six divers who found the *550*, I owe a great debt to two other divers who regularly sail aboard *Tenacious* and who have dived to U-*550*. Pat Rooney and Harold Moyers have been endlessly helpful with my research. Pat has been around deep-wreck diving and boats for more than three decades and has borne witness to both the glory and the death that surround the sport. Likewise for Harold, who also has an absolutely encyclopedic knowledge of U-boats and other ships involved in the Battle of the Atlantic. I can't count the times Harold has shot me email attachments and photos to clarify some question or detail of U-boats or of World War II.

The divers shared their decades of research with me and their libraries. Eric Takakjian presented me with shopping bags full of his personal volumes—with key pages bookmarked—on submarines, destroyers, and merchant ships. Both Eric and Joe offered up gigabytes of correspondence with researchers, survivors of the U-boat/tanker/ destroyer escort battle, emails from families of dead veterans, and letters between the dead veterans.

Joe connected me with Garry Kozak, who offered his memories of the search trips for U-*550* as well as insight into his life as a deep-sea researcher and his side-scan sonar equipment. John Rauh spoke with me about his father, Johann Rauh, the U-boat machinist who survived the battle and started a new life as an engineer in America. Mort Raphelson, the former radio officer aboard the *Pan Penn*, was gracious with both his time and sharp recollections of the tanker's last hours. I was able to talk with the family of Bob Wilcox, captain aboard USS *Joyce*; Klaus Hänert's son, Dr. Wolf Hänert, in Kiel, Germany; and the family of Friedrich Torge, *550*'s doctor. The dive team's trip to Germany in November 2013 was an adventure in itself. Its high point was meeting U-*550* survivor Albert Nitsche and hearing his reminiscences of serving in the Ubootwaffe aboard *550* as gunner and steward. The conversations with Nitsche would not have been possible had it not been for the assistance of our capable and gregarious translators Lisa Svec in the United States and Andreas Schalomon in Germany.

Families on both sides of the Atlantic were helpful in providing correspondence and interviews that document the story of the battle south of Nantucket and, even more importantly, giving us insights into the lives of exceptional men who survived a horrific battle and a devastating war and forged new and rich lives that included their former enemies.

Steve Gatto shared with me hours of video interviews that he shot with American veterans Mort Raphelson and John Hudock. Joe Mazraani's correspondence with other survivors' families, like that of John Bender, ASW officer on the *Joyce*, also helped me understand the men involved in the battle. Despite ill health Hugo Renzmann, the former engineer aboard U-*550*, and his shipmate Albert Nitsche met with the divers and me during our research trip to Germany. That meeting would have been impossible without the collaboration and help of NDR TV reporter Andreas Schmidt.

I found a helpful interview with Renzmann in the German publication *Bild*. I also found interviews with Bob Wilcox and other crewmen from the *Joyce* on Vimeo. "Eye Witnesses of World War II, U-*550*" is a moving posting by diver Mark Munro and filmmaker Rob Sibley. The video gives first-person accounts of the battle and a look at brave men who are no longer with us. U-*550* survivor Robert Ziemer spoke with me and Joe Mazraani by phone through a translator about the battle, and I found the *Peterson*'s radarman Collingwood Harris's amazing interview on the same topic (and more) at the website of the US Coast Guard Oral History Program. Of course, the deck logs and action reports from USS *Joyce*, USS *Gandy*, and USS *Peterson* clarified the timetable of the battle and the action, as the captains chose to reveal it, from each man's perspective. The post-sinking deposition of *Pan Pennsylvania* captain Delmar Leidy gave me an additional look into the events of April 15–16, 1944, as does the action report of the head of the naval armed guard on the tanker.

The amazing battle and rescue photos by Chief Petty Officer Emmett O'Hara capture the poignant last minutes of U-*550* and the desperation of its crew. The cameras of all the divers have documented essential moments and images in the search for U-*550*, giving a window into the current condition of this pristine wreck that only a few men have ever seen face-to-face.

Of course, only so much research for a book like this can come from firsthand observers. When it came to following the paper trail surrounding the ships involved in the battle of April 16, 1944, Eric Takakjian, Brad Sheard, and Joe Mazraani offered me volumes of action reports, radio messages, depositions, and interrogation reports gleaned through the Freedom of Information Act from correspondence with, and visits to, the Naval Historical Center and the National Archives.

My colleague Lisa Svec's German 600 class at Phillips Academy in Andover, Massachusetts (where Lisa and I both teach) proved enthusiastic, able, and invaluable translators of German war records as well as letters in German written by Klaus Hänert and other members of his crew. Sibylle Beckwith came to my rescue and translated a letter from Hänert written in Old German script to the family of one of his dead crewmen. It offered a glimpse into the essential humanity of the Old Man.

For a historical perspective, three books on World War II in the Atlantic were invaluable: Samuel Eliot Morison's *The Battle of the Atlantic* (Little, Brown), Clay Blair's monumental two-volume set *Hitler's U-boat War* (Random House), and legendary diver Gary Gentile's *Track of the Gray Wolf* (Avon Books). Eberhard Rössler's *The U-boat* (Cassell) has excellent photos and historical documentation of U-boat development. Likewise, there is great historical material on Type IX U-boats in Fritz Kohl and Axel Niestlé's *Vom Orignal zum Modell: Uboottyp IX C*. Niestlé's book *German U-boat Losses During World War II: Details of Destruction* also adds to the picture. While researching online one day, I came across the website of the Historic Naval Ships Association, hnsa.org. Here was an English translation of the Kriegsmarine's *The Submarine Commander's Handbook*, circa 1943. What insight it gives into the German navy's expectations for Klaus Hänert as the commander of the *550*. U-boat commander Herbert A. Werner took me into his life on a World

War II German submarine through his memoir *Iron Coffins* (Da Capo Press), as did Michael Gannon's *Operation Drumbeat* (Naval Institute Press). Lothar-Günther Bucheim is not only the author of the novel *Das Boot*, but also the creator of an amazing volume of photos and narrative called *U-boat War* (Bonanza Books), which documents a patrol on a combat U-boat in 1942 with astonishing photos. The website uboatarchive .net is a trove of information on battles, submarines, ships, and, especially for my research, crew information. Its webmaster Captain Jerry Mason, USN (Ret.), came to my rescue on more than one occasion with complete translations of the KTBs (radio reports between U-boats and headquarters). Other helpful websites include uboat.net, sharkhunters .com, and historisches-marinearchiv.de. Nothing is better at illustrating the strain of life aboard a U-boat than Wolfgang Petersen's film version of Bucheim's *Das Boot*.

Curator Steve Rosengard at the Museum of Science and Industry in Chicago and former curator Keith Gill shared their vast amounts of research with the divers and me on *U-505*. It is a national landmark and a keystone exhibit at the museum. It is also only one of two type IXC U-boats to be preserved for history and a near clone of *U-550*. The other preserved type IX is cut in three pieces and on display at the Woodside Ferry Terminal on the River Mersey in the United Kingdom.

In researching destroyer escorts, I relied on Lewis M. Andrews Jr.'s *Tempest, Fire and Foe—Destroyer Escorts in World War II and The Men Who Manned Them* (Narwhal Press), *Escort* (W. Kimber) by Denys Arthur Rayner, *The Cruel Sea* (Burford Books) by Nicholas Monsarrat, and the website of the Destroyer Escort Sailors Association, desausa.org. The 1957 film *The Enemy Below* does for DEs what *Das Boot* does for life aboard U-boats. Former destroyer skipper captain Ron Trossbach, USN (Ret.), helped me to understand the duties of a destroyer captain during combat. *A Careless Word . . . A Needless Sinking* (American Merchant Museum) by Arthur R. Moore is an excellent resource for researchers looking to find the histories of

American merchant ships sailing in World War II. Additional helpful volumes include John Keegan's *The Second World War* (Penguin Books), Nathan Miller's *War at Sea—A Naval History of World War II* (Scribner), and John Terraine's *Business in Great Waters: The U-Boat Wars, 1916–1945* (Leo Cooper). Another great source is the website usmm.org. Tim Rizzuto, ship superintendent at the USS *Slater* Historical Museum, and the museum's website ussslater.org have been highly elucidating about life aboard destroyer escorts. The website for the Naval Historical Center, history.navy.mil, was my source for the story of the capture of U-*505* and an excellent site for all things related to U.S. Navy history.

When it comes to deep-wreck diving, all the books by veteran diver Gary Gentile took me deeper into this dark, wet, cold world, but especially *The Advanced Wreck Diving Handbook* and *Deep, Dark and Dangerous: Adventures and Reflections on the* Andrea Doria (Gary Gentile Productions). Brad Sheard's *Beyond Sport Diving* (Menasha Ridge Press) and *Lost Voyages* (Aqua Quest Publications) are great vehicles for exploring some of the most famous wrecks of coastal New York and New Jersey. Although tarnished a bit by controversy about inaccuracies, Robert Kurson's *Shadow Divers* (Random House) remains a compelling read. *The Last Dive* (HarperPerennial) by Bernie Chowdhury is a heartbreaking look at the lives and deaths of the father-and-son dive team of Chris and Chrissy Rouse. It is a cautionary tale about the extreme dangers of deep-wreck diving. The book is all the more gut-wrenching for me knowing that my friends Tom Packer and Steve Gatto were on the same dive trip and actively working with others on the boat to give CPR to keep the Rouses alive before the rescue chopper arrived.

Finally, a book like this one cannot take its final shape without the help of a legion of people. First, my agent Doug Grad brought immense enthusiasm to this project. His guidance has been honed by three decades as editor and agent for some of the best-known authors of military and maritime books. Berkley Caliber senior editor Tom Colgan brought similar gusto to this book to give it a final massage before publication. He's a man with a highly developed sense of aesthetics and a great ear for rooting out awkward expressions. Our production team also included Tom's able assistant Amanda Ng, managing editor Pam Barricklow, copyeditor William Drennan, book designer Tiffany Estreicher, and production manager Joi Walker.

To all, my deep and enduring thanks.

AN OUTTAKE

Hänert's Second Letter to the Gardt Family

A second letter from the captain says that he will never forget Karl Gardt's "safe and reliable handling of the complicated technical equipment always earned the chief engineering officer's and my recognition. He was always willing to put his great strengths at our disposal."

Speaking of the depth charge attack on his U-boat, Hänert writes:

On board, almost everything fell apart and lots of water came in. Nevertheless our calm and confident chief engineer was able to bring the boat to the surface. At the surface were three American destroyers in a tight circle around our U-Boot and the Americans immediately began to shoot from all gauges at the heavily damaged, sinking boat which was inoperable and unsalvageable. In the process I sustained wounds, especially to the head, so I could only see unconvincingly out of one eye. After a bit of time it was possible for the crew, and your son Karl, to be provided with life vests and were able to leave the boat and swim in the direction of a nearby destroyer. The destroyer simply drove away without caring for the shipwrecked. Shortly thereafter, as I left the boat as the last one on board, came a second destroyer, but it only rescued those who were directly on its tail board, in total: 12 [sic].

Hänert continues:

The water was 5 degrees C. In those situations, the saving ship must swim to every single person in the water and get them out. Coincidentally, I was only a few meters away from the destroyer. But even that wouldn't have mattered had I not been a trained swimmer and hadn't been able to swim forward unhindered because my life vest had been shot to bits. In the cold water, everyone needs all of their strength, even with a life jacket, in order not to sink. (A quiet forwards swim is nothing to think twice about). I passed out as I was being carried on board, and by the time I woke up, it was too late to reproach the captain for his actions. I could only ascertain that most of my Comrades, including your son Karl, died at sea.

Your brave boy will never leave my thoughts.

With sincere regards,
Your Klaus Hänert

INDEX